National Identities and Foreign Policy in the European Union

The Russia Policy of Germany, Poland and Finland

Marco Siddi

ecpr PRESS

ROWMAN & LITTLEFIELD
INTERNATIONAL
London • New York

Published by Rowman & Littlefield International Ltd
Unit A, Whitacre Mews, 26-34 Stannary Street, London SE11 4AB
www.rowmaninternational.com

Rowman & Littlefield International Ltd. is an affiliate of Rowman & Littlefield
4501 Forbes Boulevard, Suite 200, Lanham, Maryland 20706, USA
With additional offices in Boulder, New York, Toronto (Canada), and Plymouth (UK)
www.rowman.com

British Library Cataloguing in Publication Data
A catalogue record for this book is available from the British Library

Library of Congress Cataloging-in-Publication Data

HARDBACK ISBN: 978-1-78552-279-6
PAPERBACK ISBN: 978-1-78661-110-9

∞™ The paper used in this publication meets the minimum requirements of American
National Standard for Information Sciences—Permanence of Paper for Printed Library
Materials, ANSI/NISO Z39.48-1992.

Printed in the United States of America

Other books available in the Monographs series

Agents or Bosses? Patronage and Intra-Party Politics in Argentina and Turkey
(ISBN: 9781907301261) Özge Kemahlioğlu

Causes of War: The Struggle for Recognition
(ISBN: 9781907301018) Thomas Lindemann

Cities and the European Union: Mechanisms and Modes of Europeanisation
(ISBN: 9781785521584) Samuele Dossi

Citizenship: The History of an Idea
(ISBN: 9780954796655) Paul Magnette

Civil Society in Communist Eastern Europe: Opposition and Dissent in Totalitarian Regimes
(ISBN: 9781907301278) Matt Killingsworth

Coercing, Constraining and Signalling: Explaining UN and EU Sanctions After the Cold War
(ISBN: 9781907301209) Francesco Giumelli

Conditional Democracy: The Contemporary Debate on Political Reform in Chinese Universities
(ISBN: 9781907301698) *Emilie Frenkiel*

Constraints on Party Policy Change
(ISBN: 9781907301490) Thomas M. Meyer

Consultative Committees in the European Union: No Vote – No Influence?
(ISBN: 9781910259429) Diana Panke, Christoph Hönnige, Julia Gollub

Contesting Europe: Exploring Euroscepticism in Online Media Coverage
(ISBN: 9781907301513) Pieter De Wilde, Asimina Michailidou and Hans-Jörg Trenz

Coping with Complexity: How Voters Adapt to Unstable Parties
(ISBN: 9781785521515) Dani Marinova

Deliberation Behind Closed Doors: Transparency and Lobbying in the European Union
(ISBN: 9780955248849) Daniel Naurin

Democratic Institutions and Authoritarian Rule in Southeast Europe
(ISBN: 9781907301438) Danijela Dolenec

Democratic Reform and Consolidation: The Cases of Mexico and Turkey
(ISBN: 9781907301674) Evren Celik Wiltse

The Personalisation of Politics: A Study of Parliamentary Democracies
(ISBN: 9781907301032) Lauri Karvonen

Policy Making In Multilevel Systems: Federalism, Decentralisation and Performance in the OECD Countries
(ISBN: 9781907301339) Jan Biela, Annika Hennl and André Kaiser

Political Conflict and Political Preferences: Communicative Interaction between Facts, Norms and Interests
(ISBN: 9780955820304) Claudia Landwehr

Political Parties and Interest Groups in Norway
(ISBN: 9780955820366) Elin Haugsgjerd Allern

The Politics of Income Taxation: A Comparative Analysis
(ISBN: 9780954796686) Steffen Ganghof

Regulation in Practice: The de facto Independence of Regulatory Agencies
(ISBN: 9781907301285) Martino Maggetti

Representing Women? Female Legislators in West European Parliaments
(ISBN: 9780954796648) Mercedes Mateo Diaz

The Return of the State of War: A Theoretical Analysis of Operation Iraqi Freedom
(ISBN: 9780955248856) Dario Battistella

Schools of Democracy: How Ordinary Citizens (Sometimes) Become Competent in Participatory Budgeting Institutions
(ISBN: 9781907301186) Julien Talpin

Split-Ticket Voting in Mixed-Member Electoral Systems: A Theoretical and Methodological Investigation
(ISBN: 9781785521805) Carolina Plescia

Transnational Policy Innovation: The OECD and the Diffusion of Regulatory Impact Analysis
(ISBN: 9781907301254) Fabrizio De Francesco

Urban Foreign Policy and Domestic Dilemmas: Insights from Swiss and EU City-regions
(ISBN: 9781907301070) Nico van der Heiden

Why Aren't They There? The Political Representation of Women, Ethnic Groups and Issue Positions in Legislatures
(ISBN: 9780955820397) Didier Ruedin

Widen the Market, Narrow the Competition: Banker Interests and the Making of a European Capital Market
(ISBN: 9781907301087) Daniel Mügge

Please visit www.ecpr.eu/ecprpress for information about new publications.

Contents

List of Abbreviations

AA	Association Agreement
DHA	Discourse-Historical Analysis
EEU	Eurasian Economic Union
EU	European Union
EUMM	Monitoring Mission of the EU
NATO	North Atlantic Treaty Organisation
OSCE	Organisation for Security and Co-operation in Europe
UN	United Nations
WTO	World Trade Organisation

List of Tables

Acknowledgements

This book is the outcome of the research that I started during my Ph.D. studies at the Universities of Edinburgh and Cologne and concluded as a research fellow at the Finnish Institute of International Affairs. I am indebted to Professor Luke March for his invaluable academic advice and encouragement at the University of Edinburgh. I also want to thank my doctoral co-supervisors, Professors Wolfgang Wessels and John Peterson, and the many other researchers and colleagues who commented on draft chapters. Dr Geoffrey Edwards deserves a special mention, not least because he travelled as far as Cologne, Dublin and Cagliari to discuss my work in various seminars and conferences. Professor Brigid Laffan, Dr Robert Kissack, Professor Ben Tonra and Professor Juliet Kaarbo also gave me incisive advice on the theoretical and methodological framework of the research.

I am particularly grateful to Juha Jokela, Alec Aalto, Susan Stewart, Katrin Böttger, Hans-Henning Schröder, Ludvig Zsuzsa and Szymon Kardas for the useful discussions, interviews and analytical feedback concerning the case studies for this work. The Discourse Analysis, Politics and International Relations, and Europa research groups at the University of Edinburgh were highly stimulating forums where I could present and refine my research. Thanks are also due to my colleagues in the EXACT Marie Curie programme, at the Jean Monnet Chair of the University of Cologne and at the Institut für Europäische Politik in Berlin who were a great source of moral and intellectual support.

Last but not least, I am grateful to my parents, who have taught me the importance of being hard-working, Luca and Anna, who hosted and supported me during my research trips to Germany, and Krzysztof, who greatly contributed to my interest in Poland by taking me to some of the most fascinating corners of the country. The biggest thanks go to my partner Barbara for giving me all kinds of support and tirelessly reading and commenting on everything I wrote.

Chapter One

Introduction: Identity, Memory and Russia as Europe's Other

This book explores the relationship between national identities and foreign policy discourses concerning Russia in selected member states of the European Union (EU). In doing so, it builds on previous studies that focused on European and national identities and the role of external factors in the process of identity construction. An increasingly large body of European Studies literature has explored the emergence of a shared European identity (see Bayley and Williams 2012; Checkel and Katzenstein 2009; Herrmann *et al*. 2004; Risse 2010). These works generally argue that European identity is, at best, still developing next to national identities. Following Willfried Spohn's (2005: 2) categorisation, three main perspectives can be identified in the literature. The first sees European identity as a weak addendum to strong national identities. The second assumes that European identity will unfold in the long run and restructure national identities through their gradual Europeanisation. The third hypothesises the future emergence of a variable mix of European and national identities. All three perspectives agree on the current dominance of national identities over a still weak European identity.

As these initial observations suggest, national identities play an important role in Europe and may provide a key to understanding European politics. Scholars studying nationalism have argued that we are unlikely to see the transcendence of national identities by a strong European identity (Smith 1996a: 363). Their colleagues working on memory politics, a domain that is very close to and partly overlaps with identity studies, have come to similar conclusions in their assessments of the prospects for a common European memory: national discourses are pervasive in collective memory and can scarcely be reconciled with a shared European discourse (Bell 2006: 16; Jarausch and Lindenberger 2007: 1). This is not surprising, as nation-states have a much longer history than European institutions. Linguistic, historical and cultural differences contribute to the endurance of national identities and of political constructions that draw their legitimacy from national communities.

The focus on the national level in this book should not lead to the assumption that the concept of European identity can simply be dismissed. A feeling of attachment to Europe and to the political structures of the EU is observable among both European elites and citizens, however weak and inconsistent it might be (see Standard Eurobarometer 83: 112, 123). The creation of a common European market, the removal of barriers to the free movement of citizens and numerous transnational schemes have contributed to its emergence. However, as most of the relevant scholarly literature argues, in Europe national identities and memories are still stronger than transnational ones. Studying national identities is thus important to understand both the dilemmas surrounding European identity and, most importantly, current European politics.

Social constructivist literature has highlighted the strong relationship between national identity and foreign policy discourses.[1] This book applies a social constructivist theoretical model to examine this relationship in three European states – Germany, Poland and Finland – and assess the prospects for a shared European foreign policy discourse concerning Russia. The key argument is that divergent national foreign policy approaches to Russia are the result of the different ways in which the country's national identity was constructed. However, the analysis also shows that national identity is malleable and a country's leaders can reformulate dominant narratives in order to achieve particular foreign policy goals. It is argued that national discourses on Russia can be reconciled if divisive identity narratives are marginalised and common foreign policy goals are pursued.

Relations with Russia have been chosen as a litmus test for a shared European foreign policy discourse because they have proven to be one of the most divisive issues among European Union countries (Cadier 2014; Casier 2011; David and Romanova 2015; David *et al.*, 2011, 2013; Gromyko 2015; Haukkala 2010a, 2015; Korosteleva 2016; Nitoiu 2016; Romanova 2016). In 2007, former EU trade commissioner Peter Mandelson stated that 'no other country reveals our differences as does Russia' (cited in Kagan 2008: 14). A decade later, such divisions continue to exist and are reflected in the different stances of EU member states concerning the future of relations with Russia after the Ukraine crisis (Emmott 2016; Romanova 2016; Siddi 2016a). Russia is the EU's largest neighbour, a key energy supplier and an essential, though often very controversial, factor in the European security architecture. As highlighted by the profound crisis that erupted in Ukraine in the autumn of 2013, the European Union and its member states cannot guarantee the stability of their eastern neighbours without taking Russia into account as a geopolitical factor. Furthermore, the political system built by post-Soviet Russian leaders challenges some of the European Union's founding values, particularly in the field of democracy and human rights (see Treaty on European Union Article 2; Shiraev 2013).[2]

Relations with Russia are a test for the very idea of a united EU foreign policy because they have traditionally been based on a bilateral, national dimension. The most frequent explanations for this bilateralism refer to the different economic interests and security concerns of EU member states, as well as to Russia's preference for dealing with European countries separately (see David *et al.* 2011: 183–4; Schmidt-Felzmann 2011). This book proposes an alternative understanding of the relations of the EU and its member states with Russia, one that is based on national identity. The focus on national identity provides a useful research angle

---

1. *See* Chapter Two in this volume for a detailed discussion.

2. All references to the Treaty on European Union concern the treaty version as amended by the Treaty of Lisbon.

because, in contrast with predominant analyses focusing on power politics and economics, it seeks to explain relations with Russia through an investigation of historical and cultural factors.

The conceptualisation of identity as a key element in international relations provides a much-needed alternative to realist and liberal institutionalist models framed around the notions of anarchy, balance of power and institutional cooperation. The book analyses international relations as a social construction, of which national identities are essential constituents. Drawing on constructivist literature, a theoretical model is developed highlighting the mutually constitutive relationship among national identity, interests and foreign policy discourses. In particular, the historical dimension of national identity formation is explored in order to examine its relevance in current foreign policy discourses. Hence, the book adopts a historicist approach, which assigns key importance to cultural and historical context. Foreign policy discourses are studied through discourse-historical analysis (DHA), a variant of critical discourse analysis developed by Ruth Wodak (2002a). DHA was previously used by scholars to study debates about immigration and identity politics in the media, in EU institutions and among the wider public (Krzyzanowski 2010, 2009; Oberhuber et al. 2005; Reisigl and Wodak 2001; Wodak 2009). This book constitutes the first application of the methodology to the analysis of the public discourses of national foreign policy elites.

Empirically, the book also contributes to the understanding of the current foreign policy of the EU and its member states towards its eastern neighbours. It constitutes an attempt to strengthen the strand of research focusing on the role of nationalism, identity and memory politics in EU–Russia relations. The surge of nationalist sentiment and widespread political use of history during the current Ukrainian crisis has exposed that these are powerful factors in EU–Russia relations (Luhn 2014; Siddi 2016c). This book shows that national identity and memory politics played an important role in this relationship well before the beginning of the turmoil in Ukraine. The empirical chapters highlight the significance of identity and memory politics in events that took place during the last decade in fields of extreme importance for the EU, such as energy security, the stability of the neighbourhood, Russia's democratisation and its role in the European security system. Through an interdisciplinary approach combining social constructivist theory, discourse theory and historical analysis, the book sheds light on the deep identity and cultural roots of relevant foreign policy discourses.

The focus of the empirical analysis is restricted to key foreign policy leaders (heads of state or government and foreign ministers) for reasons of feasibility and relevance. Covering thoroughly three national discursive arenas, each having thousands of participants, would not be possible within the scope of this book. However, in countries such as those under analysis, key foreign policy decisions are ultimately made by a restricted group of leaders who have received a mandate from a parliamentary majority or a majority of electors. These leaders also represent the country internationally and, thanks to their political prominence, they have the discursive power to steer the country's main foreign policy debates.

Most important for this analysis, their behaviours and decisions are influenced by the national identities in which they are embedded.[3] National identity is a very useful concept to understand the domestic construction of international politics because it encompasses and is forged by the defining cultural, historical and political constituents of a state. Its relationship with foreign policy discourses is complex. It is mutually constitutive, because national identity and foreign policy discourses influence each other. It is also malleable, because the two concepts are in constant flux and change over time. For some scholars, the notion of national identity might be elusive (see Malesevic 2011). However, it is exactly the complexity of the concept and its changing and multifaceted nature that make it a fascinating research topic. National identity is not the only element in the complex scenario of international politics, but it is certainly one that scholars cannot ignore in a comprehensive analysis.

Nations, national identity and collective memory

Constructivist scholars argue that grasping the relationship between national identity and foreign policy is essential in order to understand international relations. Before exploring why this might be so, it is fundamental to define and explore the concepts of nation and national identity. Due to their diverse uses and their confusion with concepts such as nationalism, the terms are highly ambiguous and have generated a lively discussion among academics. The most relevant debates took place among historians and sociologists who, especially from the 1980s onwards, attempted to assess the role played by nations and national identity in international politics during modern and contemporary times.

Prominent scholars such as Ernest Gellner, Eric Hobsbawm, Benedict Anderson and Anthony D. Smith used different parameters to define nation and national identity, emphasising concrete elements (for instance territory, economy), psychological and abstract factors (memories, myths) or both. Some considered the terms too ambiguous for a precise classification and adopted only working definitions (Hobsbawm 1990), others rejected them altogether as explanatory variables (Malesevic 2011). Most treated national identity as a corollary of the nation, a collective belief in belonging to a national community and to its defining elements. Although the relationship between nation and national identity is in fact more complex, a close link exists between the two concepts. To understand national identity, we thus have to grasp the concept of nation first (see Guibernau 2004: 134; Smith 1991: 9).

One of the most widely debated definitions of nation is the one provided by Anthony D. Smith (1996a: 359): 'A named human population sharing a historic territory, common myths and memories, a mass public culture, a single economy and common rights and duties for all members'. Smith's definition provides an apparently easy way out of terminological issues: it includes both the concrete

---

3. *See* Chapters Two and Three in this volume.

and the abstract factors highlighted in previous definitions of nations. However, Smith broadens the scope of the definition at the expense of clarity: does a nation need to satisfy all these characteristics to be classified as such? Which elements are more important? Furthermore, additional terminological problems arise: what is 'a mass public culture' and what is meant by 'historic territory'? Cannot diasporas constitute or be part of a nation even though they do not share a historic territory?

Smith's definition reveals one of the main confusions that occur in debates on the nature of nations: by listing 'common rights and duties for all members' as one of their key elements, it conflates the concepts of nation and state. As Montserrat Guibernau (2004: 127) argues, judicial functions pertain to the state and are not inherent in the nation. While most nations have their own states, and thus also their own judicial systems, some do not. Furthermore, due to immigration and globalisation, many states are no longer nation-states: they include sizeable minorities that are bound by the same rights and duties and yet do not lose their distinctive identity. To avoid confusion, states and nations have to be classified differently. Borrowing from Max Weber's conceptual framework, a state can be defined on the basis of its coercive powers, namely as a body that successfully claims monopoly of legitimate force in a particular territory (cited in Miller 1997: 19–20). A state has the means to enforce its rules and a legal system to discipline those who do not comply with them.

In contrast, a nation is defined more by feelings of attachment to both concrete and abstract elements, rather than in terms of powers and prerogatives. Ernest Gellner (1983: 7), a pioneer in the study of nationalism, identified two essential components of the nation, namely a shared culture – broadly meant as a system of ideas, signs, associations and ways of behaving and communicating – and its members' mutual recognition of belonging to the same nation. Gellner stressed that nations are human artefacts, social constructions deriving from people's convictions and loyalties. Benedict Anderson (1991: 6) also focused on the constructed nature of nations and defined them as 'imagined political communities'. According to him, nations are imagined because the members of even the smallest nations will never meet most of their fellow members, but the image of belonging to a single community lives in all their minds.

Anderson argued that nations are political communities because they emerged at the same time as concepts such as popular sovereignty (namely the idea that political power rests in the hands of the people), at the time of the Enlightenment and the French Revolution. The argument that nations originated with the advent of the modern age connects them closely with nationalism, namely the political principle which holds that the political and national unit should be congruent (Gellner 1983: 1). This connection generated a lively debate among academics. According to modernists such as Ernest Gellner, Eric Hobsbawm, Montserrat Guibernau and Benedict Anderson, nations emerged in modern times because they were the product of nationalism. Conversely, ethno-symbolists such as Anthony D. Smith and John Hutchinson argued that the constitutive elements of many nations, notably their foundation myths and their ethnic and cultural heritage, predated the French Revolution and the modern age (Guibernau and Hutchinson, 2004; Smith 1996a).

The academic dispute between modernists and ethno-symbolists was arguably the longest and liveliest in the field of nationalism studies so far. It is relevant to this analysis because it highlights different ways of conceptualising the nation and national identity. Modernists claim that, from the early nineteenth century on, nationalists were successful in disseminating the concept of nation thanks to mass schooling and the standardisation of national languages (Hobsbawm 1990: 10). Nationalists carefully selected pre-existing cultural elements and branded them as defining components of the nation (Gellner 1983: 55). Hence, according to modernists, nations are constructed entities and national identity is a fabrication of the modern state, which attempts to gain the support of citizens by uniting them in a single national community (Guibernau 2004: 140).

Ethno-symbolists concur that creating national identities was one of the objectives of the nationalist movement during the nineteenth century. However, they maintain that collective memories, cultural heritage and traditions developed before the age of nationalism. According to ethno-symbolists, modern nations are not simply political constructions or imagined communities, but are founded on concrete cultural elements and tend to have strong ties to pre-modern ethnic identities. Ethnic groups are considered as the precursors of nations, having 'shared ancestry myths and memories or "ethno-history", with a strong association [...] to a historic territory or homeland' (Smith 1994: 382). The emphasis on ethnicity highlights the major weakness of the ethno-symbolist approach: in order to define the nation, it introduces other concepts that are equally ambiguous. The same criticism applies to modernist definitions, which refer to the complex phenomenon of nationalism to explain the emergence of nations and national identity. Although all these concepts are interrelated, cross-references in their classification are confusing. A clear and comprehensive definition of nation and national identity should take into account the most insightful observations of ethno-symbolists and modernists, without relying on equivocal terms.

David Miller's (1997: 18, 22–7) definition of nation provides a good starting point. According to Miller, a nation is a community with shared beliefs and mutual commitment, extended in history and connected to a particular territory. It is marked off from other nations by a distinct public culture, including political principles, social norms and cultural ideals. Like Gellner, Miller argues that members' mutual commitment and recognition of one another as compatriots is an essential precondition for the emergence of a nation. This reciprocal sense of obligation is extended over time, in the past, present and future, and ensures the historical continuity of the nation. Collective memories play an important role in this respect, as they remind the members of a nation of their forebears' presumed achievements and cultural heritage.

Collective memories are instrumental to the formation of national identities. National identity can be defined as the psychological attachment of a collective to the nation and its defining elements. Shared memories and culture are the main sustaining factors of this attachment, as they constitute the core of narratives stimulating identification with the nation (Anderson 1991: 205). As Anthony D. Smith (1996b: 383) argues, 'only by remembering the past can a collective identity come into being'. Collective memories provide the 'cognitive maps and mobilising moralities of nations as they struggle to win and maintain recognition' (Smith 1988: 14). According to Smith (1996b: 384–5), vital elements of the nation such as its drive for regeneration, the sense of national authenticity, collective mission and national destiny depend on collective memory. Similarly, Eric Hobsbawm and David Kertzer (1992: 3) argue that 'nations without a past are contradictions in terms. What makes a nation *is* the past; what justifies one nation against others is the past'.

Table 1.1: Definitions: nation and national identity

Nation: a community with shared beliefs and mutual commitment, extended in history and connected to a particular territory. It is marked off from other nations by a distinct public culture, including shared political principles, social norms and cultural ideals.

National identity: the psychological attachment of a collective to the nation and its defining elements.

Source: author's own compilation

The politics of memory and national identity

While Hobsbawm and Smith are right to emphasise the importance of the past for national identity, the way in which a nation remembers its past is more complex and ambiguous than their statements might suggest. In fact, the collective memory and the past of a nation are fundamentally different concepts. The term 'collective memory' refers to the shared memories held by a community about the past (Hunt 2010: 97), an image of the past constructed by a subjectivity in the present (Megill 2011: 196). Collective memory is a discourse about historical events and how to interpret them, based on a community's current social and historical necessities (Arnold-de Simine 2005: 10; Pakier and Stråth 2010: 7). It is neither merely an accurate reflection of the past, nor the product of historical research. As Maurice Halbwachs (1992) argues, collective memories are socially framed: they form when people come together to remember and enter a domain that transcends individual memory. According to Andreas Huyssen (2003: 6), collective memory is also essential to imagine the future and give a strong temporal and spatial grounding to life.

The study of collective memory is of particular relevance at institutional level (Lebow 2006: 13–14). Political elites formulate or adopt selective discourses of past events in order to forge national identities that strengthen social cohesion. In particular, politicians try to forge national memories, a particular type of collective memory where the collective coincides with the nation (Gillis 1994: 7). National memory is disseminated primarily via political leaders' official discourses and commemorations in the realms of memory (*lieux de mémoire*), namely historical or pseudo-historical sites that are reminiscent of selected events in national memory

(Nora 1992: 7). This does not preclude the role of other unofficial actors in the forging of national memory. Individual or other group memories coexist side by side with official national memories and often influence them. However, political leaders play a decisive role in the construction and diffusion of national memory because they have easier access to mass media, which makes them highly influential. Richard Ned Lebow, Wulf Kansteiner and Claudio Fogu (2006) call the selection and dissemination of discourses on a country's past 'the politics of memory'. It involves actors using their public prominence to propagate narratives about the past which are functional to their political goals (Lebow 2006: 26–8).

Memory matters politically because it can be used by the political establishment as a source of legitimacy for its power. For instance, policy makers can make reference to events that play an important role in national memory and construct plausible historical analogies to obtain support for their policies (Bell 2006: 20; Gildea 2002a: 59; Koczanowicz 1997: 260; König 2008: 27–34; Olick 2007: 122). The inherent ambiguity of collective memories, which are in constant flux, facilitates their manipulation and mobilisation in the service of national identity formation (Berger 2002: 81; Müller 2002: 21–2; Ray 2006: 144). As Jay Winter and Emmanuel Sivan (1999: 6) have noted, political elites manipulated the past on a massive scale during the twentieth century. Manipulations of national history took place in particular after wars and regime changes, when states and new political elites attempted to restore social cohesion. Following major social dislocations, political elites tend to formulate and propagate official narratives that reflect their view of history and exclude all events and elements that do not fit with it (Hunt 2010: 110). They construct national histories as triumphant narratives, a selective retelling of the past based on accounts that stimulate strong identification with the nation (Eder 2005: 214–15).

Due to the constant influence of a multiplicity of political, historical and social factors, collective memories are not fixed; they undergo a process of gradual change and adaptation. As Pierre Nora (1989: 8) argues, national memories are constantly constructed and reconstructed in a selective way; they are 'in permanent evolution, a perpetually present phenomenon'. During the last twenty to thirty years, this process has been fuelled by a dramatic upsurge in public memory debates in North American and European societies (Huyssen 2003: 12–15). Politicians have attempted to intervene and guide these debates in a way that suited and served both their political aspirations and their conception of national identity (Gillis 1994: 3; Müller 2002: 23; Smith 2011: 235).

A widespread use of the politics of memory to forge national identities took place in almost all European countries immediately after the Second World War and again after 1989 in most East-Central European countries, following the collapse of the Soviet bloc (Assmann 2006: 260; Evans 2003: 5; Judt 1992: 96).[4] Both in 1945 and 1989, the new political elites that emerged from the ordeal of war

---

4. Following the classification adopted by Konrad Jarausch (2010: 310–11), in this book East-Central Europe includes EU member states that were located in the Soviet sphere of influence during the Cold War (Poland, the Czech Republic, Slovakia, Hungary, Romania, Bulgaria) or were part of the Soviet Union (Lithuania, Latvia and Estonia).

and from regime change needed founding myths to strengthen social cohesion at a time of economic dislocation and transformation from authoritarian to democratic forms of government (Müller 2002: 7–9). This political necessity led new leaders to search for a 'usable past' in national history and reframe it in narratives that propped up present political goals (Moeller 2003).

The national memories that were constructed in Western Europe after 1945 and in East-Central Europe after 1989 constitute the core of current national memory discourses. This is due to the fact that many of the founding myths of today's national political systems in Europe date back to these two historical moments. In countries such as the ones under analysis in this work, the images of Russia that crystallised in national memories during these periods, partly continuing pre-existing perceptions and partly based on new elements, influenced the process of national identity construction. Thus, particular perceptions of Russia as a foreign policy actor have become enshrined in national consciousness and still affect attitudes to Moscow.[5]

National memory can be conceptualised as an essential component and driving factor of national identity. Unsurprisingly, the two concepts share many of their essential features. Like national memories, national identities are multiple, malleable, contested and provide a powerful instrument for the political elites that have enough power to manipulate them. Their multiplicity derives from different conceptions of national identity across the large and diverse national community. However, states tend to propagate one particular narrative of national identity, which becomes dominant in official discourses. Individual and other group identities coexist and interact with officially endorsed versions of national identity, thereby creating alternative and competing variants that can become dominant within new historical and institutional contexts.[6]

National identities are malleable because they are influenced by domestic and external events and can change over time. Changes usually take place gradually; core constituents such as the founding myths and cultural frameworks of reference of the nation (notably in literature, the arts and music) are relatively stable. However, sudden changes in national identity discourses may also occur, particularly when historical events force upon the nation a reconsideration of its values and interests.[7] Moreover, national identities are contested because they are subject to manipulation by social groups vying for dominance and because they compete for people's allegiance with class, religious, local and supranational identities (Miller 1997: 45–6). Narratives of national identity tend to be used as political instruments because they are generally formulated and propagated by the state in order to strengthen and legitimate the existing political system (Guibernau 2004: 140).

---

5. The analysis of different national perceptions of Russia is beyond the scope of this chapter. However, Chapter Four provides a thorough discussion of Russia's role in German, Polish and Finnish collective memory and identity.

6. For instance, as shown in Chapter Four, unofficial narratives of national identity in pre-1989 Poland became part of official discourses following the fall of communism.

7. Germany after the Second World War provides a good example in this respect.

Political leaders are both the main advocates and beneficiaries of national identity construction. National identity promotes homogeneity in a community because it cuts across class and local differences and transcends divisions of rank, descent, region and profession. It therefore helps to create a strong bond between political leaders and ordinary citizens, as well as among different sections of the population (Benner 2001: 162; Greenfeld 1990: 550).

Since national identity provides a very useful tool for the unity and cohesiveness of a state, governments employ several strategies to promote it. They disseminate a specific image of the nation that usually relates to the dominant ethnic group. In addition, they confer citizenship and encourage numerous symbols and rituals that serve the purpose of reinforcing the sense of community among citizens, as well as their loyalty towards the state. National identity is constructed also through the steering of public education and the mass media. This phenomenon is particularly marked in authoritarian states but also exists in democratic countries.

Furthermore, states often attempt to strengthen national identity by creating external enemies (Guibernau 2004: 140). For instance, France and Germany constructed each other as external threats for nearly a century (from the 1860s to the 1940s) and used the image of the menacing neighbour to foster national unity in moments of crisis. Past rivalries in Franco-German relations left a trace in national identity that influenced the political debate at a later stage, as shown by the French reservations about German reunification in 1989–90 (Gildea 2002b). Similar patterns of national identity formation against an external Other, namely an actor that tends to be perceived as alien and antithetical, can be detected *inter alia* in Soviet–US, US–Chinese and Europe–Russia relations.[8]

Russia as Europe's Other

As Iver Neumann (1998: 67–112) has shown, numerous primary sources suggest that Russia has played the role of Europe's Other for more than four centuries.[9] This is not to say that Russia was the only or the main Other for Europe throughout this long historical phase. Discourses on Russia were not homogeneous all over the continent and differed depending inter alia on the social milieu, political orientation and personal experiences of observers. Nevertheless, numerous and significant patterns consistently pointing at Russia as Europe's Other can be detected throughout this period. Studying these patterns is essential and of current relevance because Russia is still central to national identity discourses and to

---

8. *See* Chapter Two in this volume for a theoretical discussion of 'othering' and of the construction of the Other.

9. On the other hand, during this period Russian leaders never questioned their country's European-ness. The often-quoted dispute between Russian 'Westernisers' and 'Slavophiles' concerned the question of whether Western Europe should serve as a role model for Russia or if Russia itself should become the leader of European (and world) civilisation. None of the sides in this controversy questioned Russia's European nature, even if some Slavophiles placed it within a broader Eurasian framework and attributed to it a global civilising mission (Tsygankov 2008: 766–70).

the debate on European identity. Analysing dominant perceptions of Russia also helps to understand present political discussions, such as the one concerning the European security order (Webber 2009).

European depictions of Russia show a tendency to portray it as a liminal case of European identity. Russians were often depicted as barbarous and deficient in terms of civility, form of government and religion (Poe 2003: 21). The first depictions of Russia as 'the barbarian at the gates', a recurrent theme in European discourses of the powerful Eastern neighbour, emerged in the descriptions of Russian soldiers during the Northern War against Sweden in the early eighteenth century. Around the same time, geographical handbooks argued that Russians were constructed as 'body and nature', whereas Europeans were constructed as 'mind and civilization'. The metaphor of the Russian *ursa major*, which associated Russia with wild nature, originated in this context. Its endurance over time is demonstrated by the fact that it is still used today in modern variants, most notably the depiction of Russia as a threatening and irascible bear (Naarden 1992: 7–27; Neumann 1998: 67–80).

During the Napoleonic wars, Russian soldiers advanced as far as Paris and, after Napoleon's defeat, Russia was accepted as a legitimate player in the Concert of Europe. However, this acceptance was relativised by the enduring perception of Russia as 'the barbarian at the gates', a country that lacked the rationality which had become a defining element of European civilisation during the Enlightenment. European liberals, democrats and socialists were particularly keen on describing Russia as a socially and economically backward power. Conversely, conservative forces saw it as a bulwark of legitimism and of the European *ancien régime* (Neumann 1998: 66–93, 96–7). The Bolshevik revolution inverted radical and conservative views of Russia. The Bolsheviks' radical political programme made the Soviet Union a threat to conservative political elites in the rest of Europe throughout the interwar period. The threat was substantiated by the fact that the Soviet Union could count on the extraterritorial presence of faithful allies, organised in European communist parties. On the other hand, numerous European radicals praised the political and economic system of the USSR, as well as the allegedly higher morality of the Soviet model (Naarden 1992: 28–39; Neumann 1998: 99–102; Service 2007: 85–96).

During the Second World War, the idea of the Russians as a barbarous civilisation was pushed to the extreme by the Nazi racial discourse, which depicted them and all other Slavic peoples as sub-humans (*Untermenschen*). The idea that Russians should be excluded from humankind, and not just from Europe, was radically new (Müller and Ueberschär 2009: 209–52). However, there was continuity between some themes used by Nazi propaganda and pre-existing discourses about Russians, such as the claim that they were a barbarous and uncivilised Asiatic people. Some of these themes also characterised discourses about the Soviet Union in the post-war period; Konrad Adenauer's 1946 statement that 'Asia stands on the Elbe' (cited in Rupnik 1994: 94) provides an excellent example in this respect. Adenauer referred to the presence of the Red Army in Eastern and Central Europe, which became one of the main determinants of

European perceptions of the Soviet Union during the Cold War. While in the inter-war period the Soviet Union had been mostly perceived as a political threat, during the Cold War it primarily constituted a military threat in the mindsets of most West Europeans. The perception of a political threat persisted in the immediate post-war period, but gradually decreased as communist parties in Western Europe lost their appeal or became critical of the Soviet Union (Neumann 1998: 99–100; Service 2007: 261–71, 379–90).

The Cold War also played an important role in the construction of European perceptions of Russia because it became the setting in which a distinct East–Central European narrative developed. This discourse, fiercely critical of both the Soviet Union and of its perceived Russian core, emerged in East–Central European countries that were located within the Soviet sphere of influence and was reflected in the writings of dissident intellectuals from the region. Milan Kundera's (1984) article 'The tragedy of Central Europe' is the most representative of these writings. Kundera, a Czech writer living in exile in France, argued that Central Europe (in which he included the nations of the former Austro-Hungarian Empire and Poland) was a part of the West that had been 'kidnapped, displaced and brainwashed [by the] totalitarian Russian civilisation'. According to Kundera, Central Europe was the cultural heart of Europe and its separation from Western Europe meant that the latter was losing its cultural identity. On the other hand, Central Europe kept defending its identity and 'preserving its Western-ness' despite the Soviet domination. The main difference between Central Europe and Russia, Kundera argued, was above all cultural, as demonstrated by the fact that the anti-Soviet revolts of 1956 and 1968 were led by local students and intellectuals. One of the key objectives in Kundera's article was that of drawing the attention of the Western world towards the oppression of East–Central European countries under Soviet influence. In order to show that these countries culturally belonged to Europe while Soviet Russia did not, he described the former as the 'vital centre of gravity of Western culture' and the latter as 'the radical negation of the modern West'.

Kundera's views on Russia were echoed by other intellectuals from East–Central Europe. Different epithets, such as 'Second World', 'authoritarian' and 'totalitarian' (as opposed to 'First World', 'democratic' and 'free'), were associated with Soviet Russia in order to differentiate it from Europe and the West. Some extreme voices in the intellectual world used racial arguments against Russia. For instance, Hungarian philosopher Mihaly Vajda (1989: 170–3) argued that Russia had made the choice to become non-European and that Russians were 'incapable of tolerating another civilization, another form of life'. Vajda also spoke of 'the Russian beast' and Russian practices of 'holocaust, imprisonment, banishment, exile', forgetting that the Holocaust was actually a page of European history, rather than a Russian crime, and that its perpetrators had spoken of Russia in a way very similar to his own.

In 1989, when the communists were ousted from their posts and the Soviet Union left its satellites free to choose their political future, new East–Central European political leaders such as Vaclav Havel started to speak of a 'return to Europe' (cited in Powers 1990). However, it soon became clear that the Central Europe to which Kundera had referred in his 1984 essay had not emerged from the Cold War as a united political or cultural entity. East–Central European countries had only managed to pass themselves off as a united entity vis-à-vis third parties by using the image of the Soviet Union as a common Other. After 1989, the new East–Central European leaders emphasised cultural differences between their countries and Russia, with the objective of creating a Self compatible with Western Europe and strenuously opposed to Russia. This strategy was meant to create the cultural preconditions, both at home and abroad, for the integration of East–Central European countries into the EU and NATO (Neumann 1998: 144, 158).

When East–Central European states joined the European Union, they brought along the legacy of four decades of resentment and confrontation with Soviet Russia. In some cases, notably those of Poland and the three Baltic States, anti-Russian feelings dated back to much earlier than the Cold War period. Anti-Russian discourses and attitudes in these countries did not vanish once their 'return to Europe' had been accomplished. Historical conflicts, the enduring fear of a resurgent Russian military might and economic issues, aggravated by the energy dependence of East–Central Europe on Russia, continued to characterise the relations of the former Soviet satellites with Moscow. Furthermore, conflicts between the new East–Central European EU member states and Russia were transferred to the EU level and risked paralysing EU–Russia relations. Poland's decision to veto negotiations on a new partnership agreement between the EU and Russia in 2006, following a quarrel over a Russian import ban on Polish meat, was the clearest manifestation of this.

Structure of the book

This introductory chapter has presented the main research themes and highlighted the significance of the topic under analysis and the intended theoretical and empirical contribution of the book. It has defined key concepts, namely those of nation, national identity and collective memory. It has also introduced the European context of the topic and showed that Russia was traditionally perceived as Other by the rest of Europe. Furthermore, the chapter has argued for the necessity of exploring identities and discourses on Russia at the national level due to the fragmented nature of European history, politics and identity construction. The next chapter examines in greater detail the significance of the Other in identity construction. It provides a survey of relevant debates in international relations theory and a theoretical framework for the ensuing empirical analysis. The focus is on social constructivist scholarship, which emphasises the importance of concepts such as identity, the construction of Others and collective memory to understand international relations. The chapter also outlines the features of DHA, the methodology adopted in this study. Subsequently, it explains and justifies the selection of case studies and of the sources for the analysis of discourses on Russia.

Chapter Three examines national identity construction in Germany, Poland and Finland, with a special focus on Russia's role as Other. It takes a *longue durée* perspective that follows the construction of national identity in the three countries approximately from the nineteenth century until the present. This perspective allows an investigation of how Russia was internalised in national identity starting from the emergence of modern national identities, with a focus on the historical events that mark key fractures in the selected countries' process of identity formation and relations with Russia. The *longue durée* approach best fits the study of national identity construction, which took place slowly, over a long time span. Dominant themes in identity discourses and discourses on Russia over time are identified and provide an interpretive key for the subsequent analysis of policy makers' discourses on Russia from 2005 to 2015. Chapters Four to Seven analyse policy makers' discourses on Russia in the selected countries in response to four major events in which Russia was a prominent actor: the controversies surrounding the construction of the Nord Stream pipeline; the 2008 Russian–Georgian war; the street protests that followed the December 2011 parliamentary elections in Russia; and the Ukraine crisis that started in the fall of 2013 and escalated with Russia's annexation of Crimea in February–March 2014.

The analysis of the relationship between these discourses and national identity constitutes the main empirical contribution of the book. It sheds light on how conceptions of Russia framed within national identity relate to contemporary foreign policy discourses, and how the latter in turn contribute to the consolidation or change of the images of Russia enshrined in national identity and memory. Furthermore, the book explores the interaction of German, Polish and Finnish leaders' discourses on Russia in the European discursive arena, and thus offers insights into the deeper, national identity roots of European foreign policy discourse. The empirical chapters also include a comparative analysis of the findings. Drawing on the comparative analysis, the concluding chapter assesses the prospects for the emergence of a shared foreign policy discourse on Russia in the EU.

Chapter Two

Theorising National Identity and Foreign Policy

This chapter outlines the theoretical and methodological framework of the book. It first explores the conceptualisation of identity in the three main grand theories of International Relations, namely neorealism, neoliberalism and social constructivism. Drawing on social constructivist literature, it presents an interpretive theoretical model that conceptualises the relationship between identity, interests and foreign policy as mutually constitutive. The chapter discusses how this relationship is studied at the discursive level, through discourse-historical analysis (DHA). Finally, it illustrates the selection of three national discursive arenas and four case studies for the investigation of official narratives concerning Russia.

National identity and European foreign policy towards Russia

As highlighted in the previous chapter, Russia is arguably the most divisive issue in European foreign policy. Divergent views often emerge when EU member states are required to formulate a foreign policy response to a major event that sees Russia as a protagonist. Different opinions have frequently led EU member states to pursue bilateral relations with Russia, rather than coordinating their policies at EU level. The response of EU member states to the 2008 Russian–Georgian war, to Moscow's energy policies and to its concerns over NATO Eastern enlargement provide prime examples of diverging European approaches to Russia (David *et al.* 2013). Despite belonging to a single economic and defence community, EU member states perceive Russia differently, particularly with regard to their security interests. The reasons for these differences go beyond neoliberal and neorealist theorisations of institutional cooperation or interstate relations in an anarchic and hostile environment. They must be investigated at the domestic level, where national identities and interests are constructed and discourses on Russia are formulated.[1]

The constructivist school of thought defines the politics of identity as one of the keys to understanding how a country's domestic dynamics interact with and affect global politics (Hopf 1998: 192). Constructivists treat identities and interests as endogenous to interaction, whereas neoliberals and neorealists consider them as exogenously given and constant. For neoliberals and neorealists,

---

1. As Henry Nau (2002: 16) argues, national interests 'begin with what kind of society the nation is, not just what its geopolitical circumstances are'.

states have uncomplicated and unchanging identities and interests, which neither affect nor are influenced by agents and structures (Laffey and Weldes 1997: 193–237; Waltz 1979). Neoliberals investigated the significance of norms and ideas in international relations, but did not explain whether and how they play a role in identity construction. Neoliberal studies tend to consider ideas and norms only as intervening factors between states seeking self-help in the anarchic international system and their subsequent actions (Wæver 2002: 21). Neoliberal approaches largely neglect the domestic level of analysis and the function that the domestic constituency plays in the formulation of foreign policy preferences. Hence, neoliberalism does not provide solid theoretical foundations to analyse the domestic construction of national identity and its interaction with international politics.

Neorealism also focuses on structures and treats states as monoliths, unproblematic units that follow the logic of self-help and power-balancing in an anarchic international environment (see Waltz 1979: 102–28). The neorealist approach to international relations does not attribute any role to domestic and social factors such as national identity in foreign policy making. Due to the lack of attention to these factors, neorealism offers a static view of international politics and is unable to explain change, particularly peaceful change (Ruggie 1998: 874–5). This deficiency is due also to the neorealists' inability to articulate a convincing framework to understand the formulation of state interests. State interests cannot be derived from the condition of anarchy, as neorealists claim, because anarchy is an ambiguous concept. In fact, neorealism handles interest formation by assumption (Ruggie 1998: 862–9).

Moreover, neorealism oversimplifies the process of preference formation and decision making. Decision makers are not always rational, as neorealists tend to assume (Legro and Moravcsik 1999: 53). They may rely on heuristics, the logic of appropriateness (Müller 2004) and the logic of practice (Pouliot 2008), in which the decision-making process is deeply influenced by the social embeddedness of actors, their identity and other cultural elements. Thus, decision-making processes are best studied within a constructivist framework that analyses the multifaceted, malleable and complex nature of identities, as well as their mutually constitutive relationship with agents and structures (Checkel 2008: 72). Table 2.1 summarises the different conceptualisations of identity in the main approaches of International Relations theory and highlights its central role in social constructivism.

National identity tends to be constructed in relation to one or more significant Others, namely actors in the international environment that are perceived as different or antithetical by the nation (or Self). It operates as a cognitive device that provides a state with an understanding of other countries, their motives, interests, probable actions and attitudes (Hopf 2002: 5). Language and discourses play an essential role in the construction of national identity and its significant Others. Dominant identity discourses are the cognitive structures through which policy makers formulate national interests and take foreign policy decisions. A country's leaders, particularly its political and intellectual elites, are the primary agents and interpreters of national identity construction, as they shape and are influenced by

Table 2.1: Conceptualisation of identity in the main theories of International Relations

	Neorealism/neoliberalism	Social constructivism
	Exogenous to theory	Endogenous to theory
	Constant	Fluid, malleable
	Does not influence agents and structures	Shapes and constitutes agents and structures
Conceptualisation of identity	Does not affect state interests, which are derived from the anarchic international system	Shapes and constitutes state interests
	Has no influence on rational decision makers	It is a cognitive device that influences decision makers' motives, actions and understanding of the world

Source: author's own compilation.

the dominant discourses of the national environments in which they are embedded (Checkel 2006: 63; Lebow 2008a: 556–64).[2]

National identity, the Other and Wendtian constructivist research

The concept of identity has been discussed widely in constructivist scholarship. The term originates from social psychology, where it describes the individuality and distinctiveness of an actor (the Self) in its evolving relations with significant Others (Jepperson *et al.* 1996: 59). Alexander Wendt transposed the concept to international relations theory and argued that identities are relatively stable (albeit subject to change in the long run) role-specific understandings and expectations about an actor that are constructed in interactions with other actors. The type of social structure that prevails in the international system depends on how actors construct their identity in relation to others. Relatively stable identities and expectations about each other develop as a result of continuous interaction (Wendt 1994: 384–96).

According to Wendt (1999), national identity formation happens at state level, but it is also influenced by international structures. In the international arena, countries define the boundaries of their Selves and those of their respective Others so as to consolidate their distinctive national traits. National interests are rooted in national identity, because an actor 'cannot know what it wants until it knows who

2.   As Jeffrey Checkel (2006: 63) argues, agents are persuasive because they are authoritative, but also 'because they are enabled and legitimated by the broader social discourse in which they are embedded'.

it is' (Wendt 1999: 231).[3] In particular, national identity determines the interests of a state based on how other actors are perceived (Wendt 1999; cf. Adler 1997, Hopf 1998). Such perceptions are profoundly influenced by historical interaction between the state and its Others. An actor that has played the role of Other over a protracted historical period becomes internalised as such in a country's national memory (Barnett 1996: 446; Lebow 2006: 3; Smith 1992: 58). In the national memory of several European states, Russia has been internalised as a significant Other (Lebow 2008a: 10; Neumann and Medvedev 2012: 13). Together with Turkey, Russia constituted the main Other against which identities were constructed in early modern and modern Europe (Neumann 1998). The concept of otherness is thus fundamental to understand Russia's role in national identity construction in European states.

The antithesis between Self and Other is a central theme in modern philosophy, social anthropology, psychology and literary theory (Neumann 1996: 141–54). In the early nineteenth century, Hegel (1999: 15–20) argued that the citizens of a state develop a collective identity as a result of conflicts with other states. In the second half of the century, Nietzsche elaborated on Hegel's thinking and stated that Self and Other are not fixed elements, but perceive each other from changing perspectives (cited in Neumann 1998: 148). Following the same line of argument, a century later Carl Schmitt (1976) claimed that political identities can best be formed in struggles against others. During the last twenty years, the dichotomy between Self and Other became a pivotal topic in International Relations theory. David Campbell (1998: 191–205) attempted to explain US foreign policy as a continuous search for new collectives to treat as Others in order to consolidate national identity and rally domestic support. Campbell argued that, following the demise of the Soviet Union, Washington identified new Others in Saddam Hussein's Iraq and China. Writing a decade later, Richard Ned Lebow (2008a: 11) asserted that American domestic and foreign policy after the terrorist attacks of 9 September 2001 showed how easy it was for political leaders to exploit the fear of Others to create solidarity at home.[4]

Ole Wæver (2002) analysed the relationship between Self and Other from an interpretive constructivist perspective, focusing on the role of discourses. According to Wæver, a collective Self is predicated on some essential political ideas, such as what constitutes a state or a nation. The Self attempts to make these ideas the core of institutionalisation in political cooperation, which produces discursive clashes with the Other. Wæver argued that these conflicts can be studied as the substance of world politics in an alternative, identity-based approach to

---

3. To emphasise the tight correlation between identity and interests, Wendt (1999: 231–2) also claims that 'interests are needs or functional imperatives which must be fulfilled if an identity is to be reproduced'.

4. The popularity of Samuel Huntington's (1997) work on the 'clash of civilisations' has shown that the dichotomy of Self/Other has become a pervasive theme in public debates. Huntington's book in itself was evidence that othering could be used as a deliberate policy to strengthen national identities.

foreign policy analysis. Further studies investigated specific aspects of the Self/ Other dichotomy. Erik Ringmar (1996: 80) highlighted the active participation of the Other in an actor's identity construction. He claimed that Others are the main recipients of the Self's narratives and determine whether such narratives are a valid description of the Self through interaction. Jennifer Mitzen (2006: 341–70) studied the use of Others in the framework of ontological security. She contended that states become dependent on security dilemmas[5] due to their reliance on routines that help consolidate their identities in relation to significant Others.

Elaborating on Wendt's theoretical framework, the essays in Peter Katzenstein's (1996) edited volume 'The Culture of National Security' further investigated the dichotomy between Self and Other. Most importantly, they offer crucial insights for the study of the relationship between identity and foreign policy. In an introductory essay, Katzenstein, Wendt and Ronald Jepperson argued that cultural and institutional elements of states' domestic and global environments shape national identity. Variations in national identity determine the security interests and policies of a state and in turn affect normative structures, namely culture and institutions (Jepperson *et al.* 1996: 53–65). These relationships can be summarised in the following model:

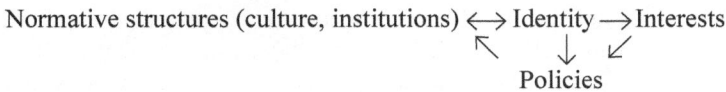

Normative structures (culture, institutions) $\longleftrightarrow$ Identity $\longrightarrow$ Interests

$$\nwarrow \quad \downarrow \quad \swarrow$$

Policies

As the model shows, identity influences policies through the determination of interests, but it can also shape policies directly as a result of a state's identity politics. The case studies in Katzenstein's volume provide convincing empirical evidence for the model. Among these, Thomas Berger's work (Katzenstein 1996: 318) argued that, because of historical experiences and how these are interpreted by domestic political actors, Germany and Japan have developed national identities which make them reluctant to resort to the use of military force.[6] Berger showed that German and Japanese post-1945 identity politics, notably the decision to construct an antimilitaristic national identity, had a direct impact both on policy making and on the domestic institutional context where defence policy is formulated (see also Bjola and Kornprobst 2007).

Robert Herman's (1996) essay on Soviet foreign policy in the late 1980s showed the interrelation between identity construction, the formation of interests and the formulation of foreign policy. Herman argued that the end of the Cold War was a consequence of Gorbachev's new thinking, which caused a radical reconceptualisation of state interests. This redefinition was determined by the

---

5. Security dilemmas refer to a condition in which one state's gain in security decreases the security of other actors (Jervis 1978: 169–70).

6. Events with enduring significance for a country, such as the Second World War for Germany and Japan, create dominant collective memories that allow the mobilisation of national identities in particular directions (Liu and Hilton 2005: 545).

emergence of a new identity in some post-Brezhnev Soviet elites, who thought that Soviet interests could best be served by overcoming the East–West division and by cooperating with the US to achieve peace and stability. The new Soviet thinking allowed progress in arms control, produced a peaceful response to the revolutions in Central and Eastern Europe and led to a democratic shift in Soviet political culture and institutions. Thus, Herman's work illustrated the effects that changes in identity can have on normative structures.

Also in Katzenstein's volume, Michael Barnett's analysis of alliances in the Middle East showed that the politics of identity often offers a better explanation than the realist logic of anarchy of the mechanisms that lead a state to identify partners and threats to its security. Most notably, Barnett (1996: 401) claimed that there is a correlation between an actor's identity and its strategic behaviour. Furthermore, Thomas Risse-Kappen's essay (1996: 397) argued that collective identities based on shared democratic values ensure the longevity of institutions and applied this logic to explain the endurance of NATO after the end of the Cold War. According to Risse-Kappen, the longevity of NATO could hardly be understood following the realist logic of balancing, as the fall of the Soviet Union meant the disappearance of the superpower which the Atlantic Alliance was supposed to balance.

Other scholars elaborated on the theoretical framework developed in Katzenstein's edited volume. Richard Ned Lebow (2008a) showed that identity construction can explain events which have traditionally been analysed in terms of power and rational choice, such as the Cuban missile crisis (see Allison and Zelikow 1999). Lebow argued that individuals, armies and political elites are committed to asserting and maintaining their identities. To achieve this purpose, they use all available means and power, which Lebow conceived not simply as material power, but also as immaterial capabilities.[7] Lebow (2008a: 552–7) also claimed that actors are reluctant to behave in ways and take decisions that do not conform to their identities, even when such behaviours and decisions appear more rational. Policies that are at odds with national identity create domestic conflict and weaken decision makers' legitimacy at home.

As Ted Hopf (2002) argued, decision makers are embedded in social cognitive structures that are shaped by national identity. National identity and political elites (the decision makers par excellence) are mutually constitutive: the latter are influenced by, contribute to create, and act based on the former (cf. Jepperson et al. 1996: 51). Hence, determining dominant identity discourses is an essential component of national politics. At the domestic level, political elites vie for control over the discursive power that is necessary to produce meaning and acquire legitimacy in a national group. However, their behaviour is also influenced by supranational structures. In particular, their foreign policy decisions are constrained and empowered by prevailing social practices both at home and abroad (Checkel 1998: 343–4; Hopf 1998: 179–96).

---

7. For instance, the authority to determine the official discourses that constitute the identity and interests of a state (see Adler 1997: 336).

The complexity of identity construction: criticism of the Wendtian approach

In order to refine the theoretical model that will be applied to this study, the most relevant criticism of the Wendtian approach will be examined and integrated in the model. This criticism concerns primarily Wendt's lack of attention to the domestic level, his positivist approach, the complexity of the use of Others in identity construction and the necessity to take into account material factors in identity-based theoretical models.

Maja Zehfuss (2001) argued that Wendt's definition of identity is problematic because it lacks complexity and does not take into consideration the domestic processes of articulation of state identity. According to Zehfuss, Wendt focused more on the boundaries of the Self than on its internal construction. He neglected identity construction at the domestic level to focus on social identities at the systemic level (see Checkel 1998: 341).[8] Zehfuss claimed that identity cannot be merely negotiated between states. Hence, the social construction of actors' identities must be studied at both the systemic and the domestic level. As Ted Hopf (1998: 196) argued, any state identity in world politics reflects the social practices that constitute identity at home. Identity politics in the domestic arena enable and constrain identity, interests and actions abroad.

Zehfuss also criticised Wendt's positivist approach. She claimed that the scientific identification of causal mechanisms cannot be applied to social sciences because identities are not logically bounded entities. They are continuously rearticulated and contested; they can be complex and multiple, which makes it difficult to use them as variables or as explanatory categories. Due to the nature and complexity of national identities, tracing direct causal links between them and foreign policy is not possible. The interaction and mutually constitutive relationship between national identities and foreign policy is best analysed as a fluid, multifaceted phenomenon.

In Wendt's theory, epistemological issues are compounded by ontological oversimplifications, such as those regarding the essence and role of the Other in national identity construction. Wendtian constructivists tend to exaggerate the significance of threatening Others. Their theorisation of a highly conflictual relationship between the Self and threatening Others has become a source of inspiration for some realists too. Alastair Iain Johnston (1999) integrated the identity variable in a realpolitik model. According to Johnston, a perceived threat to the legitimacy of the Self's cohesion, organisation and values leads to an increase in the intensity of its identity. As a result, the Self adopts a more competitive behaviour towards the Other and reacts to the threat in a realpolitik fashion. For instance, the Self becomes more sensitive and reactive to the growth of the Other's relative material capabilities as the intensity of its identity increases.

---

8.   Wendt (1994: 387) hinted at the importance of the domestic level when he argued that states depend heavily on their society for political survival. However, he failed to follow up this argument with an in-depth analysis of the relevance of domestic politics.

Johnston applied this model to explain Chinese reactions to the June 1989 protests in China, which the country's leadership portrayed as an American-led attempt to overthrow socialism and 'exterminate China' (1999: 295). At the same time as the increase in the intensity of Chinese identity discourses, Beijing raised its military expenditure and thus reacted in a realpolitik fashion to the perceived threat. Johnston's model offers an interesting perspective to explore the relationship between Chinese identity and foreign policy. However, it is marred by several fundamental weaknesses. It does not analyse identity in its complexity, but merely in terms of intensity. Furthermore, as Johnston acknowledged, there is no good indicator for the intensity of identity. He also conceded that Chinese realpolitik has deeper roots than the intensification of national identity after 1989. Furthermore, in his model identity construction is described exclusively as a process of 'devaluing external others and portraying the external environment as conflictual' (1999: 295).

However, Richard Ned Lebow (2008a) has shown that identity is not always constructed against or to exclude others. It can also form prior to the construction of the Other. In addition, the Other is not necessarily associated with negative stereotypes; positive interaction also occurs. As Ted Hopf (2002: 7) contended, identities are always relational (we understand them only by relating them to other identities) but only sometimes oppositional. Furthermore, Lebow (2008b: 473–92) convincingly argued that cultural and other differences can be overcome through assimilation and allegiance to a common humanity, which allows transcending the dichotomy between Self and Other. For instance, prominent German intellectuals such as Kant and Hegel constructed the German Self by incorporating crucial elements of the French Other (Lebow 2008a: 12). Ancient Roman identity was also built by assimilating numerous cultural elements from Greek and other civilisations.[9]

Following Lebow's argument, Erik Gartzke and Kristian Gleditsch (2006) showed that culture and identity may influence international disputes in a way that runs counter to conventional beliefs. In a study on identity and conflict, they argued that conflict is more likely among states with closer cultural ties. Hopf (2002: 8) concurred with this argument and claimed that the closest Other is often perceived as the most threatening antagonist, as it may be able to replace the Self more easily than any alternative. This conceptualisation helps explain the conflicts of the Soviet Union with communist China and Yugoslavia during the Cold War. Chinese and Yugoslav communists were condemned in Soviet discourses because they proposed a different way to the construction of state socialism, thereby challenging Moscow's primacy in the communist camp.

Lebow (2008a: 476–86) conceded that abundant historical evidence highlights the construction of a stereotyped and negative Other in conjunction with national identity formation. He also stated explicitly that Russia was mostly treated as a

---

9.   Conversely, groups or elements considered at the core of a community's identity can lose their status and even become threatening Others. Shifting US colonists' perceptions of Britain during the eighteenth century provide a good example in this respect (Lebow 2008b: 487-8).

cultural and political Other in the construction of European society. However, his warning against assuming that the Other always has negative connotations remains valid. Empirical studies have shown that Russia's role as a negative Other for Europe has often been exaggerated. Iver Neumann (1998: 67–80) has documented that Russia was portrayed as a liminal case of European identity: at times, Europeans perceived it as a threatening Other, but occasionally it was considered as a full and valuable member of the European family of nations.[10]

Both when Russia was constructed as a threatening Other and as part of the European Self, its considerable power in the international scene constituted an essential determinant of these constructions. Hence, as Ole Wæver (2002) argued, both ideational and material factors must be taken into account in the analysis of the Self/Other dichotomy. The relationship between ideas and material factors is dialectical. Material power acquires significance only in particular discursive constructions that define it as, for instance, threatening or not. As Wæver (2002: 22) noted, Wendt neglected the material aspect, which turned his theoretical approach into a culturalist explanation for inertia and continuity. The Wendtian approach is therefore unable to explain material interests and the complexity of evolving foreign policy beyond historical narrative.

A model for analysis: discursive relations between identity and foreign policy

Foreign policy discourses can be studied through a theoretical framework that allows an investigation of how they mutually interact with national identity construction. Some research on this subject has relied on similar, constructivist models. In an edited volume on EU–Russia and German–Russian relations, Iver Neumann and Sergei Medvedev (2012: 13–18) conceptualised identity as an essential constituent of foreign policy and argued that constructivist theory provides the missing link to bridge political practices with social identities. In a milestone study of interpretive constructivist research, Ted Hopf (2002) analysed the domestic construction of Soviet and Russian identities and their impact on foreign policy, focusing on the years 1955 and 1999. Hopf's work showed that domestic identities influence the understanding and formulation of strategic and economic interests. Identity discourses shaped Soviet leaders' understandings of other states and influenced their foreign policy moves, which in turn had an impact on the development of Soviet identity. Thus, deconstructing the national identity in which Soviet leaders were embedded and studying their discursive practices constitute fundamental preconditions to understanding their foreign policy decisions.

A focus on the domestic level is also essential to assess the nature of European identity. Jeffrey Checkel (2006) argued that European identity is shaped by numerous domestic elements, including deeply entrenched social discourses.

---

10. See Chapter One.

Political and societal debates largely originate and take place in national discursive arenas. For common policies to be agreed at the European level, relevant national discourses need to be coherent with each other, so that national elites and public opinions share similar viewpoints (see Liu and Hilton 2005: 542). A constructivist approach to the study of European identity and policies should therefore integrate the European and the national levels of analysis (Checkel 2006: 68–9). This work attempts to integrate the two levels of analysis by assessing how national identity discourses interact and relate to each other in the European context.

In order to do this, the book elaborates on the model developed by Katzenstein, Wendt and Jepperson and discussed above. The relationship between national identities and foreign policy discourses on Russia is studied as the interaction of discursive formations, rather than as a causal concatenation of variables. The association between national identity and foreign policy discourses is conceptualised as complex, dialectical and mutually constitutive (see Prizel 1998: 12–37). In the model, foreign policy discourses reflect and in turn constitute the essence of national identity. National identity provides the cultural context for national interest formation and for a country's behaviour in the international arena. It is in turn influenced by international structures and by the pursuit of national interests therein. Hence, an updated model for this analysis would look as follows:

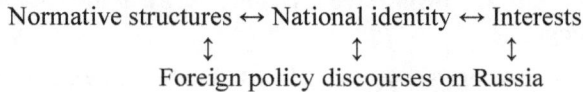

$$\text{Normative structures} \leftrightarrow \text{National identity} \leftrightarrow \text{Interests}$$
$$\updownarrow \qquad\qquad \updownarrow \qquad\qquad \updownarrow$$
$$\text{Foreign policy discourses on Russia}$$

The arrows in the model represent mutually constitutive discursive relationships. Numerous identity and foreign policy discourses exist in each national context. This work focuses on dominant official discourses formulated by heads of state or government and foreign ministers, as these actors are the main decision makers in the realm of foreign policy. Their discourses matter most because they are formulated in institutional settings that are authoritative and conducive to persuasion (Checkel 2004: 240). Dominant media discourses are occasionally referred to in order to contextualise policy makers' statements and reconstruct the main Russia-related themes in public debates. These debates influence the social cognitive structure in which policy makers are embedded and help us understand the domestic roots of their discourses about Russia (see Hopf 2002: 20).

Decision makers' agency, namely their capacity to act and influence dominant discourses and policies, is central to the model adopted for this analysis. As argued, national identity guides and constrains decision makers' choices. However, national leaders can also make selective and instrumental use of particular identity discourses in order to achieve specific foreign policy goals. For instance, decision makers who intend to strengthen economic relations with Russia will emphasise narratives portraying it as a good and reliable partner. Conversely, politicians who oppose the partnership with Russia, or who attempt to strengthen domestic consensus by constructing negative external Others, will rather stress identity discourses portraying it as threatening and unreliable.

National identity and foreign policy narratives are studied both at the domestic level, in their process of national formation and contestation, and in their interaction with international structures. In this latter regard, the focus is on interaction with Russia and its construction as an Other in national identity. Russia is not considered a priori as a negative Other against which national identity is constructed. The investigation of the historical construction of national identities shows that, occasionally, positive interaction occurred in the past between Russia and the three countries under analysis.[11] Furthermore, the boundaries between Self and Other are treated as blurred and not as sharply delimited. For instance, in spite of their historical rivalry, post-1945 Poland and Russia followed parallel paths of social and economic development, which are reflected in some similar national identity narratives today (for example, those expressing a rejection of communism as a political model or emphasising the role of religion in society).

While Russia is a significant Other for the three countries under investigation, it is by no means the only one. For a long historical period, France and Sweden were at least equally important Others for Germany and Finland respectively. Today, due to its double role as Other in the international arena and as the country of origin of millions of immigrants, Turkey may be an even more critical Other for Germany. Furthermore, Polish identity construction was affected by interaction with several significant Others, including Germans, Ukrainians, Lithuanians and Jews (Prizel 1998: 38–152). Hence, the analysis of Russia's role as Other in Polish identity and foreign policy discourses has to take into consideration this tangled web and the fact that additional Others may often influence and even feature more prominently in these discourses.

The theoretical model adopted in this work investigates both the cultural and the material factors constituting national discourses on Russia within a constructivist framework. Material power is seen as acquiring significance only within particular discursive constructions. For instance, Polish leaders have considered Russia's energy power both as a positive factor, as after the Polish–Russian agreement to build the Yamal–Europe pipeline in the early 1990s, and as a national threat, as shown by Warsaw's overt hostility to the Nord Stream pipeline (Castle 2006; Prizel 1998: 132). Polish national identity, notably its construction of the Russian and German Other, provides the key to understand radically different perceptions of the same material power.

Discourse analysis and the discourse–historical approach

In this work, 'discourse' is defined as a form of social practice, a specific type of language use in social interaction, both in speech and in writing. Discourses are socially constructed and have a mutually constitutive relationship with social structures. Discursive practices contribute to sustaining, reproducing and transforming social structures. They reflect and affect power relations through

---

11. See Chapter Four.

their representation of the world. No discourse can be fully understood without taking into account the context in which it was produced; it is meaningful only in its cultural, historical and ideological embedding (Wodak 1996: 14–19).

Most important for the purpose of this study, discourses on a country's identity and external Others are of essential relevance to the formulation of foreign policy (Wæver 2005: 35). As Ruth Wodak (2002b: 66) has noted, a dialectical relationship exists between discursive practices and the field of action in which they are embedded. Accordingly, policy makers' discourses on Russia affect their country's foreign policy towards Russia. Discursive practices are constructed domestically in hegemonic struggles for political and moral–intellectual leadership. They are instrumental in perpetuating, justifying or transforming national identities. They also involve the formation of social antagonism, most notably the exclusion of threatening Others. Discourses about external Others – like all discourses – are fluid and should be studied as flexible, historically bound constructs. Hegemonic discourses become dislocated when they prove unable to explain new events (de Cilla *et al.* 1999: 157; Torfing 2005: 15–16).

Discourse analysis, particularly its discourse–historical approach, offers a suitable methodology to study national discourses on Russia and their relationship to foreign policy in their evolving, historical dimension. DHA is an interpretive and explanatory methodology that systematically reduces the number of possible readings of a text by identifying its cultural and historical embedding. It deconstructs texts and relates them to their social and ideological background (Wodak 1996: 19). As a variant of critical discourse analysis, DHA investigates social processes from which texts originate and within which social actors create meanings, with the aim of exposing power relations and changing discursive structures.

Three concepts are essential in critical discourse analysis: power, ideology and history (Wodak 2002a: 3). In discourse theory, power is defined as 'the political acts of inclusion and exclusion that shape social meanings and identities and condition the construction of social antagonisms and political frontiers' (Torfing 2005: 23). Power rests in the hands of social groups that formulate dominant discourses and can thus demarcate the boundaries of identity. This means that power and identity discourse are intrinsically linked. As discourse is shaped by dominant social structures and groups, it reflects their ideology. The role of ideology, meant as the system of political and cultural beliefs of an actor, must therefore be recognised and deconstructed in discourse analysis (van Dijk 2002: 117).

Critical discourse analysis has a contextual and historicist view of discourses. It seeks to place them against their historical background in order to understand how they evolve and to investigate political attempts at restructuring them (Torfing 2005: 14). DHA pays particular attention to the historical dimension of discourse. By integrating knowledge about the historical sources and the background in which discursive events are embedded, it provides a comprehensive interpretation. Accordingly, the analysis of Russia's role in German, Polish and Finnish national identity formation in the next chapter serves the purpose of delineating the historical framework of current discourses on Russia. Furthermore, DHA explores how discourses are subject to diachronic change. Hence, the historical background is studied as a factor affecting the development of discourses over time (Wodak 2002b: 65; see de Cilla *et al.* 1999: 156).

DHA is interdisciplinary, as it draws on the methods and thematic focus of both political science and history. It is problem-oriented, because it focuses on specific social themes (in this study, the role of Russia as Other in national identity and foreign policy discourses) and not exclusively on linguistic issues. It is applicable to different genres of text, including political speeches and newspaper interviews, which are the main primary sources for this work. Texts and discourses are not studied in isolation; relationships with other texts (intertextuality) and discourses (interdiscursivity) are also investigated (Wodak 2002b: 69–70).

Most of the textual analysis involves tracing the development of key concepts and themes, including their historical origins and relationship to other subjects (see Wæver 2005: 36). Key concepts and themes identify semantic macrostructures that play a fundamental role in communication and interaction. They reflect what a discourse is about globally speaking and exemplify its most important information; they epitomise the gist of a discourse, namely the essence that an audience retains from it (van Dijk 2002: 101–2). Language users are unable to memorise and process all meanings in a discourse; they reorganise them into a few global meanings. Key themes are often explicit in titles, headlines or summaries of a text. Sometimes they are not observable directly, but can be inferred through a careful analysis of the text (van Dijk 2002: 102; Wodak 2002b: 66).

The process of identifying key themes in a text is affected by the subjectivity of the analyst and involves the risk that different analysts detect different themes in the same text. However, this risk can be minimised by examining a large number of texts and by using the background knowledge acquired from the investigation of relevant scholarly literature. Dominant themes should be clearly detectable in many texts, if they are indeed dominant. Furthermore, the texts chosen for analysis must be formulated by individuals with sufficient discursive and societal power to construct dominant narratives. For instance, they can be speeches of key policy makers or articles in mainstream newspapers with a broad readership.

Undoubtedly, there is no single reading of texts, and diverging selections of key themes are also possible if the number of primary sources under analysis is large. However, the deconstruction of numerous and authoritative texts will at the very least offer sufficient data for a plausible interpretation of key themes. In this work, the plausibility of the interpretation is augmented by the fact that it is guided by and can be confronted with the findings of existing scholarly literature on national identity and discourses on Russia. As Teun van Dijk has noted, no complete discourse analysis is possible, as a thorough examination of even a short passage may require months and hundreds of pages of explanation. However, a satisfactory investigation of key themes in discourses can be performed if specific structures are selected for closer analysis (van Dijk 2002: 99). Accordingly, in this work the focus will be restricted to the textual extracts concerning descriptions and interpretations of Russia's domestic and foreign policy.

Critical discourse analysis usually involves a normative dimension. It is often applied to study social problems and the role of discourse in producing power abuse or domination by scholars who are keen on unmasking and modifying existing power relations (van Dijk 2002: 96; Wodak 2002b: 70). The pragmatic potential of the methodology is one of its interesting and useful aspects, but it is not a *conditio sine qua non* for its application. In particular, DHA allows an exploration of the cultural and historical roots of dominant discourses but does not necessarily require a normative approach aimed at changing dominance relations. Accordingly, this work analyses the construction of discourses on Russia and their relationship with foreign policy making without advising on how to change them. The main aim is that of exposing the different nature of discourses on Russia in European countries, as well as the deep identity and historical roots of such differences.

DHA in practice

The methodology adopted for the empirical analysis is based on Wodak (2002b). Its main features are summarised in Table 2.2.

Table 2.2: The main features of DHA

Based on interpretation/hermeneutics
Problem-oriented
Interdisciplinary
Historical context analysed and integrated into the interpretation of texts and discourses
Moves back and forth from theories to empirical data
Investigates intertextual and interdiscursive relationships
Focuses on multiple genres of text
Incorporates fieldwork and ethnography

Source: author's own compilation, based on Wodak (2002b).

DHA is based on the premise that causal models do not match the complexity of the real world. In order to provide a thorough reading of multicausal and mutually constitutive phenomena, such as the relationship between national identity and foreign policy discourses, researchers have to rely on their knowledge and interpretive skills. As Wodak (2002b: 65) argues, the researcher 'makes use of her or his background and contextual knowledge and embeds the communicative or interactional structures of a discursive event in a wider frame of social and political relations, processes and circumstances'. Furthermore, Wodak states that only interdisciplinary research can make complex social relationships transparent. Following this approach, this work combines International Relations theory with discourse theory and historical analysis to perform an in-depth investigation of national discourses concerning Russia. Social constructivist theory and historical analysis are applied throughout the empirical part of this work in order to substantiate the interpretation of discourses. The historical dimension of discursive actions and the social and political background in which discursive events are embedded are integrated in the analysis.

Wodak also suggests incorporating fieldwork and ethnography, whenever possible, in order to explore the subject under investigation from a closer perspective. Due to the time constraints of this research, this was done only partially and with the sole purpose of acquiring background for the historical and textual analysis. Fieldwork included an investigation of how the German, Polish and Finnish nations, and their historical relationship with Russia, are portrayed in the main history museums in the respective national capitals. Table 2.3 lists the museums where fieldwork took place.

Table 2.3: Museums where national identity construction was analysed

Location	Museum
Berlin, Germany	• German Historical Museum (*Deutsches Historisches Museum*) • German–Russian Museum (*Deutsch–Russisches Museum*)
Warsaw, Poland	• Warsaw Uprising Museum (*Muzeum Powstania Warszawskiego*) • Museum of Independence (*Muzeum Niepodległości*) • Museum of the Polish Army (*Muzeum Wojska Polskiego*)
Helsinki, Finland	• National Museum of Finland (*Suomen kansallismuseo*)

Source: author's own compilation.

While the examination of narratives presented in these museums provided useful background material, the analysis of national identity construction and of historical discourses on Russia is based mostly on secondary literature. Relying on secondary sources could be methodologically problematic, as some of their findings may be debatable and require further research. However, a study of the construction of three national identities across centuries based entirely on primary sources is beyond the scope of this work. Furthermore, issues related to the reliability of secondary literature can be tackled by including different conceptual histories and by verifying the quality of their primary analysis. This can be done through the examination of a few key primary texts to which secondary sources refer and a subsequent comparison of the researcher's reading with the one presented by the conceptual history (see Hansen 2006: 84).

The investigation of secondary literature serves the purpose of identifying dominant discourses on Russia over time, which helps situate current discourses within a broader historical framework. Most importantly, it provides in-depth background information and hence a solid foundation for the ensuing interpretive textual analysis. As Lene Hansen (2006: 83) argues, 'the writing of good discourse analysis of primary texts requires knowledge of the case in question, and knowledge comes, in part, from reading standard works on the history, processes, events and debates constituting a foreign policy phenomenon'. The analysis of secondary literature complements the interpretive theoretical framework outlined in the previous chapter, which requires thorough historical and contextual grounding.

After examining the secondary literature, I analysed primary sources, with a focus on the presence of historically constructed images of Russia in foreign policy discourses. For each text under investigation, information concerning its immediate context was sampled. Who is the author? When was the text produced? Which contemporary events does it make reference to? What is the target audience? Relevant political, historical and sociological background is incorporated in the analysis. The text genre was examined too, as it may provide important indications on how the text should be read. For instance, a speech delivered by a foreign minister in front of an audience of diplomats is likely to be much more cautious in terms of wording and judgements than a pre-election speech or a newspaper interview. Following Hansen (2006: 86), both highly formal texts and texts with more clear articulations of identity are included in the analysis, reflecting the broad spectrum of genres in foreign policy discourse.

Once this preliminary and background information on the text was acquired, I identified dominant discourses. In order to detect dominant discourses, their essential constituents were traced in texts: recurrent arguments, the corresponding semantic structures (the use of specific verbs, nouns and adjectives to construct meaning) and the logical outcome of an argument in terms of policy making. For instance, in the case study on Nord Stream, recurrent claims about the importance of energy relations with Russia, its construction as a 'reliable' and 'indispensable' partner and frequent statements supporting the building of the pipeline clearly highlighted the dominant German discourse.[12] I also explored interdiscursivity and intertextuality. Based on the dominant discourses, I formulated research questions specific to the text and to its linguistic constructions. Questions generally asked were: how is Russia defined linguistically (with what adjectives, images, metaphors or other figures of speech)? What does Russia do in these discourses: that is, how is Russia presented as an actor? With texts that had a normative dimension, I asked: in the speaker's opinion, how is Russia to be addressed?

The next step concerned the analysis of discursive strategies and of specific linguistic markers that constitute dominant themes and discourses (*see* also Table 2.4). Discursive strategies are systematic ways of using language in order to achieve a particular social, political, psychological or linguistic aim (Wodak 2002b: 73). Membership categorisations in order to construct in-groups and out-groups are examples of discursive strategies. For instance, peoples are categorised as Europeans and non-Europeans with cultural or geographic arguments, with the use of figures of speech such as metaphors (asserting that something is the same as an otherwise unrelated object) or synecdoches (when a term for a part of something is used to refer to the whole or vice versa: for instance, calling Russia

---

12. See Chapter Four.

'Asia'). Other discursive strategies such as predication (defining the action, state or quality of the subject) are used to label social actors in positive or negative ways. For instance, the previously mentioned category of non-Europeans can be labelled with stereotypical attributions of positive or negative traits. In the texts under analysis, Russia was labelled as 'strategic partner', 'a threat', 'a friendly neighbour' or 'inherently imperialistic'.

Perspectivation, namely the ways speakers contextualise their perspectives and show their relevance to the interpretation of a fact, is another frequently used discursive strategy. It aims at expressing involvement and positioning the speaker's point of view through, for instance, reporting an event that the speaker witnessed and on which he or she claims to have inside knowledge. Out of all discursive strategies, argumentation is possibly the most fundamental. It is used to justify positive or negative attributions and to bolster the main message or purpose of a text. Argumentation can be studied through an analysis of topoi, namely content-related parts of a discourse that connect the arguments with their logical conclusion (Wodak 2002b: 74). For instance, in one of the texts analysed, the speaker advocated engaging Russia (as opposed to marginalising it) and argued that his country (Finland) and Europe would obtain economic and security benefits out of cooperation (Kanerva 2008a). He also claimed that engaging Russia would have positive effects for the preservation of the Baltic Sea and allow his country to fulfil its historical role of bridge builder between Europe and Russia. His conclusion was that appropriate policies should be followed in order to make sure that cooperation takes place. The topoi connecting his arguments and conclusion are economic usefulness, security, environmentalism and history, namely all the semantic and argumentative fields leading to the conclusion that adequate policies should be taken to engage Russia.[13]

Table 2.4: Discursive strategies: objectives and devices

Strategy	Objectives	Devices
Nomination/categorisation	Construct in-groups (Self) and out-groups (Other)	Inclusive or exclusive metaphors and synecdoches
Predication	Label social actors in positive or negative terms	Stereotypical evaluations and attributions of negative or positive traits
Perspectivation	Expressing involvement and positioning the speaker's point of view	Personal and strongly subjective reporting of an event
Argumentation	Justify positive or negative attributions; bolster the main message in a text	Topoi connecting arguments to their logical conclusion

Source: author's own compilation, based on Wodak (2002b).

---

13. For a selection of topoi frequently used in discourses, see Wodak (2002b: 74).

Once dominant discourses and themes, discursive strategies, linguistic markers and topoi were identified, I interpreted the meanings resulting from the analysis and, with reference to my theoretical model, I addressed the research questions. After comparing across texts and discourses, I made an extensive interpretation concerning the role of national identity and of historically constructed images of Russia, thereby assessing their relevance to current foreign policy discourses. The whole procedure is summarised in Table 2.5.

Table 2.5: Steps in the application of DHA

1	analysis of secondary literature and identification of dominant themes in national identity and historical discourses on Russia;
2	sampling of information on the immediate context of the text (author, target audience, events referred to), including its political, historical and sociological background;
3	analysis of text genre;
4	identification of dominant discourses and themes in the text;
5	analysis of interdiscursivity and intertextuality;
6	formulation of text-specific research questions, focusing on linguistic constructions;
7	analysis of discursive strategies and linguistic markers (topoi);
8	interpretation of the meanings resulting from the analysis with reference to the theoretical model; all so that:
9	based on the analysis of all texts, an extensive interpretation can be made concerning the role of national identity and historically constructed images of Russia in foreign policy discourses.

Source: author's own compilation, based on Wodak (2002b).

Selection of national discursive arenas and case studies

The selection of case studies for this analysis involves two aspects. First, due to the impossibility of investigating national identity construction and discourses on Russia in all EU member states within the scope of this work, a few national discursive arenas have been selected for in-depth study. Second, specific policy areas and events have been chosen for the analysis and comparison of national discourses on Russia.

The discussion of distinct East–Central European narratives concerning Russia in Chapter One highlighted the dangers of assuming the existence of a homogeneous EU discursive arena. As Iver Neumann (1998) has shown, occasionally it is possible to identify similar discourses on Russia across European countries, particularly in intellectual circles, which constitute the main subject of Neumann's analysis. However, a thorough investigation must take into account the national level. The history of the European continent is profoundly divided along national lines, and European countries had remarkably different relations with Russia, which presupposes different national discourses.

Geography and history, particularly the nature of political relations in the past, are the main discriminants when examining the interaction between European countries and Russia. These two factors are closely interlinked. States that are closer to Russia's borders also tend to have deeper and more complex historical relations with Russia than those that are located further away. There are exceptions to this observation: despite its considerable distance from Russia, Britain had intense and controversial relations with it from the early nineteenth century until the present, mostly due to the two countries' great power status and geopolitical competition (see Ewans 2004; Keith 2006). However, this exception does not apply to most other West and South European countries. Their historical involvement with Russia was much more limited than that of Central and East European states.

In order to explore the relationship between identity and foreign policy discourses on Russia, this work considers case studies of nations that both had deep historical interactions with Russia and are geographically close to it. This is likely to produce results that are more relevant analytically and that can be compared more easily. The countries under analysis were not selected in order to show that national identity has a strong correlation with foreign policy discourses. A large body of constructivist literature has already shown that this correlation exists. The central questions in this work are more specific: how does this correlation manifest itself in selected European countries with regard to Russia? Can European foreign policy discourses thus constructed be reconciled at the European level?

Since the focus is on the relationship between national identity and discourses on Russia, it is best to select countries where Russia is likely to have played a role in national identity construction, hence those geographically close to and with deep historical interactions with Russia. Furthermore, as we want to compare different foreign policy discourses within the EU, it is fundamental to focus on member states which traditionally have a different foreign policy stance towards Russia. The analysis can thus explore how national identity constructions in which Russia played a role are related to different national foreign policy discourses. Conversely, if the investigation focused on countries chosen for their geographical spread within the EU, it would risk coming to the tautological conclusion that national identity is an important factor in foreign policy discourses on Russia only or mostly in states that are closer to it. Geography, and not national identity, would likely be the main or the only determining factor.

This explains why large and influential EU member states such as France, Italy and Spain were not included in the analysis. A preliminary consultation of secondary sources confirmed that Russia did not play an important role in their national identity construction (see Bedani and Haddock 2000; Boyd 1997; Gildea 2002a, 2002b; Isnenghi 2010; Kamen 2008; Nora 1992). Their cooperative, largely unproblematic relations with Moscow were mostly the result of commercial interests, rather than of deeply engrained identity narratives (see Leonard and Popescu 2007: 31–6). Investigating foreign policy discourses in one of these countries could be useful to highlight how, by contrast with EU member states that are closer and had deeper historical interactions with Russia, national identity and memory do not hamper current relations. However, this analysis is beyond the scope of this book, which focuses on how different constructions of Russia in national identity influence foreign policy discourses. Furthermore, examining more than three national discursive arenas in some depth is not possible within the constraints of this work.

Germany, Poland and Finland have been selected as the focus for this analysis because they best satisfy the analytical criteria outlined above. Tsarist and Soviet Russia was a neighbouring power for most of their modern history, which is still true of Poland and Finland today. Russia and Germany shared a border from 1871 (1815, if we consider Prussia as Wilhelmine Germany's predecessor) until 1918 and again in 1939–41. Although there was no shared border during the Cold War, the presence of Soviet troops and political advisors throughout East–Central Europe and in East Germany practically meant that Soviet Russia was for Germans both a neighbouring and an occupying power from 1945 until the early 1990s. The three countries under consideration had deep and controversial historical relations with Russia during their modern history, including several armed clashes and the occupation of part of their territory by Russian or Soviet troops. We can thus assume that Russia played a role in national identity construction. This assumption is verified through a review of secondary literature in Chapter Four.

Furthermore, the countries selected for analysis are particularly active in current relations with Russia, both at bilateral level and within the EU. Their active roles vis-à-vis Russia contributes to making them interesting and relevant case studies. Within the EU, Germany has had a leading role in shaping energy and economic policies towards Russia (Högselius 2013; Makarychev and Meister 2015; Siddi 2016a; Timmins 2011). Poland has been one of the most active member states in advocating policies concerning the shared neighbourhood of the EU and Russia in Eastern Europe. For instance, it was one of the main supporters of the Eastern Partnership, a policy that aims to intensify the EU's relations with post-Soviet countries in Europe (excluding Russia) (Cichocki 2013; Copsey and Pomorska 2014). Finland has been the main promoter of the EU's Northern Dimension, a framework to address environmental and health issues in border areas between Russia and North European EU member states (Etzold and Haukkala 2011; Haukkala 2010a: 152–6).

Although all countries under analysis had controversial relations with Russia in the past, their current foreign policy stances towards Moscow differ considerably. German foreign policy makers tend to be less critical and more positive about Russia, whereas Polish leaders often have overtly hostile overtones (Krumm 2012a; Reeves 2010; Siddi 2016a). Within the EU, Germany and Poland epitomise the member states' two main and contrasting approaches to Russia (Stewart 2012: 165). The German approach tends towards accommodating Russia and is followed by West and Central European member states such as France, Italy, Spain and Austria. The Polish approach is much more sceptical towards Russia and is generally followed by East–Central European member states (particularly the Baltic States), occasionally joined by Britain and Sweden. The Finnish position is somewhere in between and reflects an apparently neutral pragmatism (Etzold and Haukkala 2011: 253–4; Stewart 2012: 187). These divergences may be due to dissimilar ways of internalising historical experiences in national identities and to the different nuances of past and current bilateral relations with Russia (see Schmidt-Felzmann 2011). Hence, a detailed analysis of Russia's role in national identity construction and of the broader picture of bilateral relations is a precondition for the study of current discourses on Russia.

In order to have a common basis for analysis, the book focuses on national policy makers' discourses on Russia concerning four major international and domestic events in which the Kremlin was directly involved between 2005 and 2015. These are the construction of the Nord Stream pipeline, the 2008 Russian–Georgian war, the post-electoral street protests that took place in Russian cities from December 2011 until the late spring of 2012 and the Ukraine crisis (from its inception until the end of 2015). This selection of events allows the study of discourses on Russia in three areas that are of utmost relevance to the relationship between the European Union and Russia: the security of Russian energy supplies to the EU, the stability of the shared neighbourhood and the development of democratic institutions in Russia (see Haukkala 2010a: 1).

Arguably, other international events and Russian domestic developments might have provided interesting case studies. For instance, a focus on discourses about the US plan to deploy a ballistic missile defence system in East–Central Europe would allow an exploration of different German and Polish perceptions of Russia in the field of security.[14] Nonetheless, this topic was not selected as a case study because it was not of direct relevance for Finland. Moreover, national security debates concerning Russia are already examined in the chapters on the Russian–Georgian war and the Ukraine crisis. Narratives about Dmitry Medvedev's modernisation agenda would offer further material to analyse the reception of key Russian domestic developments in the countries under investigation. However, by the time the empirical research for this book began (late 2012), the modernisation agenda no longer seemed a priority for the Russian government (Makarychev and Meister 2015). Therefore, the authoritarian shift following the Russian parliamentary elections of December 2011 appeared as a more topical domestic development.

The empirical chapters focus on narratives about events that took place in the European context. Discourses about Russia's involvement in non-European issues, such as the negotiations on Iran's nuclear programme and the Syrian civil war, could be analysed to assess how identities influence perceptions of Russia's role in the global arena. While this is a promising avenue for further research, the decision was made to focus on policy issues that are of immediate relevance to EU–Russia relations. The events under investigation were among the most controversial issues in EU–Russia relations since Vladimir Putin's rise to power in 1999. In the three countries selected for analysis, they sparked lively debates on the nature of Russia's domestic and foreign policies. These debates offer an ideal context to identify dominant national narratives on Russia.

---

14. The plan was strongly opposed by Moscow and led to disagreement between the German and Polish governments (Meier 2007).

Source selection

The book analyses public texts, mostly speeches and interviews of top state officials (heads of state or government and foreign ministers) recorded in the electronic archives of national foreign ministries and in prominent national newspapers. The choice of focusing on public texts, as opposed to private or internal documents, is motivated primarily by the theoretical foundations of this work. The contestation among different national identity discourses and narratives on Russia takes place in the public sphere, where their advocates compete for dominance. Hence, the analysis attempts to identify official discourses that are dominant there. Discourse analysis is the best methodology for this investigation because it focuses on public texts (Wæver 2002).

Focusing on public texts and discourses that are easily accessible ensures several methodological advantages. Easy access to sources ensures the transparency of the research, as it allows a quick verification of the plausibility of interpretations and the cogency of arguments (Blaikie 2010: 217; Bryman 2008: 380). This is particularly relevant when studying foreign policy. In foreign policy making, a lot tends to be hidden and every interpretation of an actor's actions and speeches may be subject to questions such as: is this what the actor really thinks, or is it just the image that he or she intends to convey in public? Actors' thoughts, motives and secret intentions would be extremely difficult to determine without privileged access to a wide range of reliable private sources and people acquainted with the actors in question. As Ole Wæver (2002: 26) convincingly argued, 'if one sticks rigorously to the level of discourse, the logic of the argument remains much more clear – one works on public, open sources and uses them for what they are, not as indicators of something else'. Therefore, the main focus of research is not what actors really believe, but what arguments and linguistic codes they use in public and what discourses become widely shared or dominant in the public arena. These discourses have practical relevance, as they condition possible policies. Policy is strongly related to discursive structures because decision makers need to be able to justify policy choices in public and reconcile them with the self-image of the state (Wæver 2002: 27).

Focusing exclusively on discourses of top state officials may result in an analysis that does not reflect all the complexities involved in identity construction and the formulation of foreign policy. Other actors at lower levels in the power chain or civil society also play a role in shaping identity and foreign policy discourses. Business and other advocacy groups (such as religious, environmental and pacifist organisations) lobby governments to take foreign policy decisions that conform with their economic or social objectives. Scholarly literature has highlighted in particular the role of epistemic communities in influencing decision makers (Adler 1992; Davis Cross 2013; Haas 1992 2004; Sebenius 1992; Zito 2001). Epistemic communities are networks of professionals with recognised expertise and policy-relevant knowledge in a particular area. The members of an epistemic community share a set of normative and causal beliefs, which shape their analysis of possible policy actions and desired outcomes. Overarching agreement on policies is an essential prerequisite for a group of experts to be considered as part of the same epistemic community. Prominent think tanks, regulatory agencies and governmental policy research bodies provide ideal locations for members of an epistemic community to gain leverage over policy choices. Former political leaders, diplomats, judges, high-ranking military officials, bankers and international lawyers often become part of these expert groups and use their prestige and expertise to influence decision makers (Davis Cross 2013: 155–9; Haas 1992: 2–4).

In the countries under investigation, prominent think tanks that work closely with national governments – such as the German Institute for International and Security Affairs, the Centre for Eastern Studies in Poland and the Finnish Institute of International Affairs – are likely to influence the decision-making process concerning relations with Russia.[15] To cite only a few examples regarding Germany, former political leaders such as Gerhard Schröder, Joschka Fischer and Helmut Schmidt and national advocacy groups that have strong commercial interests in Russia (such as the *Ost-Ausschuss der deutschen Wirtschaft*) have been particularly vocal in the debate on German–Russian relations (see Meister 2014). In order to have a more complete picture of all national identity and foreign policy narratives, the discourses of epistemic communities, advocacy groups and civil society organisations would have to be investigated. However, covering three whole national discursive spaces is practically impossible and a bias towards a selected category of actors is inevitable. Within these constraints, the choice of focusing on discourses of leading state officials is motivated by the fact that they are the main foreign policy actors and they steer relevant public debates (Wæver 2002: 42).

The sources selected for this analysis are essentially excerpts of these public debates. They are policy makers' interviews targeted to a broad audience or transcripts of policy makers' speeches made in meetings with other state officials and with civil society. All of them were publicly and freely accessible at the time when the empirical research was performed. They can be thought of as snapshots of dominant discursive constructions concerning national identity, foreign policy and relations with Russia. The electronic archives of the Finnish, German and Polish foreign ministries proved essential to retrieve foreign ministers' speeches. Additional sources were investigated for transcripts of speeches and interviews given by other top state officials who were particularly active in foreign policy making in the case studies under consideration. For Finland, the Eilen Archive and Chronology of Finnish Foreign Policy (curated by the Finnish Institute of International Affairs) was used to retrieve speeches by Finnish prime ministers and presidents of the republic. For Germany and Poland, the official online archives of the speeches, interviews and press conferences held by the German federal

---

15. Researchers focusing on Russia and EU–Russian relations at these institutes were consulted during both the data collection and the drafting of this work. These discussions contributed to steering the research and sharpening the interpretive analysis.

chancellor, the Polish prime minister and the Polish president of the republic were consulted. Furthermore, several interviews and statements made by top German, Polish and Finnish officials were retrieved from prominent European and North American mass media.

In order to identify relevant texts in large databases such as the online archives of the German and Finnish foreign ministries, the German federal chancellor and the Eilen Archive and Chronology of Finnish Foreign Policy, search functions on the websites were used. Texts (articles, interviews, speeches, press releases and travel reports) dating from the period 2005–15 and including the terms 'Russia', 'Nord Stream', 'Georgia' and 'Ukraine' were preselected for further analysis. This data collection procedure allowed for the retrieval of material from similar databases (institutional websites) for the three countries under consideration. However, while numerous relevant texts could be retrieved from German and Finnish databases, fewer primary sources were available on Polish institutional websites. Hence, in order to gather a similar body of material for the analysis of Polish discourses, an additional search was carried out. Further texts were found in the international press (in English, German and French) by retrieving interviews with Polish foreign policy makers that were mentioned in the news section of Polish institutional websites. German and Finnish archives normally reported the full text of national leaders' interviews, whereas Polish archives did not. Therefore, retrieving interviews of Polish officials directly from the press compensated for this deficiency, while keeping the scope of the sources under analysis the same for the three countries.

Table 2.6: Sources for the analysis of foreign policy makers' discourses on Russia

Germany	Poland	Finland
Foreign ministries' electronic archives		
Online archive of federal chancellor speeches, press conferences and interviews	Online archives of prime minister and president of the republic speeches, press conferences and interviews	Eilen Archive and Chronology of Finnish Foreign Policy
Newspaper interviews and open letters		

Source: author's own compilation.

The texts under investigation date from 2005 to 2015. More specifically, the analysis of texts concerning the Nord Stream project starts from 2005, the year when the building of the pipeline was agreed upon and started, and stretches until 2012, when construction works were completed. Between these dates numerous international controversies arose concerning the political and economic significance, the security implications and the environmental impact of the pipeline. The investigation of discourses regarding the August 2008 war in Georgia focuses primarily on texts dating from the summer of 2008 (the peak of the crisis), but a few later texts are also examined. The analysis of narratives concerning the street protests in Russia centres on the period between early December 2011, when the first post-electoral mass demonstrations took place, and December 2012. Although the demonstrations became smaller after May 2012 (following Vladimir Putin's third inauguration to the presidency of Russia), the relevant debate continued in some of the countries under analysis, mostly due to the repressive measures that Russia adopted in the summer and autumn of 2012.[16] Finally, the chapter on the Ukraine crisis focuses on the period from Russia's annexation of Crimea until the end of 2015.

Conclusion

This chapter has argued that social constructivism provides the best theoretical approach to examine the relationship between national identity and foreign policy discourses. Following social constructivist theory, national identity reflects historical relations with Russia and influences foreign policy narratives in the countries under analysis. Conversely, neorealist and neoliberal approaches largely ignore the importance of identity and interaction with the Other in the formulation of foreign policy discourses. Building on the insights of positivist constructivist scholarship from the 1990s and its subsequent criticism, the chapter developed an interpretive constructivist model for the ensuing empirical analysis. In the model, identity is conceptualised as a multifaceted and fluctuating construct, hard to measure or quantify. Its relationship with foreign policy is best studied as the interaction of discourses, both at the domestic level (where foreign policy is formulated) and in the international arena. This relationship is complex and mutually constitutive. Concretely, this means that national identity narratives both influence and are shaped by interaction with Russia.

The relationship between national identity and top national leaders, the primary agents in foreign policy making, is also mutually constitutive. The leaders of a country are embedded in social cognitive structures shaped by national identity. Hence, they are reluctant to enact policies that do not conform to it. However, as they are also the main agents in the construction of national identity, they sometimes develop new narratives that complement and further develop dominant identity discourses. This in turn contributes to explaining the malleability of national identity. The chapter also highlighted the relevance of a discursive approach to the study of national identity, foreign policy and the construction of a country's external Others. It argued that the DHA, a variant of critical discourse analysis, provides an appropriate methodology because it focuses on the historical dimension of discourse. It is therefore functional for the investigation of the relationship between deep-rooted national identity narratives and foreign policy discourses about Russia. In addition, its focus on discursive strategies allows for

---

16. As Hansen (2006: 87) argues, the focus on periods of international or domestic crisis, and hence of increased political and media activity, is likely to make the selection of texts for discourse analysis more manageable. Moreover, it allows the study of the evolution of discourse in the face of important developments on the ground.

a systematic analysis of the linguistic and rhetorical tools that are used in the construction of Russia as the Other.

Three national discursive arenas within the EU (Germany, Poland and Finland) were chosen for closer inspection. This selection was based on the depth of the countries' historical interactions with Russia, their active role in current relations and the representativeness of the main national positions towards Russia within the EU. As the selected countries play an important role in EU–Russia relations and epitomise the member states' main stances towards Russia, the analysis also offers insights about influential discourses on Russia at the EU level. Furthermore, four key events in which Russia played a major role in recent years were selected in order to provide a common basis for the analysis of discourses in each national arena. These events concern key policy areas in EU–Russia relations, namely energy security, the security and stability of the shared neighbourhood and the development of democratic institutions in Russia.

Chapter Three

National Identities in Historical Perspective

As Chapters One and Two have highlighted, national identity is a complex construction that involves a large number of cultural and historical factors. Deconstructing national identity and examining its main components is essential in order to understand its relationship with a country's foreign policy. This chapter analyses the historical construction of German, Polish and Finnish identity, with particular focus on discourses that are considered most relevant to national foreign policy towards Russia. The main argument is that, in the last two centuries, Russia was a prominent Other in national foreign policy discourses and perceptions of Russia played an important role in national identity formation. The chapter draws on the scholarly literature on German, Polish, Finnish identity and foreign policy and on original material collected during fieldwork in the countries under investigation. National identity construction is studied in a *longue durée* perspective. The focus is on the period starting from the nineteenth century, when modern national identities began to be constructed. The *longue durée* approach highlights the historical roots of current national identities and foreign policy behaviours. It thereby provides a historically grounded and substantive interpretive framework for the discourse analysis in the following chapters.

While the discussion below is by no means an exhaustive analysis of the three national identities, it hopes to provide the essential framework to understand and interpret them, most notably their mutually constitutive relationship with national foreign policy. For each of the three countries under analysis, the dominant themes and historical trends of national identity construction are investigated alongside their relationship with contemporary foreign policy. The role of Russia as Other in identity formation and the evolution of national discourses on Russia are analysed in greater depth in distinct, yet strongly interconnected, sub-sections.

Democracy, stability, multilateralism: the historical construction of German identity

Well into the second decade of the twenty-first century, Germany appears as one of the most successful countries in Europe, with well-established democratic institutions, a strong economy and a leading role in the EU. The Berlin Republic seems to have successfully combined political stability and a strong economic performance, after nearly a century of wars, dictatorships and territorial division.[1]

---

1. The term 'Berlin Republic' is used to distinguish post-reunification Germany from the country's previous republican experiences: West Germany, which had Bonn as its capital (1949–90), and the Weimar Republic (1919–33) (see Wittlinger 2008).

Democracy, economic prosperity, the respect of human rights and the rejection of war as means to solve international disputes have become an integral part of German identity (see Berger 1996; Bjola and Kornprobst 2007). These values influence German foreign policy discourses, notably the country's strong support for multilateralism and its normative approach to international affairs (Risse 2007). Governments in Berlin believe that their foreign policy priorities can be achieved best within the framework of the EU, which explains their strong pro-European orientation (Banchoff 1999).

Some International Relations scholars have attempted to define the nature of post-reunification German foreign policy by developing concepts such as that of civilian power (Harnisch and Maull 2001). Civilian powers are defined as states that actively promote the 'civilising' of international relations through efforts to constrain the use of force, strengthen the rule of law and promote international cooperation. The endorsement of participatory forms of decision making, social equity, sustainable development and interdependence are also important features of civilian powers (Harnisch and Maull 2001: 3–4). However, this conceptualisation leaves important questions unanswered. How does a country develop a specific type of foreign policy discourses? In what historical and cultural context can concepts such as that of civilian power be understood?

The historical construction of German national identity is illuminating in this respect. The dominant identity discourses that constitute current German foreign policy have been constructed as a rejection of the national experience between 1871 and 1945 and of the East German dictatorship (Jarausch and Geyer 2003: 235–40). The record of the united Germany between 1871 and 1945 is widely considered as catastrophic, as it is associated with two world wars, economic instability, a brutal dictatorship and, most importantly, genocide. Militaristic and chauvinistic Imperial Germany (1871–1918), the economically and politically unstable Weimar Republic (1919–33), let alone the racist and genocidal experience of the Third Reich (1933–45), could provide no positive reference for the identity of post-1989 reunified Germany.

In 1945, the German nation had no 'usable past' (Moeller 2003a) from which to reconstruct its political identity.[2] Foreign occupation and the existence of two radically different German states after 1949 further complicated the emergence of a new sense of national identity. East German authorities drew a thick line between the Third Reich and the newly founded German Democratic Republic (GDR). Official rhetoric portrayed GDR citizens as either anti-fascist heroes or victims of the Nazi regime, who had finally been united under the first socialist state in German history (Fulbrook 1999: 55–9; Naimark 1995). It also attempted to construct a separate identity based on anti-fascism and hostility to the capitalist Western world. However, most East German citizens never fully accepted

---

2. While in 1945 Germany had no 'usable past' in political terms, a large part of German cultural and artistic heritage was not discredited by the catastrophic outcome of national unity until 1945 and — together with the shared language — continued to constitute a powerful unifying factor in the following decades.

the official narrative. In fact, East–West competition and the GDR authorities' obsession with defining their country in opposition to West Germany acted as a constant reminder of all-German commonalities among East German citizens (Fulbrook 1999: 198).

In West Germany, the dynamics of national identity construction were more complex. In the first post-war decade, the focus was on material and economic reconstruction. The swift achievements in these fields, including the so-called economic miracle (*Wirtschaftswunder*), created a feeling of identity based on collective working ethics and the resolve to rebuild a country that lay in ruins (James 1989: 177–95). In foreign policy, alignment with the US and support of European integration were seen as absolute priorities in order to be accepted as a full member of the Western community. The issue of coming to terms with German history, particularly with the recent past, proved more controversial. Although the Bonn Republic accepted paying reparations to Israel in 1952, public debates on the Nazi past did not gain momentum until the early 1960s (Herf 1997: 334–72).

From the 1960s onwards, memory of the Holocaust became a dominant public and institutional discourse, as well as a crucial constitutive element of West German identity and foreign policy. The sense of responsibility for genocide prevented attempts to positively define West German identity and to reassess German history in less negative or exculpatory terms.[3] In foreign policy, the rejection of unilateralism and the support of European and Western integration appeared even more as the only possible course of action to re-establish the country's reputation (Banchoff 1999: 273–4). West German attitudes to national identity and foreign policy choices led many intellectuals to argue that, by the 1970s, the country had become a post-national democracy. According to this view, West Germans had learnt from the past and moved beyond the ideas of nation and nationalism (Berger 1997: 77–108; Jarausch and Geyer 2003: 240; Winkler 1996).

This interpretation was seriously challenged by events in East and West Germany in 1989–90. Reunification brought about attempts to renationalise German history and identity (Berger 1997: 198–221). The fall of the Berlin Wall clearly showed that a German nation had survived Cold War divisions. Undeniably, the existence of two German states with different political and economic systems left material and cultural traces in post-1990 united Germany (see Arnold-de Simine 2005; Herf 1997; Kocka 1996; Weidenfeld 2001). The Wall fell when East and West Germans were growing apart in practice, but the West German government and the majority of GDR citizens still believed in the unity of the nation in principle (Fulbrook 1999: 23). Although elements of a distinct GDR identity survived

---

3.   Conservative historians Ernst Nolte and Andreas Hillgruber attempted to relativise German responsibility for the Holocaust by presenting it as a reaction to Bolshevism (Nolte 1986) and by comparing it to the suffering of German expellees from East-Central Europe (Hillgruber 1986). Their claims sparked a vitriolic exchange with left-leaning intellectuals such as Jürgen Habermas and Hans-Ulrich Wehler, known as the *Historikerstreit* (historians' quarrel). The debate took place on the pages of prominent national newspapers (*Frankfurter Allgemeine Zeitung and Die Zeit*) and was followed with great interest by the West German public (Berger 1997: 91–2; Knowlton and Cates 1993).

among its former citizens and sometimes resurface in nostalgic filmic and cultural representations, they do not overshadow dominant identity discourses and are contested by competing narratives that focus on the authoritarian and repressive nature of the East German regime (Arnold-de Simine 2005; Sabrow 2009).

While reunification revived the feeling of a German national identity, it neither reawakened the extreme nationalism that had characterised the history of Germany in 1871–1945, nor did it mark a sudden departure from pre-1989 West German identity and foreign policy discourses. The latter became dominant also in the reunified Germany. Memory of the Holocaust and the suffering inflicted upon other nations during the Second World War plays a central role in the collective identity of the united Germany (Langenbacher 2010: 43–9; Wilds 2000; Wittlinger 2011: 139–40). If anything, debates on these issues have become deeper and more prominent since the 1990s, including social groups that had been neglected earlier (such as Soviet prisoners of war and forced labourers, Roma and Sinti, homosexuals).[4] The erection of numerous monuments commemorating the victims of National Socialism in the reunified Berlin has led some authors to label it as 'the capital city of remorse' (in German, *Hauptstadt der Reue*; see Reichel 2005).

The experience of the East German dictatorship constituted a further controversial issue which the Berlin Republic had to come to terms with in order to forge a united national identity. The trials of GDR officials and border guards in the 1990s and the social issues and economic difficulties resulting from reunification ensured that the East German past was present in public debates in both the 1990s and the 2000s (Ahonen 2011; Gellner and Douglas 2003). Despite the already cited nostalgia for some aspects of life in the GDR, dominant discourses and historical analyses have drawn an unequivocally negative balance for the East German regime (see Fulbrook 1995, 2011; Hodgin and Pearce 2011; Jarausch 1999; Jarausch and Geyer 2003: 77–81; Klessmann 1999; Langenbacher 2010: 54–7). This contributed to reinforcing the stress on democracy and human rights and the rejection of any form of totalitarianism in German identity discourses.

Although the national past has remained mostly a source of contrition and collective responsibility for the perpetration of unprecedented crimes, in the second post-reunification decade the Berlin Republic felt confident enough to address the issue of German suffering during and in the aftermath of the Second World War. This concerned in particular the expulsion of approximately twelve million ethnic Germans from East–Central Europe between 1945 and 1950, the rape of thousands of German women in the last months of the war by Allied soldiers, the carpet bombing of all main German cities and the internment of millions of Wehrmacht soldiers in Soviet camps (Langenbacher 2010: 49–54; Moeller 2003a). German suffering had been largely a taboo in mainstream public and institutional

---

4.   These debates were fuelled by the appearance of new studies, films, documents and exhibitions. Among the most important are the Goldhagen controversy concerning the responsibility of ordinary Germans in the Holocaust, the exhibition on the crimes of the German army in the Soviet Union organised by the Hamburg Institute of Social Research and the Walser-Bubis quarrel over the building of the Holocaust memorial in central Berlin (see Weidenfeld 2001: 30–2).

debates since the 1960s. It returned forcefully to mainstream discourses in 2002 with the publication of Günter Grass's novel *Crabwalk* and Jörg Friedrich's *The Fire: The Bombing of Germany 1940–1945*. During the following years, a lively memory debate on German suffering took place, fuelled by numerous television productions and new publications (Langenbacher 2010: 51; Wittlinger 2008: 10; Zehfuss 2006: 222–6).

This memory received institutional endorsement in 2008 through the creation of the *Bundesstiftung Flucht, Vertreibung, Versöhnung* (Federal Foundation Flight, Expulsion, Reconciliation). The foundation was given the task of setting up and curating a museum that would commemorate the expulsion of ethnic Germans from East–Central Europe in the wider context of Nazi racial policies and of other forced resettlements in twentieth century Europe.[5] Chancellor Merkel's endorsement of the project and her simultaneous, unambiguous acknowledgement of Germany's historical responsibility reflect her willingness to encourage a discussion of multiple national memories and identities, without relativising the role of the Holocaust and Germany's criminal policies in the Second World War (Wittlinger 2008: 22). The focus on German suffering during the last decade has not significantly altered the nature of dominant German identity and foreign policy discourses. If anything, it strengthened their pacifist and anti-totalitarian components by emphasising the pernicious consequences of aggressive and unlawful policies (see Langenbacher 2010: 50).

The long way to Ostpolitik: Russia in German identity and foreign policy discourses

During the nineteenth and twentieth centuries, Russia was a significant Other in German identity construction. German perceptions of Russia were predominantly negative, emphasising its presumed social and economic backwardness and threatening military power. However, a counter-narrative that relativised these negative views also existed, notably in particular social milieux and historical periods. A significant strand of German official discourses emphasised the necessity of a cooperative approach to Russia that took into account its strategic importance for Germany and in the international arena. From the late 1960s onwards, these discourses constituted a cooperative West German foreign policy stance towards the Soviet Union that has become enshrined in the concept of Ostpolitik. The term literally means 'Eastern policy' and generally refers to Germany's foreign policy towards its Eastern neighbours (see Ash 1993: 34–5). It acquired a more specific meaning in the context of Cold War detente, when West German Ostpolitik established a tradition of cordial bilateral contacts that has remained an important element of reunified Germany's policy towards Russia. The coexistence of deeply rooted stereotypes and the Ostpolitik tradition has resulted in an ambiguous relationship, which Russia's role in German identity discourses can help us to understand.

5.　Details are available on the foundation's website, www.sfvv.de (accessed on 19 July 2016).

Negative perceptions of Russia in German intellectual and policy-making elites date back at least to the sixteenth century. In 1549 German diplomat and writer Sigmund von Herberstein published a book describing the country as a brutal authoritarian regime and its people as backward and wretched. As Russia was largely unknown in Western Europe at the time, the book became a major source of knowledge (von Herberstein 2010; see Schröder 2012: 97). Criticism of Russia in German discourses became dominant in the nineteenth century and was fuelled by popular publications such as Astolphe de Custine's 'Empire of the Czar'. Published in 1839, it portrayed the Tsarist Empire as a corrupt, inefficient and despotic police state (de Custine 1989). Contemporary German liberals were particularly critical of Russian autocracy and the overall backwardness of the Tsarist Empire. For them, Russia was a threat to German and European liberal values (Schröder 2012: 99).

Conservatives tended to be less contemptuous of the Tsarist political system. Between 1847 and 1852, Prussian agricultural expert August von Haxthausen published a report on his trips to Russia, describing it as a well-ordered patriarchal monarchy. Von Haxthausen's (1972) publication promoted a competing, more positive discourse on Russia and was particularly popular among the German aristocracy, which considered the Tsarist Empire as a bulwark against revolution and democracy. However, sympathetic conservatives were also convinced of Germany's cultural superiority and looked down on the Russian social and economic model. Stereotypes about Russia, such as its image as an underdeveloped and uncivilised country, were widespread throughout German society. Negative views were only partially mitigated by the appreciation of Russian literature, music and art (see Schröder 2012: 99–100).

At the end of the nineteenth century, the Tsarist Empire's alliances with France and Britain led to a shift in perceptions among German conservatives also, who no longer considered Russia as a political ally. Dominant discourses in political and intellectual circles portrayed it as a backward colossus that threatened German culture and simultaneously offered a vast expanse for the extension of German power and civilisation.[6] These discourses provided the rationale for Berlin's annexationist policy during the First World War and, in a more extreme and racist variant, during the Nazi–Soviet war (see Liulevicius 2000). In Wilhelmine Germany, publicist Johannes Haller (1917) described the Tsarist Empire as an Asiatic, Tatar state, a true heir of the Golden Horde poised for a war of conquest and pillage. After the Bolshevik revolution, racial discourses intertwined with political ones. The German elites and middle class associated the 'Bolshevik threat' with Jewish commissars and savage Slavs that were keen to commit atrocious crimes and enslave Europe. On the other hand, a sizeable minority (mostly radicals and communists) viewed the Soviet Union as an economic and social model. From the opposite side of the political spectrum, some conservatives remained sympathetic

---

6. Until 1945, German academia contributed to this line of thought. The scholarly discipline of *Ostforschung*, focusing on the European territories east of Germany, justified Berlin's expansionist aims in East–Central and Eastern Europe with pseudohistorical arguments (Mühle 2003).

to Russia, in spite of its communist regime, because they saw it as a partner in their fight against the Versailles system. These competing and more positive views resulted in the coexistence of diverse discourses and approaches to Russia in Weimar Germany also (see Schröder 2012: 100–3).

Following Hitler's rise to power, racist and anti-Bolshevik discourses became omnipresent; the Nazis silenced all competing views. From the start of the war with the Soviet Union (June 1941), the Nazi regime incessantly disseminated propaganda that described Russians and other peoples of the Soviet Union as 'sub-humans' (*Untermenschen*). German racial policies in the East built on and radicalised pre-existing anti-Russian stereotypes. The military defeat of the Third Reich frustrated Nazi plans to enslave and exterminate Slavic peoples. However, Goebbels' propaganda had a longer lasting impact on German mindsets. The image of Russians as uncivilised Asians, threatening German and European values, persisted in post-war West German discourses (Schildt 2003: 158).

In the 1950s and 1960s, the Soviet Union was the main Other against which West German identity was constructed. The Bonn Republic pursued transatlantic integration and shifted Germany's geopolitical self-perception from being part of Central Europe to full membership of the capitalist and democratic West (see Schröder 2012: 106). As West Germany left behind the historical enmity with France and Britain, the Soviet Union and its satellites became the only neighbouring foes. Perceptions of Russia were not positive in the German Democratic Republic either. Most GDR citizens considered East German official rhetoric on Soviet–German friendship hollow, particularly after the Soviets used tanks to repress popular protests against low living standards in East Germany in June 1953 (Knopp 2003; Ostermann 2001).[7]

The presence of Soviet troops and Moscow-friendly regimes on German soil and in bordering countries allowed West German politicians to focus public debates on the contemporary communist and Russian threat and avoid confrontation with the Nazi past. Soviet Russia was described as a totalitarian state that menaced the West with both its military might and its alleged cultural backwardness (see Schröder 2012: 107–9). The overtly racist discourses on Russia of the early post-war years lost momentum only gradually from the 1960s onwards, when the focus of West German debates shifted to Nazi crimes, most of which had been committed in Eastern Europe and the Soviet Union. Chancellor Willy Brandt's genuflection in the former Warsaw ghetto in 1970 and his cooperative Ostpolitik with the Soviet Union epitomise the shift in official West German identity narratives and policies towards the Soviet bloc (see Ash 1993: 298–300).

Brandt's Ostpolitik enhanced trade exchanges between West Germany and the Eastern bloc and resulted in a series of treaties, signed between 1970 and 1973, which improved diplomatic relations between Bonn and Soviet Russia. Negative discourses on Russia did not disappear among West German political elites (Hildermeier 2003: 41; see Satjukow 2008). However, the Soviets were no

---

7. Furthermore, the violence of Soviet soldiers against German citizens, especially in the first months of occupation, had left many East Germans embittered (Naimark 1995: 470).

longer perceived as aggressive and uncivilised Bolsheviks; the image of a peaceful neighbour that could become an economic partner gained momentum (Schildt 2003: 169; see Albert 1995; Thumann 1997). Ostpolitik created a new, powerful discourse showing that cooperation was possible and beneficial to both Moscow and Bonn. It marked a turning point in West German policies towards Russia that was eventually endorsed by all political forces. Leaders of the conservative opposition to Willy Brandt declared their approval of Ostpolitik in the mid-1970s and did not change course when they won elections and became the ruling majority in the 1980s (Schildt 2003: 171; see Marx 1990).

A further positive turn in German discourses on the Soviet Union took place in the late 1980s, when Mikhail Gorbachev's reforms in Moscow improved dramatically the image of the USSR in the West. Dominant West German discourses about the Soviet Union abandoned the emphasis on economic and social stagnation, which had characterised the Brezhnev years, and stressed profound change. West German politicians and German civilians on both sides of the Iron Curtain acclaimed Gorbachev for his role in ending the Cold War and allowing the reunification of Germany. West German leaders took pride in arguing that peaceful transformation in Eastern Europe had taken place as a result also of their cooperative Ostpolitik with the Soviet Union. Furthermore, Chancellor Helmut Kohl developed a personal friendship with Gorbachev, thereby establishing a tradition of cordial relationships between Russian and German leaders that lasted for nearly two decades. In the euphoria of reunification, the image of Russia as the aggressive Other disappeared and left room for optimism and hope for further democratic change in the Eastern bloc (Ahrens and Weiss 2012: 149–50; Krumm 2012: 115–17).

The collapse of communism in Russia and East Germany brought the end of ideological controversies, but Russian capitalism and democracy turned out to be very different from the German variant. Boris Yeltsin's violent confrontation with the Russian parliament in October 1993 and the beginning of the war in Chechnya a year later ended German optimism about democratisation and the rule of law in Russia. The image of destitute masses of Russian citizens, juxtaposed to that of a few opulent oligarchs who had enriched themselves with shady privatisations of state-owned assets, became prominent in the German media. Russian politicians were also perceived with increasing scepticism (Krumm 2012: 118–19). By the mid-1990s, the euphoric German discourse about Gorbachev and Yeltsin's reforms gave way to the realisation that Russia was failing to democratise (Ahrens and Weiss 2012: 153). As the First Chechen War (1994–6) unmistakably showed, mass violations of human rights were commonplace in post-communist Russia also. In this context, deep-rooted German discourses on Russia as a socially and economically backward state became dominant again. In addition, the discourse on Russia as a chaotic country with a corrupt government and a crumbling social structure gained prominence. From a German viewpoint, the military and political threat at the time of the Cold War was replaced by the risk of Russia's complete economic and social collapse, with spillover effects that would reach far beyond the country's borders (Ahrens and Weiss 2012: 150). As Yeltsin's health worsened and Russia was hit by a disastrous financial crisis in 1998, critical perceptions overshadowed the positive image that Moscow had acquired by facilitating German reunification and ending the Cold War.

Vladimir Putin's rise to power in 1999 and Russia's economic growth during his first two presidencies was accompanied by a new shift in German perceptions. Critical discourses about the lack of democracy, the maltreatment of journalists and gross violations of human rights in Chechnya remained prominent in the German press. However, Putin was also ascribed the merit of economic and political stabilisation, an achievement that is valued highly in Germany due to the deeply engrained memory of the consequences that instability had on the country in the 1920s and 1930s (see Ahrens and Weiss 2012: 152). Hence, negative perceptions were accompanied by a more positive discourse about Russia's economic and social development, which was exemplified by Chancellor Gerhard Schröder's friendly approach to Moscow and personal relationship with Putin. As was shown by a study of articles published in 2003 in *Der Spiegel* and *Stern*, the two main German weekly magazines, German news coverage of Russia became more differentiated (Daniliouk 2006). Optimistic evaluations of Russia were juxtaposed to critical assessments, particularly in the conservative press.

A study of editorials on Russian domestic and foreign policy published between 2001 and 2008 in the two most widely read and authoritative German dailies, *Süddeutsche Zeitung* and *Frankfurter Allgemeine Zeitung*, provides further evidence for diversity in German discourses about Russia (Ahrens and Weiss 2012). Overall, assessments remained negative, particularly on issues such as Chechnya, democracy, freedom of the press, the rule of law and Russia's handling of Islamic terrorism within its borders. However, the theme of Russia as a stable and important actor in the international arena was dominant in 40 per cent of foreign policy editorials. The dominant discourse that emerges from the editorials describes Russia as an undemocratic country with internal problems, but also with a key international and economic role that made Germany's cooperation with Moscow inevitable.

Table 3.1: Dominant themes in German identity discourses

National identity discourses	Discourses on Russia
Democracy and human rights	Ostpolitik
Economic prosperity and stability	Authoritarian, corrupt, socially and economically backward
Rejection of war as means to solve disputes	Economic partner
Pro-European Union and multilateralism	Key actor in international arena

Source: author's own compilation.

Martyrdom and heroism: the historic construction of Polish identity

After two centuries of nearly uninterrupted foreign occupation and tutelage, Poland recovered its full independence in 1989. Since then, the country has pursued a

West-oriented foreign policy that led it to join NATO and the EU (in 1999 and 2004, respectively). However, the long periods of foreign occupation have left a profound impact on the construction of Polish identity. Post-1989 identity and memory discourses have focused on the suffering and heroic resistance of the Polish nation under the German and Russian yokes (Orla-Bukowska 2006). Narratives constructed during the nineteenth and twentieth centuries frequently re-emerge in current public discussions and interact with debates concerning Poland's foreign policy. In 1990, the decision to restore 3 May as a national holiday established an ideal link between post-communist Poland and the Polish–Lithuanian Commonwealth of the eighteenth century. On 3 May 1791, the Commonwealth had adopted a constitution that can be regarded as Europe's first democratic constitution (Davies 1996: 699). Four years later, the Commonwealth was partitioned between Austria, Prussia and Russia and ceased to exist. It took 123 years before an independent Polish state re-emerged. During this period, a modern Polish national identity was constructed and many debates that still characterise Poland's self-image as an international actor were started (Porter 2000).

In the early nineteenth century, Polish intellectuals relocated the idea of the nation to a spiritual plane, where it could continue to survive in the absence of a nation-state. According to contemporary romantic nationalists, Poland was a community defined by moral principles, rather than by political structures. This conception of the nation was inclusive and left room for cultural, religious and ethnic diversity. Tyranny, rather than a specific country or nation, was identified as the main Other. Catholic Poland was also considered as a Christian rampart (*antemurale christianitatis*), ready to sacrifice itself for Western civilisation ('for your freedom and ours', as a contemporary Polish romantic motto emphasised). These ideas provided the foundations for the 1830 uprising in the part of Poland occupied by the Russian empire, while Russia came to be seen as an embodiment of tyranny (Porter 2000: 16–22, Prizel 1998: 40–1).

The failure of the 1830 uprising was the first major defeat for Polish romantic nationalists. Although the Poles considered their fight against Tsardom fundamental for Western civilisation, other European nations did not join in the battle. The commitment that Polish volunteers had shown in the fight for the freedom of other nations (for instance, during the American Revolution and the Napoleonic wars) remained unreciprocated. The theme of unrequited commitment to the Western cause was dominant in Polish identity discourses well into the twentieth century, when it was further radicalised into accusations of outright betrayal addressed to the West (Prizel 1998: 41–2, 72–3). Polish elites started to see their nation as the 'Christ of nations', an image propagated in particular by the national poet Adam Mickiewicz after the 1830 uprising (see Mickiewicz 1833). According to this interpretation, the Polish nation sacrificed itself for the sake of all other nations; one day, like Jesus Christ, it would resurrect. Mickiewicz's metaphor appealed to the Poles' deep religious sentiment and aptly combined political and religious imagery to foster faith in national rebirth.

The hopes of romantic nationalists suffered a fatal blow in 1863, when another major uprising was crushed in Russian Poland and the Tsar launched policies of cultural and linguistic Russification (Stauter-Halsted 2001: 244–6; Porter 2000: 15).[8] After 1863, the ideals of Polish romantics were gradually displaced by those of positivists. With the advent of Positivism, the definition of the nation became more focused on Polish culture and language. Positivists believed that national minorities in the former territories of the Commonwealth (notably Lithuanians, Ukrainians, Jews and Belarusians) would converge towards Polish culture and language due to Poland's cultural superiority. In this conception, the nation was no longer an ideal and spiritual entity (as for romantics), but rather an ethnic and linguistic community. The positivist reconceptualisation of the nation paved the way for ethnonationalism, an aggressive and more exclusive form of nationalism (Prizel 1998: 40–50). Ethnonationalism was advanced by political organisations that originated in the 1880s, most notably the National League of Roman Dmowski. Its nationalist discourse was authoritarian, xenophobic and anti-Semitic. Thanks to the gradual politicisation of the peasantry in the last years of the nineteenth century, ethnonationalism quickly became a mass movement (Porter 2000: 125–6, 136–55).

In the period when ethnonationalism was dominant in Polish discourses (from the late 1890s until the 1940s), it influenced dramatically the relationship between the Poles and their neighbouring nations. Jews, who numbered several million in the former territory of the Commonwealth, were depicted as an alien body that had to be either expelled or polonised. They were the first community to be considered as irredeemable Others, but by the end of the nineteenth century Polish nationalists applied similar discourses to the Germans, Russians, Lithuanians and Ukrainians also (Porter 2000: 158–77). Ethnonationalists became convinced that a Polish state had to be rebuilt within the Commonwealth boundaries (stretching over most of today's Lithuania, Belarus and Ukraine), but with the Poles as a dominant ethnic group. Poles were also seen as having the messianic task of educating ethnic Ukrainians, Belarusians and Lithuanians, with the ultimate objective of polonising them (Prizel 1998: 52–67).

Between 1918 and 1939, Poland temporarily became independent. As ethnonationalist leaders were appointed to leading positions in the new state, their narratives became dominant in official discourses. Although national minorities constituted one third of Poland's interwar population, they were marginalised and had hardly any representation in political institutions (Prizel 1998: 62–7; see Brubaker 1996: 416–30). Ethnonationalist policies irremediably soured relations between the Poles and their neighbouring nationalities. In the 1990s, when Poland finally regained full independence, its foreign policy with Lithuania, Belarus, Ukraine and Russia was still constrained by the image that the country had projected towards its Eastern neighbours in the heyday of ethnonationalism (Snyder 2003; see Fedorowicz 2007).

The interwar Polish state was dismantled abruptly in 1939, when Nazi Germany and the Soviet Union partitioned the country. The brutal Nazi and Soviet

---

8.   In 1866–7 Russian was established as the mandatory language for the teaching of all subjects in all Polish secondary schools, with the exception of religion (Porter 2000: 79–80).

war occupations strengthened and radicalised Polish perceptions of Germany and Russia as hostile Others. Since the Second World War is the key episode in current national memory, resentment towards both Germany and Russia has continued to be perpetuated in dominant discourses until today (Ruchniewicz 2007). Polish characterisations of their Second World War experiences can be clustered around the themes of suffering and heroism. Discourses on suffering stress that Poland was the first country to be attacked by Nazi Germany (and simultaneously by the Soviet Union), experienced the longest foreign occupation in the war and endured enormous material losses and the worst human losses as a proportion of its total population (nearly 6 million deaths out of a pre-war population of nearly 35 million). This discourse was influenced by and perpetuated nineteenth-century narratives on national martyrdom that portrayed Poland as the 'Christ of nations'.

The discourse on Polish heroism is closely linked to that of suffering and stresses that the nation strenuously opposed the Nazis (Ruchniewicz 2007: 19). The opening of the Warsaw Rising Museum, which was inaugurated in the Polish capital in 2004 and immediately drew thousands of visitors every month, highlights the enduring relevance of the discourse on heroism. As the official website states, the museum is 'a tribute from Warsaw's residents to those who fought and died for an independent Poland and its free capital'.[9] The historical event has been turned into a founding myth of post-1989 Poland, regardless of its disappointing outcome, the large number of civilian casualties and the ensuing destruction of Warsaw. Poland's wartime experience led to a revival of the discourse on Western betrayal and the unreciprocated support to the cause of freedom. Poles felt betrayed in 1939, when the United Kingdom and France provided no military assistance during the German invasion, and particularly at the Yalta conference in 1945, when the Western Allies agreed to leave Poland in the Soviet sphere of influence (Prizel 1998: 73–4). The Western decision to accommodate Moscow's requests left Poles with the conviction that the United States' foreign policy would always prioritise the Soviet Union. This fear motivated Polish foreign policy makers swiftly to use the window of opportunity of the 1990s and apply for NATO integration, while Russia was focusing mostly on internal problems (Snyder 2003: 110–11).

The outcome of the Yalta conference and Poland's swift Sovietisation after the Second World War led Polish intellectuals and the political opposition to reassess the country's role in the international scenario (Prizel 1998: 75–87). Poland's communist leaders attempted to develop a socialist, pro-Soviet identity but were largely perceived as alien and imposed on the country by a foreign power. Next to the official communist discourse, prominent oppositional discourses originated in the underground and in émigrés communities. The literary–political émigré magazine *Kultura* was one of the leading forums for the discussion of Polish identity and the future role of Poland in the international arena. From the 1970s onwards it prepared the conceptual background for the foreign policy of post-communist Poland (Snyder 2003: 220). In a fundamental break with

9. See website of the Warsaw Rising Museum, www.1944.pl/en/ (accessed 5 February 2013).

Poland's interwar foreign policy, *Kultura* advocated the acceptance of existing borders (although Poland had lost most of its pre-1939 Eastern provinces), the recognition of post-communist Ukraine, Lithuania and Belarus as equal nations and the rejection of any division of Eastern Europe into spheres of influence with Russia. By accepting its post-war territorial losses in the East, Poland would be less exposed to German territorial claims in the West based on 1939 borders.[10] By the late 1980s, *Kultura*'s foreign policy ideas had become widely accepted among the Polish underground opposition (Snyder 2003: 220–5).

The success of *Kultura*'s ideas had been made possible also by their endorsement by the Polish Catholic Church and the Vatican. This endorsement was fundamental to promoting the new international self-image of Poland among the masses, as the Church enjoyed widespread support in civil society. Due to the protracted lack of independent state structures, the Polish Catholic Church became the main repository of the country's national identity, particularly under communism. In popular perceptions, the Polish Catholic Church was one of the main factors leading to the end of communist rule in Poland. With the support of the Vatican, where Polish cardinal Karol Wojtyła became Pope in 1978, the Catholic trade union Solidarity became a mass movement and challenged the regime, eventually leading to its demise in 1989. The metaphor of Poland as the 'Christ of nations' gained momentum once again: after decades of martyrdom, the nation finally resurrected (Ash 2002). The Church also retained a prominent role in identity politics after the recovery of full independence in 1989 (Prizel 1998: 90–1, 229–30). According to a 2005 survey, Catholicism in Poland is linked to national pride; Poles are very religious and trust the Church more than any other institution, except for the army (McManus-Czubinska and Miller 2008: 147–8; see Sidorenko 2008: 119).

After 1989 the theme of the 'return to Europe', meant as joining the achievements of post-war Western Europe (Snyder 2003: 291), became dominant. Polish governments made EU and NATO integration their primary foreign policy goals. In order to achieve these aims, Warsaw adopted the policy of reconciliation with its neighbours conceptualised by *Kultura* and embraced a rhetoric that stressed so-called European standards (Snyder 2003: 256–8; see Curry 2008: 186–7). The ethnonationalist, xenophobic and anti-Semitic discourses of the interwar period lost dominance, but they did not disappear and remained widespread in important sections of the Catholic Church, right-wing political parties and public opinion in general (Bikont 2012). The fact that by 1990 Poland was almost a mono-ethnic state, having lost most of its interwar national minorities, made previous ethnonationalist discourses about threatening internal Others anachronistic. However, deep-seated perceptions of Western Europe as a treacherous ally and of Germany and Russia as Poland's historical enemies survived (Orla-Bukowska 2006: 181–7). Between 2005 and 2007, when the right-wing party Law and Justice formed a coalition government with the far right, these perceptions constituted the

---

10. In 1945, the former German provinces of Silesia, most of Pomerania and part of East Prussia were annexed to Poland; ethnic Germans living there were expelled.

backbone of a virulent official discourse (Reeves 2010). The strong anti-German and anti-Russian rhetoric of the mid-2000s showed that, for a considerable part of its leadership, Poland still lived in an insecure international environment, where it was threatened by its historical Others.

Russia in Polish identity discourses: the eternal Other?

Throughout Poland's modern history, Polish identity discourses constructed Russia and Germany as aggressive and threatening Others. Poland's post-1990 rapprochement to Germany and European integration has not cancelled negative images of its Western neighbour, which are strongly rooted in national memory. However, they have contributed to reconciliation and to the belief that a new era in Polish–German relations has begun (see Langenbacher 2008: 74–5). In this context, Russia has become the dominant Other in official Polish discourses.

Russian domination over Poland was the longest the country ever experienced, stretching from 1795 to 1918 and then again (under the Soviet banner) from 1939 to 1941 and from 1945 to 1989. It was also the one that ended most recently and is generally considered by Poles as the most economically damaging for the country. Dominant Polish discourses describe the Russian partition zone in 1795–1918 as the least developed (by contrast with the German and Austrian zones) and blame the Russians for having imposed a repressive and inefficient economic and political model after 1945 (Zarycki 2004: 604). Soviet tutelage during the Cold War is seen as the continuation of Tsarist domination and the terms 'Russia' and 'Russians' are used as metonymies for 'Soviet Union' and 'Soviets' (Orla-Bukowska 2006: 203).

Russia plays a key role in the narratives about Polish heroism and martyrdom. The discourse on Polish heroism was constructed mostly in the context of wars and uprisings against Russian domination. The 1830 and 1863 uprisings against the Tsarist Empire, the Polish–Soviet war of 1920 and the anti-communist uprisings of 1956, 1968, 1970 and 1980 are considered as a *continuum* in a two-century-long tradition of anti-Russian struggle (Loew 2008: 87–95; Ruchniewicz 2007: 11–12). Particular importance is attributed to the 1920 Polish–Soviet war. The decisive battle of the war, fought at the gates of Warsaw, is commonly referred to as 'the miracle at the Vistula', as it averted a Bolshevik victory that had seemed inevitable (see Orla-Bukowska 2006: 204). It is commemorated every year on 15 August, which is also Army Day and Assumption Day. Due to the concurrence of the 'miracle' with the religious festivity, the victorious battle has acquired a quasi-religious significance for the Poles. It also fosters the romantic image of Poland's resurrection after it sacrificed itself to defend Europe and Christianity, and hence the themes of Poland as 'Christ of nations' and as *antemurale christianitatis*.

Within the martyrdom discourse, Russia plays a key role as the oppressor that crushed nearly all Polish attempts to regain freedom. Most notably, it is portrayed as the brutal, dictatorial power that partitioned Poland with the Nazis in 1939 and exterminated nearly 22,000 Polish officers in the Katyn massacre in April 1940. The massacre and the Nazi–Soviet pact have been widely discussed in public only in post-1989 Poland, as both topics were taboo under communism (Paul 2010).

According to surveys conducted in 2006 and 2007, most Poles consider the events of 1939–40 as the main reason why Russia should feel guilty and issue an official apology to Warsaw (Levintova 2010: 1357). Post-Soviet Russia, however, has refused to take responsibility for Stalinist crimes. In 2010 Russian president Dmitri Medvedev suggested that Warsaw lacked moral grounds to demand an apology for Katyn, as interwar Poland had been responsible for comparable crimes against the Soviet Union, such as the death of 16,000–20,000 Soviet prisoners of war in Polish detention camps (cited in Feklyunina 2012: 444). Polish narratives reject such comparisons and the dispute concerning responsibility for Katyn has not ended. In fact, the death of former Polish president Lech Kaczynski in a plane crash in April 2010, while he was going to commemorate the seventieth anniversary of the Katyn massacre, contributed to the continued prominence of the topic in public discourse. The ensuing debate on responsibilities for the plane crash showed that mutual distrust and hostility are still important factors in Polish–Russian relations (Shuster 2011).

Russia's enduring role as Poland's threatening Other has turned the country into a negative reference point for the construction of the Polish Self and for Poland's understanding of its role in the international arena. According to Tomasz Zarycki (2004), in Polish discourses Russia fulfils the function of relativising Poland's distance from the West. Russia is perceived as inherently undemocratic and as an inferior imitator of European civilisation (see Prizel 1998: 82–5). Polish discourses orientalise Russia: they describe it as a less civilised and backward country, with a tradition of despotism linked to strong Asiatic influences. The ensuing feeling of cultural superiority allows Poles to strengthen their European identity, construct themselves as Central Europe and feel closer to Western European civilisation (see Said 1978). Polish identity narratives portray Russia as inherently imperialistic. Post-communist Russia's use of energy politics to achieve political objectives is constructed as a continuation of Tsarist and Soviet expansionist policies by different means. Arguably, the image of Russia as a potential threat has been the backbone of Polish foreign policy after 1989 and the main reason for Poland's pursuit of EU and NATO membership (Zarycki 2004: 607–14).

After the collapse of communism, relations between Moscow and Warsaw improved only slightly and briefly when Red Army soldiers left their bases in Poland and Russian president Boris Yeltsin initially agreed to Polish NATO membership (Snyder 2003: 245–6). By September 1993, Yeltsin had changed his position and vehemently opposed Warsaw's accession to the Atlantic Alliance. Poles perceived his volte-face as the demonstration that post-Soviet Russia was still imperialist and wanted to retain a sphere of influence by constraining Polish foreign policy choices (Zarycki 2004: 609). Furthermore, the Russian parliamentary crisis of October 1993, which Yeltsin ended by having tanks fire at the Parliament, revived the argument that Russia was inherently undemocratic and would not change course despite the end of communism. After the crisis, a survey showed that 70 per cent of Poles considered Russia a military threat (Snyder 2003: 278).

For the rest of the 1990s, while Poland prepared for Western integration and Russia faced repeated economic crises, Polish–Russian diplomatic relations were restricted to the bare minimum. In 2002 Vladimir Putin finally travelled to Poland, nine years after the last official visit of a Russian president (Feklyunina 2012: 438). However, the renewed activism of Russia's foreign policy under Putin, combined with its rapid economic growth in the years 2000–8, reawakened deep-seated Polish fears of the powerful Eastern neighbour. In 2004, Poland and Russia got involved in the political crisis that followed the presidential election in Ukraine. Warsaw and Moscow resented each other's attempts to influence political developments in a neighbouring state. The following year was marred by a series of bilateral crises, culminating in a Russian ban on the import of Polish meat and dairy products. In response, Poland (an EU member since 2004) vetoed the start of EU–Russia negotiations on a new partnership and cooperation agreement (Feklyunina 2012: 439). Furthermore, Putin's invitation of his Polish counterpart Aleksander Kwasniewski to the May 2005 celebrations of the Soviet victory in the Second World War revived the Polish public debate on Soviet crimes in Poland during the war (Onken 2007).

Polish official discourses about Russia became further radicalised due to the 2005 electoral victory of the profoundly anti-Russian and anti-German Law and Justice party of Lech and Jaroslaw Kaczynski. The Law and Justice governments made constant use of historical analogies to address foreign policy issues with Germany and Russia. In 2006 Polish defence minister Radoslaw Sikorski dubbed the Nord Stream gas pipeline connecting Russia to Germany via the Baltic Sea (thereby circumventing Poland) a 'new Molotov–Ribbentrop pact' (cited in Castle 2006). A year later, Law and Justice foreign minister Anna Fotyga publicly called Russia and Germany Poland's 'historic enemies' (cited in Reeves 2010: 522). The government's decision to host elements of the US anti-missile shield on Polish territory, describing them as an anti-Russian guarantee, further spoiled relations with Moscow (Ozbay and Aras 2008).

A study of articles concerning Russia published between 2000 and 2007 on *Gazeta Wyborcza*, the largest-circulation Polish daily, and on *Rzeczpospolita*, the third-largest, reveals that historical stereotypes and rivalry were still dominant in Polish discourses (Levintova 2010). Russia was described mostly as aggressive, authoritarian, corrupt and xenophobic. Bilateral relations were framed negatively, particularly in the energy sector, where Russia was considered an unreliable supplier. The worst criticism concerned the field of memory politics, most notably Russia's refusal to condemn the Yalta agreement and take responsibility for the Katyn massacre and the 1939 invasion of Poland. Russian political elites were portrayed very negatively and identified with the whole country. Only under themes such as culture and arts was Russia portrayed in a more positive light (see Zarycki 2011).

After the end of the Law and Justice governments, Polish–Russian relations started to improve. In October 2007, centre-right candidate Donald Tusk won the elections and became prime minister. The Tusk government sought partial reconciliation with Russia by adopting a pragmatic approach on economic issues and by fostering dialogue on sensitive topics such as the Katyn massacre. Anti-Russian discourses did not disappear but were toned down, at least at official level.

The Russian ban on the import of Polish meat and dairy products was swiftly lifted and Poland removed its veto on the negotiations of the EU–Russia partnership and cooperation agreement. Some progress was made also in discussions regarding historical controversies. In 2010 a forum of prominent Russian and Polish experts appointed by their respective governments produced a joint publication addressing sensitive issues, including the Katyn massacre and the origins of the Second World War (Feklyunina 2012: 438–41).[11] According to surveys, the number of ordinary Poles seeing Russia as friendly modestly rose from 9 per cent in 2005 to 19 per cent in 2011 (Feklyunina 2012: 445). For the first time in the history of Polish–Russian relations, in April 2010 the Russian and Polish prime ministers jointly commemorated the Katyn massacre (Schwirtz 2010).

However, the atmosphere of reconciliation generated by the joint commemoration was marred by the aftermath of the plane crash in which Polish president Lech Kaczynski died. The Polish right overtly blamed Russia for the plane crash and constructed a discourse juxtaposing Russian past and (alleged) present crimes, which swiftly became dominant. This discourse became more virulent in 2011, when a Russian enquiry commission published a report exculpating the Russian authorities from responsibility for the accident. Conspiracy theories blaming Russia for a 'new Katyn' became omnipresent in the Polish media (Shuster 2011). Hence, Poland's reconciliation with Russia under Tusk was only partial and has proven to be fragile. Profoundly anti-Russian discourses have remained prominent both at official and unofficial level and are often voiced by Law and Justice, which has regained the political control of the country following its victory in the 2015 parliamentary and presidential elections. Furthermore, relations with Moscow have become extremely tense following Russia's annexation of Crimea and destabilisation of Ukraine in 2014.

Table 3.2: Dominant themes in Polish identity discourses

National identity discourses	Discourses on Russia
National martyrdom (Christ of nations)	Imperialist and aggressive
National heroism	Brutal occupying power for most of Poland's modern history
Catholicism	Oriental, undemocratic and corrupt
Euro-Atlanticism	Relativising Poland's distance from the West
Unreciprocated commitment to the West	Partner in pragmatic foreign policy

Source: author's own compilation.

---

11. The forum was named 'Group on difficult issues' and its work was published under the title *White Spots – Black Spots: difficult Issues in Russian-Polish Relations* (Feklyunina 2012: 440). Furthermore, Andrzej Wajda's movie on Katyn, produced in Poland, was shown on Russian television, which greatly contributed to ordinary Russians' awareness of the massacre (Ash 2011).

Nordicity along the East–West continuum: the historical construction of Finnish identity

Finnish national identity has been constructed around the concepts of marginality, Nordicity and the historical necessity to locate the country along an East–West continuum. These conceptualisations do not merely concern geography; they have profound cultural and political significance and have shaped the way Finns perceive their country and its role in the international arena. They were constructed during the last two centuries within historical frameworks that allowed Finland to become first an autonomous entity within the Russian empire, then a fully independent country.

The year 1809 is a key date in the construction of Finnish national identity. After nearly six centuries of Swedish control, the Grand Duchy of Finland was created as part of the Tsarist Empire, with autonomous institutions and a distinct legal and administrative system (Tiilikainen 1998: 120–2). Within this political context, Finns could develop for the first time a feeling of national belonging based on a common language and the rediscovery of their cultural heritage.[12] The lack of full political independence was not perceived as an obstacle to the emergence of the nation at this stage. Finland was considered as a young nation in the process of maturation. Within this discourse, the autonomy acquired under Russian tutelage was seen as a considerable step forward from the period of Swedish domination. Key figures of the Finnish national movement such as Yrjö Sakari Yrjö-Koskinen and Johan Vilhelm Snellman argued that the nation could still be constructed within Russian imperial structures by focusing on the cultural sphere and temporarily renouncing ambitions of independence (Browning and Lehti 2007: 697).

The dichotomy between the cultural and the political conception of the nation, each gaining the upper hand in different historical periods, has remained a key element of Finnish identity until today (Joenniemi 2002). In the nineteenth century, the emphasis on cultural identity was also part of a discourse portraying Finland as a small nation that needed the protection of a stronger, benevolent Other while it developed a distinct identity. Simultaneously, Finnish nationalists used the peripheral location of the Grand Duchy in the Tsarist Empire and its administrative autonomy to relativise Finland's political dependence on Russia. Being marginal meant being distinct from the rest of the empire. Marginality and the notion of being a small country at the mercy of neighbouring great powers became dominant traits of Finnish identity and of Finland's self-image in the international arena (Browning and Lehti 2007; Tiilikainen 2006).

Towards the end of the nineteenth century, the Russification campaigns and increasing repressiveness of the Tsarist government led to a gradual rethinking of Finnish national identity and its relationship with Russia. While the Finnish leadership attempted to accommodate Russian requests and retain political

---

12. In 1835 the *Kalevala* was published, a national epic of Finland and one of the main works in Finnish literature. It had a profound impact on virtually all aspects of Finnish cultural life.

autonomy, a new conception of national identity, based on ethnicity and exclusive boundaries, became widespread (Joenniemi 2002: 198). According to this view, national identity could not be based simply on cultural distinctiveness and political autonomy; Finns had to strive for full independence and the creation of a nation-state. The Russian revolution provided the opportunity to disentangle the country from the crumbling Tsarist Empire. In December 1917 Finland proclaimed its independence.

The newly born Finnish state immediately experienced a bloody civil war between the political right and the left, which led to the radicalisation of national identity discourses. The victory of the right in Finland and the success of the Bolsheviks in the Russian civil war brought about fundamental changes in Finnish self-images and perceptions of the international role of Finland. The Soviet Union was orientalised and constructed as the main national threat, while Finland was portrayed as an outpost of Western civilisation (Joenniemi 2002: 199). From this time, locating Finland somewhere along a continuum between East and West became a permanent feature of national identity discourses (Browning and Lehti 2007: 691). In the following decades, the country was alternately depicted as a Western, anti-Soviet bastion or as a bridge between East and West, with the function of bringing Russia closer to the latter.

In the interwar period, ethnonationalism dominated Finnish political discourses. It was accompanied by the formulation of expansionist foreign policy ideas, such as the creation of a Greater Finland extending to Eastern Karelia and Siberia. The Finns' confidence in their ability to stand on their own and confront larger neighbours was temporarily bolstered by the successful defensive campaigns of the Winter War against the Soviet Union (1939–40). Eventually, however, such confidence was shattered by the entanglement in the broader geopolitical struggle between Nazi Germany and the USSR and, most importantly, by the defeat in the Second World War (Vehviläinen 2002). The harsh conditions imposed by the Soviets at the end of the war, including the loss of considerable portions of national territory and a large indemnity, led Finnish leaders to reject the political course of the interwar years and reformulate the foreign policy of the country (Browning 2008: 169–78).

Dominant post-war discourses stressed that the involvement in great power politics had had catastrophic consequences for Finland. Hence, the idea of Finland as a small nation that should adopt a pragmatic policy and stay aloof from geopolitical struggles remained central in foreign policy making throughout the Cold War. Pragmatism in foreign policy meant primarily accommodating the requests of the Soviet Union, the powerful neighbour with which Finland shared a border of over 1,000 kilometres. In 1948 a treaty of friendship, cooperation and mutual assistance with the Soviet Union was signed. While maintaining good relations with the USSR, Finland became a neutral state. This pragmatic foreign policy doctrine became known as the Paasikivi–Kekkonen line, from the names of Juho Paasikivi, who became president in 1946 and is credited with having started it, and his successor Urho Kekkonen, who was in office from 1956 until 1981 (Browning 2008: 169–71; Tiilikainen 1998: 146–51). The key objective of the

Paasikivi–Kekkonen line was the preservation of independence and territorial integrity, which appeared seriously threatened at the end of the Second World War. The idea of the nation as sovereign and linked to a specific territory survived the defeat in the war against the USSR and was a key foreign policy tenet throughout the Cold War. This conception also constituted the pragmatic essence of 'Finlandisation', a termed coined in the German scholarly debate during the Cold War that referred to the policy of securing sovereignty through appeasement of the Soviet Union (Jokela 2010: 56).[13] Following this policy line, Finland would accommodate Soviet requests and obtain in return Soviet acceptance of its independence, political system and free market economy (Browning 2008: 176).

The choice of neutrality in the East–West confrontation was also pragmatic and supportive of Finnish foreign policy interests. It sent a positive message to both Cold War camps. For the communist world, it meant that Finland would stay neutral in international crises, despite its adherence to Western values. The 1948 treaty with the Soviet Union was a further guarantee that Helsinki was interested in maintaining good relations with the Eastern bloc. For the West, neutrality was a message of belonging: it could be read as evidence that Finland had been forced to accommodate Soviet interests, but while doing so it kept Western political and economic structures. As the Cold War unfolded, Finnish neutrality evolved from a defensive policy for the preservation of sovereignty to an opportunity to acquire an active role in mediating the East–West conflict. Finland was constructed as a successful bridge builder within the framework of detente between the two blocs. The signature of the Helsinki Final Act at the 1975 summit of the conference on security and cooperation in Europe, held in the Finnish capital, was arguably the greatest success of the Finnish policy of bridge building between East and West (Tiilikainen 1998: 153–6).

The policy of neutrality allowed Finland to become active and construct a distinct identity in other fields of world politics too, where some room for manoeuvre existed outside the East–West conflict. Most notably, the country became a prominent supporter of 'internationalist solidarism' (Browning 2007: 33), namely the efforts to bridge the economic gap between rich and poor states. Finland was a fervent advocate of the United Nations (UN) and, together with the other Nordic countries (Sweden, Norway and Denmark), provided 25 per cent of the military personnel deployed in UN operations during the Cold War (Browning 2007: 35). Alongside the focus on international solidarity, Finland shared with its Nordic neighbours the domestic model of egalitarian social democracy (portrayed as a third way between communism and capitalism) and the international image of being a peaceful and highly modern society. These three elements became the foundations of a Nordic identity through which Finland constructed its international role during the Cold War (Browning 2007: 32–5).

When the Cold War ended, the main tenets of Nordic identity and of Finland's self-image were challenged by the new geopolitical reality. The idea of the Nordic

---

13. In Finland the term 'Finlandisation' has acquired a negative meaning, indicating an excessive willingness to appease the Soviet Union (see Browning 2008: 207; Jokela 2010: 56).

countries as the most peaceful region of Europe and as the main supporters of international solidarity became somewhat anachronistic, particularly as the EU started to be constructed as the main guarantor of peace in the continent and became the largest provider of development aid. Most importantly, the end of the East–West confrontation called into question the significance of a model that was alternative to the blocs of the Cold War. Domestically, it made little sense to define the Nordic social democratic model as a middle way between Western European capitalism and Eastern European communism, as the latter no longer existed. In foreign policy, Finland had to face the fact that it no longer appeared useful to define its identity in terms of an East–West continuum. The changed international scenario caused a temporary identity crisis in the country (Browning 2007: 36–43; Tiilikainen 1998: 159; see Wæver 1992).

The crisis was, however, solved in a relatively short period through the combination of a new identity discourse and the adaptation of pre-existing discourses. The new narrative argued that Finland could finally return to the West and to Europe, after being forced to stay at their margins in order to retain its sovereignty during the Cold War (Browning and Lehti 2007: 704). This was exemplified by the first Finnish foreign policy moves after the end of the Cold War. The 1948 treaty with the Soviet Union expired in 1992 and Finland applied for membership of the EU, which was granted after nearly 57 per cent of Finns voted in favour in a referendum held in October 1994 (Joenniemi 2002 186). The shift in Finland's foreign policy identity brought about by accession to the EU could be reconciled with pre-existing identity discourses. The EU was conceptualised as an entity that did not intrude on the Finnish social model, national security policy and Nordic identity (Joenniemi 2002: 204). Within the EU, Finland also attempted to keep its Cold War role as a bridge builder to Russia. The northern dimension, a Finnish initiative launched in 1998 to coordinate the cross-border policies of the EU with Norway, Iceland and particularly Russia, provides the best example of these attempts (see Haukkala and Ojanen 2011: 159–61).

By stressing interdependence and the need for cooperation among the countries involved, the northern dimension sought to blur the boundaries between the European (and Finnish) Self and the Russian Other. In particular, it endeavoured to harmonise the EU's views and policies with those of its partners. For instance, during the 1999 Finnish presidency of the European Union, northern dimension partners were invited to present position papers prior to the European Council summit in Helsinki; their stance influenced the drawing up of a relevant EU action plan (Haukkala 2005: 287–8). Despite the EU's declared objective of creating a common foreign and security policy for its members, Finland did not relinquish its neutrality in the military field. The Finnish security discourse was partially reframed in terms of alignment. Helsinki conceded that it had aligned with the West and the EU politically and economically, but continued to adhere to military non-alignment (Jokela 2010: 61). This position has constantly enjoyed the support of the majority of Finns, which highlights how strongly the country's public opinion has internalised military neutrality as part of national identity. Surveys conducted in the years 1996–2008 revealed that a proportion of Finns oscillating between 58 and 79 per cent believed that Finland should remain neutral (Möller and Bjereld 2010: 371).

The ease with which Finland adapted its foreign policy identity to the new post-Cold War conditions may be understood through the country's historical tendency to adjust itself to changing foreign policy scenarios in order to survive (Joenniemi 2002: 209). The awareness of being a small nation with limited room for independent manoeuvre in foreign policy has continued to be a key characteristic of Finnish political identity (Tiilikainen 2006). However, Finnish policy makers have also framed Finland's foreign policy flexibility in more positive terms. A discourse on Finland as a young, future-oriented nation that quickly adapts itself to the challenges of the modern world has emerged, somewhat in continuation with the country's early nineteenth century depictions (see Joenniemi 2010: 56). Locating Finland at the economic centre of the globalised world, in spite of its small size and geographic marginality, is the main aim of the current discourse (Browning and Lehti 2007: 708).

Russia in Finnish discourses: economic partner and security deficit

The discussion of Finnish national identity construction has highlighted the prominent role of Russia and the Soviet Union in Finnish history and foreign policy choices. By contrast with dominant Polish narratives, Russia has not always been portrayed as a threat in Finnish discourses. In fact, for most of the nineteenth century a majority of Finns considered the Tsarist Empire as a benevolent Other that allowed Finnish culture and national identity to blossom (Joenniemi 2010: 48). Russia's benevolence was contrasted with the previous period of Swedish government, during which Finns had enjoyed less autonomy and cultural independence. The positive experience under the Tsarist Empire constituted an important precedent for later Finnish leaders who made the case for peaceful coexistence and close cooperation with Russia (Browning 2003: 53).

The positive memory of the early Tsarist period is, however, counterbalanced by that of the conflicts that characterised bilateral history in the first half of the twentieth century. The Russian Revolution allowed Finland to break away from the Tsarist Empire and acquire full political independence, but it also created an ideological and military threat east of the newly born Finnish state. With the rise of Finnish ethnonationalism in the 1920s and 1930s, a new narrative depicting Russians in overtly racist terms (as evil, treacherous and culturally inferior) became prominent. The border with the Soviet Union was considered a civilisational demarcation between European and Asian culture (Browning 2007: 700). The radicalisation of negative discourses about the Soviet Union reached a peak during the Winter War (1939–40), when the Red Army attempted a full-scale invasion of Finland. The unexpected and strenuous Finnish defence saved the country's independence and became one of the key national myths. In this narrative, the Russians play the role of brutal aggressors against whom the whole country united. The loss of the region of Karelia to the Soviet Union and the resettlement of its inhabitants to other areas of Finland were constant reminders of the pain inflicted by the Soviets (see Forsberg 1995; Vehviläinen 2002). The desire to avenge Soviet aggression led Finland to participate in the German attack against the Soviet Union in 1941.

Military defeat eventually stimulated a reconsideration of Finland's stance towards its powerful Eastern neighbour. The virulent anti-Soviet discourses of the interwar years were considered responsible for the outbreak of a war that Finland could not win. They had also legitimised Soviet security concerns and subsequent military action. Finland's post-war leaders concluded that criticism of the USSR had to be curtailed in order to avoid a new confrontation (Browning and Lehti 2007: 700–1). Since the Soviet victory and the geopolitical realities left no alternative, the majority of Finns supported this policy line. Finland's economic success, the development of an alternative social model and its global role as a peace-maker translated into constant support for a neutral, Soviet-friendly foreign policy throughout the Cold War. Criticism of the Soviet Union was self-censored and the country was publicly described as an important partner for Finland (see Vihavainen 2006: 31). Threat perceptions did not disappear, but they were not voiced at official level.

The collapse of the Soviet Union and the expiry of the 1948 treaty have changed the nature of Finland's relations with its eastern neighbour. Finnish media and public opinion have often criticised Russia openly in the post-Cold War period. The post-war policy of appeasement towards the USSR no longer provides a model for Finnish foreign policy and has been retrospectively condemned by some politicians. However, at official level rhetoric has not changed dramatically. There are no prominent bilateral controversies left unsolved from the past. Even the wartime loss of Karelia, which has remained part of Russia, is no longer considered as an important issue by the majority of Finns. When Finnish politicians refer to their country's historical relationship with Russia in public, they tend to emphasise positive moments, such as the development of Finnish national identity under Russian rule in the nineteenth century and the special Finnish–Soviet relationship during the Cold War (Vihavainen 2006).

Finnish perceptions of a security threat emanating from Russia still exist. Evidence for this is provided by Finland's continued reliance on territorial defence and a relatively large army of reservists. Finnish political and military leaders do not openly mention Russia as a threat, but they refer to it indirectly, often speaking in code and with euphemisms such as 'Finland's security deficit' (Forsberg 2006: 143). Some scholars go as far as arguing that the image of a Russian threat is still present in Finnish psyche and is an essential component of the grand national narrative (see Medvedev 1999: 104). However, a majority of Finns has been in favour of friendly or non-confrontational relations with Moscow (see Forsberg 2006: 148). After the crises and instability of the 1990s, Russia has become again an important trade partner for Finland. Within the EU, Finland is one of the main advocates of a policy of pragmatic engagement with Russia. Finns consider maintaining a positive dialogue with Moscow essential in order to avoid confrontation at their country's borders (Etzold and Haukkala 2011: 253–4).

Furthermore, Helsinki has retained positive bilateral relations with Moscow, which guarantee a safe channel of communication whenever the EU proves unable to formulate a shared policy towards Russia (Haukkala and Ojanen 2011: 165; see Vihavainen 2006: 45). Finland's reluctance to abandon its military non-alignment and join transatlantic security structures is evidence of the importance that is still attributed to bilateral relations with Russia. Most Finnish leaders and public opinion believe that a change in the security policy of the country would alienate Russia, thereby producing more security drawbacks than benefits (see Giles and Eskola 2009). Hence, Finland has upheld its pragmatic policy towards Moscow and has reconciled EU membership with its traditional role as bridge builder between the West and Russia.

Table 3.3: Dominant themes in Finnish identity discourses

National identity discourses	Discourses on Russia
Moving along an East–West continuum (bridge builder to East/Western outpost)	Benevolent Other
Marginality	Economic partner
Nordicity (egalitarian model, international solidarity, multilateralism) and Europeanism	Finland's security deficit
Neutrality/military non-alignment	
Finland as a young and modern nation	

Source: author's own compilation.

Conclusion: national identities and historical discourses as interpretive frameworks

This chapter showed that current German, Polish and Finnish national identities are the result of a *longue durée* process of construction that extends well into the nineteenth and twentieth centuries. The analysis emphasised that, following the experience of National Socialism and of GDR Soviet-style communism, German identity has been constructed around the rejection of authoritarianism and war. Economic prosperity, political stability, democracy and multilateralism in international politics (notably the advocacy of policies agreed upon at EU level) have become key tenets of German identity. In Poland, national identity narratives have focused on the themes of martyrdom and heroism. The martyrdom narrative focuses on the country's loss of independence and foreign occupation from 1795 until 1918, during the Second World War and throughout the Cold War. The heroism narrative stresses that Poland never accepted its loss of independence and consistently fought for its freedom, in spite of overwhelming hostile forces and the indifference of Western democracies. During the periods of foreign occupation and tutelage, the Catholic Church and Catholicism acquired fundamental importance as key constituents of Polish identity, providing ideological and institutional support for the political forces fighting for independence. On the other hand, Finnish identity construction was profoundly influenced by the country's geographical location and its geopolitical implications. Narratives of marginality and Nordicity played an essential role, with the latter acquiring particular importance during the Cold War. In this historical phase, Finland closely identified with the Nordic model, including an egalitarian society, support for international solidarity and multilateralism as a way to address international disputes. Most importantly, Finland was conceptualised as a country moving along an East–West continuum, belonging to the West ideologically but simultaneously acting as a bridge builder towards the East, namely Russia and the Soviet Union. This self-perception as mediator between East and West also contributed to turning neutrality into a key factor of the country's post-1945 identity.

Russia emerged as an important Other in national identity narratives in the three countries under investigation. However, constructions of Russia varied significantly from country to country and over time. In the nineteenth and twentieth centuries through to the Cold War, most German discourses dismissed Russia as authoritarian, corrupt and backward. While these narratives still play a role in post-reunification Germany, new discourses have emerged, portraying Russia as an essential economic partner and as a key international actor that Germany must engage. The Ostpolitik discourse, advocating dialogue and partnership with Russia, has been particularly influential from the 1970s onwards. By contrast, Russia was constructed as the main negative Other in Polish identity throughout Poland's modern and contemporary history (sharing this role with Germany until 1945 and for brief spells in the early 1990s and mid-2000s, at times of tension between Poland and Germany). Dominant Polish narratives have portrayed Russia as imperialist, aggressive, undemocratic, oriental and therefore unaware of the Western values that Poles claim to cherish. Only in recent years, during the tenure of Donald Tusk as prime minister (2007–14), has a more positive discourse on Russia emerged, highlighting its role as potential partner in a pragmatic foreign policy. Dominant Finnish narratives alternated positive and deeply negative representations of Russia. In the early nineteenth century, Russia was considered mostly as a benevolent Other that emancipated Finland from Swedish oppression and allowed it to become autonomous. As a result of the policies of Russification in the latter part of the century and the Bolshevik revolution, dominant discourses changed radically. Soviet Russia was seen as the most formidable threat to Finnish independence, a perception that was strengthened after the Soviet aggression in 1939. Both positive and negative discourses survived after the Second World War, but were reformulated in more moderate terms. Russia was portrayed both as an essential economic partner and, due to its military might, as the chief source of Finland's security deficit.

Hence, the analysis of national identity and historical narratives on Russia revealed considerable differences across the three countries under investigation. Table 3.4 summarises the dominant discourses as they emerged from the analysis in this chapter. In the following chapters, these findings are used as an interpretive framework to examine foreign policy makers' speeches and statements on Russia between 2005 and 2015. It is possible that some of the identity constituents and narratives listed in Table 3.4 may have a stronger reflection than others in the foreign policy speeches under analysis. With the passage of time, some identity discourses that played a role in foreign policy making in the past may have lost importance, while others may have emerged in a slightly different form, adapted to present circumstances. While allowing for these eventualities, the analysis refers to key elements in *longue durée* national identity formation and historical discourses on Russia to deconstruct and provide one way of understanding foreign policy makers' speeches.

Table 3.4: Dominant themes in German, Polish and Finnish identity discourses

	German discourses	Polish discourses	Finnish discourses
National identity discourses	Democracy and human rights	National martyrdom (Christ of nations)	Moving along an East–West continuum (bridge builder to East/Western outpost)
	Economic prosperity and stability	National heroism	Marginality
	Rejection of war as means to solve disputes	Catholicism	Nordicity (egalitarian model, international solidarity, multilateralism), Europeanism
	Pro-European Union and multilateralism	Euro-Atlanticism	Neutrality/Military non-alignment
		Unreciprocated commitment to the West	Finland as a young and modern nation
Discourses on Russia	Ostpolitik	Imperialist and aggressive	Benevolent Other
	Authoritarian, corrupt, socially and economically backward	Brutal occupying power for most of Poland's modern history	Economic partner
	Economic partner	Oriental, undemocratic and corrupt	Finland's security deficit
	Key actor in international arena	Relativising Poland's distance from the West	
		Partner in pragmatic foreign policy	

Source: author's own compilation.

Chapter Four

The Nord Stream Pipeline and European Energy Security

This chapter investigates German, Polish and Finnish foreign policy makers' discourses on the Nord Stream pipeline project and the energy relationship between the European Union and Russia in the years 2005–12.[1] Dominant narratives are analysed with reference to the key elements of national identity construction and the historical perceptions of Russia that were illustrated in Chapter Three. The analysis shows that national narratives diverged considerably and that identity provides a useful interpretive framework to explain this diversity. The chapter opens with a concise survey of the broad policy context in which discourses on Nord Stream and energy relations with Russia were formulated. This background contextualises the case study and shows its significance for the relations with Russia of both the EU and its member states. In the following sections, the main German, Polish and Finnish discourses are analysed. Each section includes a brief introduction to the national political context and the main official actors that were involved in the construction of dominant discourses on Nord Stream and energy relations with Russia. Finally, the chapter compares national discourses on the energy relationship with Russia and shows why this is a highly contentious topic among EU member states.

The Nord Stream project

The debate concerning the energy security of the EU and its member states has been one of the liveliest in European foreign policy circles since the mid-2000s. The demand for fossil fuels in EU member states is considerably larger than domestic production. In 2005, EU member states imported most of their gas and oil from a few neighbouring countries, notably Russia, Norway and Algeria. Russia was the EU's main energy partner, accounting for 40 per cent of the EU's total gas imports and 36 per cent of its oil imports (Aalto and Westphal 2008: 7). Faced with declining domestic production and increasing demand, most EU member states were concerned with securing energy imports from non-EU countries. Due to the EU's plans to reduce emissions of carbon dioxide, gas (as a less polluting fossil fuel than oil and coal) became an increasingly important component of the European energy mix.

---

1. Namely the period from the signature of the agreement to build the Nord Stream pipeline until the completion of its construction.

As the longest standing gas provider to Europe and holder of the world's largest gas reserves, in 2005 Russia was an essential energy partner for many European countries (Högselius 2013). Most Central and Eastern European states were heavily reliant on imports of Russian gas. In the three countries under analysis, this reliance varied. It was highest in Finland, where 100 per cent of imported gas came from Russia, and lower but nevertheless very significant in both Poland and Germany, with respectively 63 and 45 per cent of total gas imports coming from Russia (Aalto and Westphal 2008: 8).

Russian gas was channelled to EU member states through pipelines. However, only Finland, Estonia and Latvia had direct pipeline connections with Russia. Russian gas reached the markets of other EU member states after crossing the territory of Ukraine and Belarus, two former Soviet republics that also depended on imports of Russian energy supplies. Most of the gas (around 100 billion cubic metres a year) was channelled to Central Europe via the Brotherhood pipeline, through Ukraine. The Yamal–Europe pipeline, built in the late 1990s to transport Russian gas to Poland and Germany via Belarus, provided an alternative route, but with a lower capacity (around 20 billion cubic meters per year) than Brotherhood (Högselius 2013: 212–13). As long as Russia's relations with Ukraine and Belarus were good, Russian gas supplies to Europe via the Brotherhood and Yamal–Europe pipelines appeared secure.

The situation changed in the mid-2000s, when diplomatic relations between Russia and Ukraine became tense and Russia's state-owned energy company Gazprom announced its intention to increase the price of gas sold to Kiev.[2] Until then, Russia had sold its gas to Ukraine at heavily discounted prices (Balmaceda 2012: 138). The Ukrainian government attempted to resist price increases. Its frequent disputes with Gazprom led to several disruptions in the flow of Russian gas to the EU; the most serious ones were those of January 2006 and January 2009. As a result, the security of Russian gas supplies to Central and Western Europe became increasingly dependent on the status of Russian–Ukrainian relations (Balmaceda 2012; Pirani 2012). Both Russia and some EU member states attempted to address the issue. On 8 September 2005 Gazprom and the German energy companies BASF and E.ON signed an agreement for the construction of a North European gas pipeline (renamed Nord Stream in 2006) connecting Russia and Germany via the Baltic Sea.

The government of German Chancellor Gerhard Schröder was particularly enthusiastic about the project and gave financial guarantees to cover part of its cost. In December 2005, a few weeks after the end of his mandate as chancellor, Schröder became chairman of the Nord Stream board. Nord Stream thus appeared as a German–Russian corporate project with strong governmental backing in both countries. However, both before and after the Russian–German deal of September

---

2. Tensions were due mainly to the Orange revolution in Ukraine in November 2004 and Viktor Yushchenko's election to the Ukrainian presidency in January 2005. The Russian leadership considered Yushchenko hostile to Russia's interest and backed Kremlin-friendly candidate Viktor Yanukovych.

2005, the project saw the involvement of other European actors. The planning for a pipeline connecting Russia to Central Europe via the Baltic Sea started in the mid-1990s as a Russian–Finnish initiative. Finnish companies Neste and Fortum were involved in the planning process until 2004. In 2000 the European Commission declared the North European gas pipeline a project of European interest. Between 2007 and 2010, the Dutch company Gasunie and the French GDF Suez acquired stakes in the project (Smith 2012: 122–3).[3]

The Nord Stream project involved key energy companies of Western and Central European EU member states but had no stakeholder in the East–Central European countries that joined the EU in 2004. In fact, the pipeline was designed and built following a route that circumvented not only Belarus and Ukraine, but also the three post-Soviet Baltic states (Estonia, Latvia and Lithuania) and Poland. Despite Gazprom's argument that this choice had been made in order to avoid transit fees, the governments of Poland and the Baltic states considered the pipeline to be politically motivated. Russia and the EU member states supporting Nord Stream, particularly Germany, were accused of making deals that were detrimental to the interests of East–Central European states and to EU plans to build a shared European energy policy (Westphal 2008: 109). According to this argument, Nord Stream created a preferential energy corridor from Russia to Germany and Western Europe, allowing Russia to use its gas exports to East-Central Europe as a political lever (by reducing supplies and increasing costs at its discretion while leaving gas flows to West European countries unaffected). Poland and the Baltic states feared that they would be increasingly exposed to Russian political and economic influence, a prospect that awakened anti-Russian collective memories and parallels with their subjugation to the Soviet Union during the Cold War (Grigas 2013). The debate on Nord Stream became heavily politicised, with identity and memory politics playing a major role in its development.

In the Nordic EU members, the debate focused primarily on the environmental consequences of the pipeline. Nord Stream was to cross the Finnish, Swedish and Danish exclusive economic zones and posed a potential threat to the already fragile Baltic Sea ecosystem. In October and November 2009, after years of analyses concerning the pipeline's environmental impact, the Danish, Swedish and Finnish authorities granted the authorisations to build the necessary infrastructure in their exclusive economic zones (Aalto and Tynkkynen 2008; Smith 2012: 124–6). The construction of the pipeline began in early 2010 and gas started to flow in September 2011. On 8 November 2011, the official inauguration of Nord Stream took place in the presence of German Chancellor Angela Merkel, Russian President Dmitri Medvedev, French and Dutch Prime Ministers François Fillon and Mark Rutte and European Commissioner for Energy Günther Oettinger. The construction of the pipeline was completed in October 2012.

---

3. Following the entry of GDF Suez in the consortium in March 2010, Nord Stream stakes were divided as follows: Gazprom 51 per cent, Wintershall (subsidiary of BASF) 15.5 per cent, E.ON 15.5 per cent, Gasunie 9 per cent and GDF Suez 9 per cent.

A pipeline in Europe's interests: German leaders' discourses

The Nord Stream pipeline and energy relations with Russia were a central theme in numerous speeches and newspaper interviews by German political leaders throughout the period under analysis. Between 2005 and 2012, Germany had three governments. The first one had a centre-left majority, with social democrat Gerhard Schröder as chancellor and Green Party leader Joschka Fischer as foreign minister; its mandate ended in November 2005. Angela Merkel, a member of the centre-right Christian Democratic Union, was chancellor in the second and third governments, covering the whole remaining timeframe of analysis (November 2005–December 2012). During her first government, which lasted until October 2009, Merkel was in a coalition with the centre-left Social Democratic Party. Frank-Walter Steinmeier, a leading member of the social democrats, covered the post of foreign minister. In October 2009, following new parliamentary elections, Merkel formed a coalition with the centre-right Free Democratic Party. Its leader, Guido Westerwelle, became foreign minister in the new government.

The analysis focuses on speeches and interviews made by Merkel, Steinmeier and Westerwelle. Schröder was still in power when the agreement on the construction of Nord Stream was signed (8 September 2005). However, his party lost the parliamentary elections only ten days later (18 September) and his government had to step down the following November. The archives that were consulted do not include any statements on Nord Stream by Schröder or Fischer dating from the period September–November 2005 (between the signature of the construction agreement and the end of their mandate). Hence, the analysis starts from the speeches and interviews given by Chancellor Merkel and Foreign Minister Steinmeier after the formation of the new government in November 2005.[4]

Table 4.1: German foreign policy leaders, 2005–15

Chancellor	Foreign Minister
Angela Merkel (November 2005–15)	Frank-Walter Steinmeier (November 2005 – October 2009, December 2013–15)
	Guido Westerwelle (October 2009 – December 2013)

Source: author's own compilation

Three main narratives emerged from the analysis. The first one emphasised that Russia was a reliable energy partner and referred to the long history of German–Russian energy cooperation since Brandt's Ostpolitik (see Högselius

---

4. The speeches and statements of German federal presidents were not included in the analysis because the federal president does not play a major role in foreign policy making. The German constitution gives the federal president only ceremonial functions in foreign policy, such as the conclusion of international treaties and the accreditation of foreign envoys; see Article 59 of the Basic Law for the Federal Republic of Germany, full text available at www.btg-bestellservice.de/pdf/80201000.pdf (accessed 5 August 2016).

2013; Lippert 2011). Hence, it advocated a pragmatic approach to German-Russian energy relations: as Russia was a reliable partner and could export the gas that Germany and the EU needed, projects such as Nord Stream contributed to Europe's energy security. The second narrative stressed the European dimension of Nord Stream and German energy policy towards Russia. Within this discourse, German initiatives were presented as consistent with EU policies and objectives. The third narrative took a normative approach and linked themes such as the respect of human rights, democratic freedoms and European values to the debate on German–Russian and EU–Russian energy relations.

Russia as reliable energy partner: history, pragmatism and interdependence

The discourse on Russia's reliability as an energy partner was prominent throughout the period under analysis, regardless of the speaker's political affiliation. The case for Russia's reliability tended to be constructed through the discursive strategy of argumentation and was bolstered by references to German–Russian energy cooperation from the 1970s onwards. As the argument went, Russia had been a reliable energy partner for decades, even at the height of the Cold War, when Europe was divided into competing political and military blocs; hence, there was no reason to doubt Russia's reliability in much less strained times. In this discourse, history is the topos that connects the argument (Russia is a reliable energy partner) to its logical conclusion (energy relations with Russia should be developed and strengthened).

In the texts retrieved, the discourse on Russia's reliability appeared first in an interview given by Foreign Minister Frank-Walter Steinmeier (2006a) to the German news broadcasting radio RBB Inforadio on 14 October 2006. Steinmeier argued that Germany never had any reason to doubt Russia's reliability as an energy supplier. In the same interview, he highlighted the German tradition of Ostpolitik towards Russia and argued for 'Annäherung durch Verflechtung' (convergence through economic interlocking), a phrase that is reminiscent of Willy Brandt's Ostpolitik motto 'Wandel durch Annäherung' (change through rapprochement). Hence, Steinmeier constructed parallels between the policy of his government and the German Ostpolitik of the 1970s, which is positively framed in German identity as a historical example of constructive cooperation with Russia (*see* Chapter Three).

Steinmeier made selective use of the history of German–Russian energy relations by evoking exclusively the memory of peaceful cooperation in the latter part of the Cold War and after the fall of the Soviet Union. This memory narrative aimed at providing evidence for Russia's reliability as an energy partner. This emerged, for instance, from his interview with the German business news magazine *Wirtschaftswoche* on 22 January 2007. In the interview, the German foreign minister talked of the 'long tradition in energy and economic cooperation' between his country and Russia (Steinmeier 2007a). He also used the discursive strategy of predication, most notably through stereotypical evaluations, to label

Russians in positive terms, namely as reliable partners ('the Russians are partners with whom you can speak frankly and who keep their word').

On the other hand, Steinmeier harshly criticised arguments comparing his Russia policy to that of interwar Weimar and Nazi Germany. His speech at Viadrina European University on 26 October 2006 illustrates this stance. A few months earlier, Polish Defence Minister Radoslaw Sikorski had compared the Nord Stream pipeline to the Nazi–Soviet pact of 1939 (cited in Castle 2006). With implicit reference to Sikorski's statements, Steinmeier emphasised the inappropriateness of using catchwords such as 'Rapallo' (an allusion to the German–Soviet treaty signed in 1922, when both Germany and the USSR had revanchist aspirations in Eastern Europe) and 'Hitler–Stalin pact' to describe present German–Russian relations (Steinmeier 2006b). The symbolic location where Steinmeier's speech was held, a European university founded on the German–Polish border shortly after the end of the Cold War, was functional to his argument: it suggested that Germany was seeking reconciliation with all its eastern neighbours within, as he put it, 'a united Europe that has learned from past experiences'.

Positive references to the history of German–Russian energy relations surfaced also in later speeches made by Chancellor Angela Merkel. In a joint press conference with Russian President Vladimir Putin on 1 June 2012, Merkel stated that Russia was 'a reliable [energy] supplier' and that Germany 'had experienced this for decades' (Merkel 2012a). Merkel's argumentation aimed at strengthening the case for Germany's energy partnership with Russia and for the construction of the Nord Stream pipeline, which she described as a successful 'German–European project'. In a speech made on October 2012 at the German committee on Eastern European economic relations (*Ost-Ausschuss der deutschen Wirtschaft*), an influential business group advocating the interests of German companies in Eastern Europe, Merkel claimed that the gas deals between West Germany and the Soviet Union in the 1970s greatly enhanced German–Soviet relations. Moreover, she portrayed German economic involvement in the USSR as a 'success story' (Merkel 2012b).

The history of German–Russian energy cooperation was used as an argument for adopting a pragmatic approach in relations with Russia. Steinmeier (2007a) argued that relations with Russia had to be assessed in 'realistic' rather than 'overly emotional' terms, bearing in mind both past cooperation and Europe's future energy needs, as well as the 'undisputable fact' that Russia 'is and will remain Europe's neighbour'. Moreover, he argued, Europeans had to confront the reality that Russian energy supplies would acquire increasing importance for the EU due to the depletion of other import sources. Hence, as he stated in an article published in the German magazine *Internationale Politik* in March 2007, 'for the EU Russia is an indispensable partner of strategic significance' and 'the key factor in our energy supply, above all in the field of gas' (2007b). Following from this line of argument, Steinmeier (2008a) described the Nord Stream project as 'sensible, economically viable' and motivated by 'sheer economic necessities'.

The German foreign minister portrayed EU–Russia energy relations as an example of positive interdependence: a relationship from which both sides could benefit. This view was best articulated in his speech at the French Institute of International Relations (an influential, Paris-based think tank) in February 2008. Steinmeier (2008a) argued that Russia and Europe were 'economically dependent on each other [...] Russia needs the income from fossil fuels exports to the EU and the EU needs secure and stable energy supplies from Russia'. Following this argument, Nord Stream strengthened the current interdependence and was 'a very important contribution to Europe's energy security'. Through the use of perspectivation, Steinmeier expressed his personal conviction that EU–Russia relations were mutually beneficial ('I feel very inclined to follow the reasoning of interdependency supporters') and again referred to 'historical experience' to bolster his view.

Interdependence and pragmatism featured prominently also in Merkel's rhetoric on energy relations with Russia. On 8 November 2011, at the inauguration ceremony of the Nord Stream pipeline, Merkel (2011) argued that EU gas importers and Russia would 'benefit equally from the pipeline'. The pipeline itself was the 'expression of a long-lasting cooperation that offers great economic opportunities'. These opportunities, as Merkel (2012a) explained in a joint press conference with Putin in June 2012, were particularly important 'for many German companies that have signed long-term contracts with Russia'.

The long-term German economic interests in the Russian energy market contribute to explain the pre-eminence of pragmatism and of a cooperative approach in German official discourses on Russia throughout the period under analysis. However, most of the speeches under investigation did not focus on the bilateral dimension of German–Russian economic relations. German foreign policy makers juxtaposed national interests to European interests and, consistently with Germany's pro-European and multilateral foreign policy identity, attempted to frame discourses on German energy policy within a broader European context.

Europeanising Nord Stream and German–Russian energy relations

In the texts analysed, German foreign policy makers portrayed the Nord Stream project as a European endeavour and rebuffed criticism describing it as a German–Russian pipeline. Argumentation was the main discursive strategy used to emphasise the presumed European nature of Nord Stream. The key argument was that, in addition to Germany and Russia, other countries and foreign companies had become involved in the Nord Stream project. It was claimed that the pipeline would bring profits to a diverse group of European actors and contribute to European energy security. Economic usefulness is the topos that connects the argument (Nord Stream is a profitable European project) to its logical conclusion (Nord Stream should be supported by the EU and its member states).

This discursive strategy emerges in Steinmeier's interview with RBB Inforadio on 14 October 2006. Steinmeier (2006a) argued that Germany's energy policy with Russia was functional to European interests and cited the Nord Stream pipeline as an example. According to him, the participation of a Dutch company in the Nord Stream consortium and Britain's interest in extending the pipeline to its territory demonstrated that the project 'does not just satisfy a specific German interest but also strengthens European energy policy'. The same argument was repeated in his interviews with the prominent Polish daily *Gazeta Wyborcza* on 10 December 2007 (Steinmeier 2007c) and on 17 June 2009 (Steinmeier 2009a), as well as in his talk at the French Institute of International Relations in February 2008, where he emphasised that French, Dutch, British and Danish companies had ordered large quantities of Russian gas via Nord Stream (Steinmeier 2008a). Furthermore, in an interview held in February 2009 with another large-circulation Polish daily, *Rzeczpospolita*, Steinmeier (2009b) stated that Nord Stream was originally a Finnish project, thereby implying that German companies merely took over a corporate initiative started in another EU member state.

Steinmeier's successor as German foreign minister Guido Westerwelle continued to portray German energy policy with Russia as consistent with EU policy. In a speech delivered in October 2010 at a prominent German think tank, the German Council on Foreign Relations, Westerwelle (2010a) argued that Germany's policy towards Russia was 'integrated into an overall European approach'. Hence, he claimed that 'The old and persistent suspicion that Germany was implementing its policy on Russia without consulting our [Germany's] immediate neighbours and other partners has been allayed'. The concerns of other EU member states about Germany's alleged unilateralism were negatively qualified ('old and persistent suspicion') and deemed unfounded. In a speech held a few days earlier at the German Committee on Eastern European Economic Relations, Merkel (2010) used an even harsher tone, defining criticism against Nord Stream as 'multifarious stereotypes' that her government had managed to 'dismantle'.

By contrast, in most German policy makers' speeches, the semantic field associated with Nord Stream was unambiguously positive and emphasised its correlation with European policies. This is illustrated by Merkel's (2011) speech at the inauguration ceremony of the pipeline, in November 2011. Through the discursive strategy of predication, she qualified Nord Stream as a 'strategic project […] exemplary for the cooperation between Russia and the European Union', an 'outstanding example' for the construction of a 'robust partnership with Russia' and 'setting new standards for European energy partnerships'.

The European-ness of Nord Stream was also constructed through the discursive strategy of categorisation, which aims at defining in-groups and out-groups through the selective use of language and figures of speech. In German foreign policy makers' speeches on Nord Stream, categorisation was used to construct a European energy community as an in-group that included both the European Union and Russia. This categorisation was built up progressively and became more forceful over time. In the earlier texts, Steinmeier emphasised the pipeline's European nature by stressing that it was not a national or bilateral project, as argued by its critics. In his speech at the French Institute of International Relations of February 2008, Steinmeier (2008a) claimed that Nord Stream was 'a European, not a German project'. He reiterated this point also in an interview with *Gazeta Wyborcza* in June 2009, when he stated: 'I hear time and again that Nord Stream is a German–Russian project. No, it is a European project for more energy security' (Steinmeier 2009a). Similarly, in October 2010 Merkel (2010) defined the pipeline a 'European–Russian project' and in, June 2012, as 'a German–European project' (2012a), thereby simultaneously emphasising the European dimension of the project and Germany's leading role in it.

In Merkel's later speeches, the tone and content of the discourse on Nord Stream's European nature became more assertive. The chancellor argued that, if the pipeline did not fully comply with EU standards, the latter should be adjusted accordingly. This argument was made with reference to the EU's third energy package, namely the legislation that stipulates a different ownership for energy production and energy transmission networks (a controversial provision for Nord Stream, as Gazprom is both the gas producer and main owner of the pipeline).[5] In her speech at the inauguration of Nord Stream, Merkel (2011) raised this issue with EU Energy Commissioner Günther Oettinger, arguing that 'The third energy package is not immediately understandable for someone outside Europe [...] And, dear Günther Oettinger, perhaps we should change what we are not able to explain to others'.

Merkel reiterated this point in her speech at the German Committee on Eastern European Economic Relations in October 2012. Addressing once again Commissioner Oettinger, who was sitting in the audience, she stated: 'Indeed, dear Günther Oettinger, we must admit: the European Union's actions also sometimes confuse our partners. I am thinking about the legendary discussions on why someone who owns a pipeline [...] cannot ship gas through it' (2012b). Using the discursive strategy of perspectivation, Merkel clearly positioned herself against the application of the EU's third energy package to the Nord Stream pipeline. However, she was not dismissive of European rules and attempted to reconcile them with the project. For instance, in a joint press conference with Putin in November 2012, she argued: 'I will continue to lobby, including in Brussels, for using the pipelines we have, rather than ending up – so to speak – without gas' (2012c). In accordance with Germany's pro-European foreign policy identity, Merkel attempted to keep her policy on Nord Stream within the EU framework.

Energy, democracy and European values

In many of the speeches under analysis, German policy makers discussed the issue of democracy and human rights in Russia alongside or within the context of energy relations. This is particularly true of speeches held in the period until late 2010, which attempted to reconcile the view of Russia as an economic partner with Germany's concern for the respect of democratic values and human rights. This approach to relations with Russia reflects the interaction of two key narratives of German national identity, namely the centrality of democracy and human rights and the construction of Russia as an economic partner (*see* Chapter Four). In German

---

5.   See website of the European Commission: www.ec.europa.eu/energy/en/topics/markets-and-consumers/market-legislation (accessed 7 August 2016).

policy makers' speeches, these narratives were reconciled with the argument that energy cooperation was functional to the strengthening of democracy and human rights in Russia, as it created the economic prosperity in which these principles could be implemented and a positive atmosphere for dialogue. Hence, the German identity narrative advocating democracy and human rights was used instrumentally to support economic cooperation with Russia. Humanitarianism and economic advantage are the topoi connecting the argument with its logical conclusion that the EU should support energy cooperation with Russia.

This line of argument emerged clearly in Foreign Minister Frank-Walter Steinmeier's interviews and speeches. Steinmeier (2006a) argued that the EU–Russia energy partnership should lead to the strengthening of democracy and 'European values' in Russia. Moreover, he claimed that 'a wise and correct policy' towards Russia had to address both human rights and business, which in his opinion were not mutually exclusive. This argument was further developed in his article on EU–Russia relations published in the German magazine *Internationale Politik* in March 2007. Steinmeier (2007b) claimed that there was 'no contradiction between our [the EU's] interest in expanding economic relations and the respect of human rights and the rule of law'. Energy cooperation, he argued, could be developed into a much broader partnership where it was possible also to address 'issues on which we [the EU] do not always share the same opinion [as Russia]'.

On the question of reconciling the energy partnership with the promotion of democracy and human rights in Russia, foreign minister Guido Westerwelle adopted the same approach as his predecessor. In his speech at the German Council on Foreign Relations in October 2010, Westerwelle (2010a) stated that 'regarding Russia as a partner is the best way to solve problems', including 'shortcomings in Russia's society and mode of governance'. In an interview with the German daily *Der Tagesspiegel* in November 2010, Westerwelle (2010b) argued that the economic partnership with Russia should be expanded to include the legal system and domestic reforms.

In the speeches made by the German policy makers under analysis after 2010, energy cooperation and questions of democracy and human rights in Russia tended to be discussed separately, with very few exceptions. This might be due to the deterioration in democratic and human rights standards in Russia following the parliamentary elections of December 2011, which may have made German leaders reluctant to discuss the energy partnership within the context of Russia's increasing authoritarianism. Internal developments in Russia from December 2011 seemed to refute the argument previously made by German leaders that increasing economic and energy relations would lead to improvements in democratic and human rights standards (*see* Chapter Seven).

From Molotov–Ribbentrop to economic nonsense: Polish leaders' discourses

The Nord Stream project sparked a heated debate in Polish society and among the country's political leaders, most of whom argued that the pipeline undermined

Poland's interests. The analysis focuses on discourses of Polish prime and foreign ministers who were in power from the signing of the Nord Stream agreement until the end of 2012. The speeches of President of the republic Lech Kaczynski are also investigated, as he was very vocal and prominent in the debate on energy relations with Russia throughout his mandate (2005–10). Conversely, his successor Bronislaw Komorowski (to August 2015) did not become significantly involved in the debate on Nord Stream; none of the 323 entries on the Polish presidential website concerning Komorowski's speeches and activities referred to the pipeline.

In the period under analysis, Poland had four prime ministers and four foreign ministers. The mandates of the first two prime ministers (Marek Belka and Kazimierz Marcinkiewicz) and foreign ministers (Adam Rotfeld and Stefan Meller) were very short, covering only the period until May–July 2006.[6] Since the archives consulted had no speeches by these policy makers addressing Nord Stream or energy policy towards Russia, the analysis will focus on the discourses of their successors. These were Prime Minister Jaroslaw Kaczynski and Foreign Minister Anna Fotyga, both members of the right-wing party Law and Justice, which in May 2006 formed a coalition government with the far-right parties Self-Defence of Polish Farmers and League of Polish Families. Following the October 2007 parliamentary elections, Jaroslaw Kaczynski and Anna Fotyga were succeeded respectively by Donald Tusk and Radoslaw Sikorski, both members of the more moderate centre-right party Civic Platform. Tusk and Sikorski were re-elected for a second mandate in October 2011.

Table 4.2: Polish foreign policy leaders, 2005–15

Prime Minister	Foreign Minister	President of the Republic
Jaroslaw Kaczynski (July 2006 – November 2007)	Anna Fotyga (May 2006 – November 2007)	Lech Kaczynski (December 2005 – April 2010)
Donald Tusk (November 2007 – September 2014)	Radoslaw Sikorski (November 2007 – September 2014)[7]	Bronislaw Komorowski (August 2010 – August 2015)
Ewa Kopacz (September 2014 – November 2015)	Grzegorz Schetyna (September 2014 – November 2015)	Andrzej Duda (August 2015 onwards)

Source: author's own compilation

The main discourse in Polish foreign policy makers' speeches between 2006 and 2007 emphasised that Russian leaders used fossil fuel resources to achieve political aims, notably to strengthen their influence on the countries that depended

---

6. Meller left his post in May 2006, followed by Marcinkiewicz in July 2006.

7. Before joining Tusk's government and becoming a member of Civic Platform, Sikorski had been the defence minister in Kaczynski's government (from October 2005 until February 2007). Following his change of political allegiance, Sikorski's rhetoric on Russia and Nord Stream became more moderate, as shown in the analysis below.

on energy imports from Russia. It stressed Russia's historical role as a geopolitical threat for Poland and constructed parallels between Russia's past and present policies. During the same period, another dominant narrative focused on the lack of solidarity among EU member states with regard to their energy policy towards Russia. As the argument went, the agreement to build Nord Stream highlighted the self-serving logic guiding the policies of some EU member states, which supported the pipeline in spite of its negative impact on the energy security of other members. The discourse on the lack of EU solidarity is reminiscent of a dominant theme in Polish identity narratives, namely Poland's unreciprocated commitment to the Western cause (*see* Chapter Three). In the context of the Nord Stream debate, Polish leaders argued that their commitment to build a shared EU energy policy was not reciprocated by Germany and other EU members supporting the construction of the pipeline.

The two discourses introduced above also played an important role in official speeches and interviews after 2007, particularly in President Lech Kaczynski's statements. However, following the change of government in November 2007, another dominant discourse emerged. Tusk and Sikorski adopted a more pragmatic tone with regard to energy relations with Russia and emphasised the need for cooperation. They voiced their opposition to the Nord Stream project mostly with economic arguments, while references to historical rivalries and Russia's hostile geopolitical intentions were downplayed.

History, geopolitics and the political use of energy

The discourse on Russia's political use of energy was ubiquitous in Polish leaders' speeches during the right-wing government of Jaroslaw Kaczynski (July 2006 – November 2007). In this period, all the main institutional posts concerned with Poland's foreign policy making (prime minister, foreign minister and president of the republic) were held by members of the ultraconservative and deeply anti-Russian Law and Justice party (see Reeves 2010). The main argument within this discourse emphasised that Russia abused its role as chief energy supplier of Eastern European countries in order to exert political pressure on them. In particular, it was argued that Russia made energy deals with Western European EU member states (most notably Germany) which undermined the interests of East–Central European members. According to this view, Nord Stream was one of such deals. Memory politics played a prominent role in this discourse. Comparisons with Soviet Russia's former domination of Poland and with Nazi–Soviet plans to partition Eastern Europe were made in order to bolster the main argument. History is the topos linking the argument with its logical conclusion, namely the claim that Russia intended to re-establish a sphere of influence over Eastern Europe.

Radoslaw Sikorski's interview with the German magazine *Der Spiegel* on 1 May 2006 exemplifies the prominence of memory politics in this discourse. Sikorski, then defence minister in Jaroslaw Kaczynski's right-wing government, argued that the Nord Stream agreement was reminiscent of the Molotov–Ribbentrop pact because it was 'geopolitically targeted against Polish interests' (cited in Kloth

2006). The comparison with the Nazi–Soviet agreement to partition Poland, an event deeply engrained in Polish identity as one of the worst national catastrophes, highlights both the deeply anti-Russian posture of Kaczynski's government and the strong interaction between Polish identity and foreign policy discourses on Russia. Sikorski made instrumental use of the national identity narrative about Polish victimhood in the Second World War to pursue current political interests.

The analogy between Russia's energy policy and past Soviet policies towards Poland emerged clearly also in Prime Minister Jaroslaw Kaczynski's interview with the German daily *Handelsblatt* in October 2006. Kaczynski (2006) claimed that Poles

> do not want to be afraid that, at some point, someone will shut off our [Poland's] supply [of gas]. The older and adult generations of Poles can still remember well that, twenty-five or thirty years ago, they were asking themselves the question: will the Russians invade us or not?

Kaczynski's reasoning suggested that, for many Poles (including himself, as a member of the older generation) Russia appeared as threatening to Poland's independence as the Soviet Union was in the 1980s; at the time, a Soviet military invasion of Poland to crush the anti-communist opposition movement appeared as a likely prospect (*see* Chapter Three). Kaczynski juxtaposed Russia's energy power to the military threat emanating from the Soviet Union. Linguistically, the analogy between Soviet and Russian foreign policy is emphasised by Kaczynski's metonymic use of 'Russians' in lieu of 'Soviets'.

Sikorski and Jaroslaw Kaczynski's line of argument and discursive strategy were echoed by President Lech Kaczynski in an interview with *Der Spiegel* in March 2006. Lech Kaczynski stated that the reasons for building the Nord Stream pipeline were 'purely political' and that the project 'starkly contrast[ed] with Polish interests' (Kaczynski 2006a). Although the historical interpretive framework was not as explicit as in Sikorski and Jaroslaw Kaczynski's interviews, it can also be inferred easily from Lech Kaczynski's statements. The Polish president argued that he was 'very vigilant when it came to the German–Russian relationship' and, when asked whether Russia and Germany posed the greatest danger for Poland, he replied: 'That's certainly a true statement if you look at the history books'.

Polish foreign policy makers' perception of Russia as a historical and geopolitical threat also influenced their assessments of EU–Russia energy relations. In a letter to *The Financial Times* published in May 2007, Sikorski stated that the Nord Stream pipeline was 'the most outrageous attempt by Mr Putin to divide and damage the EU' because it gave Russia the 'ability to decouple old and new members by differentially turning off the tap' (Sikorski *et al.* 2007).[8] Through the use of perspectivation and a harsh anti-Russian rhetoric, Sikorski argued that Nord

---

8. The letter was co-authored with Maciej Olex-Szczytowski, an adviser to the foreign minister, and Jacek Rostowski, then adviser to the Bank of Poland and later minister of finance in Tusk's government.

Stream would enable Russia to keep gas flows to Central and Western Europe unaltered while it simultaneously used its energy power to re-establish a sphere of influence in East–Central Europe. Hence, the pipeline was 'an economic and geopolitical disaster for the Union'. According to Sikorski, EU member states could avert the threat of Russia's divide and rule policy only by showing solidarity with each other.

Nord Stream and European solidarity

The discourse on European solidarity played a central role in Polish leaders' speeches criticising the Nord Stream pipeline, particularly during 2006 and 2007. Within this discourse it was claimed that, although Poland had joined the EU and was fully committed to its values, it was still not treated as an equal by other EU members.[9] This criticism was addressed particularly to Germany, which was blamed for supporting the Nord Stream project in disregard of Polish interests. In its handling of the Nord Stream question, it was argued, Germany showed no European solidarity to Poland and prioritised its partnership with Russia. Russia was portrayed merely as a negative factor, hostile to EU principles and eager to disrupt European solidarity. This discourse aimed at exposing the irreconcilability of Nord Stream and German–Russian energy policy with the EU's values. Europeanism, meant as the commitment to EU values and policies, is the topos linking the key argument (Nord Stream undermines EU values) with its logical conclusion (Germany and the EU should withdraw their support of Nord Stream).

The discourse on European solidarity featured prominently in Lech Kaczynski and Sikorski's interviews in 2006 and 2007. The arguments of both politicians were based on the presumption that Russia used gas as a political instrument. In an interview with *The Financial Times* in November 2006, Kaczynski (2006b) claimed that Russia's political use of energy was inherent in its possession of vast natural resources ('Russia has enormous energy resources, and it is difficult not to take advantage of them'). Hence, Russia's energy policy and the Nord Stream pipeline were portrayed as a test for European solidarity.[10] In their comments on Nord Stream, Sikorski and Kaczynski concurred in the opinion that there was not enough solidarity in the EU on energy policy and put the blame on Germany. For instance, Sikorski argued that 'To first make a decision and then offer consultations is not our idea of European solidarity [...] We are shocked that Germany would do something that [...] is geopolitically targeted against Polish interests' (cited in Kloth 2006).

9. This emerged for instance in Foreign Minister Anna Fotyga's interview with *The New York Times* on 14 August 2007, www.nytimes.com/2007/08/14/world/europe/14iht-poland.4.7116334.html?_r=0 (accessed 7 August 2016). Fotyga claimed that 'Poland's status is not equal to other EU and NATO member states'.

10. See also Anna Fotyga's statement to *The New York Times* on 14 August 2007: 'The gas pipeline [Nord Stream] undermines European solidarity and questions our ability to have an equal voice'.

Lech Kaczynski (2006b) made a similar argument in his interview with *The Financial Times*.

> Question: do you expect that Germans will understand Poland's issues when it comes to energy?

> Lech Kaczynski: We do understand the need for compromise, but it cannot be that in this area a single European country, even a very powerful one, decides on a particular solution, almost as if it had stepped momentarily outside of the Union, and then says it will not change even if that solution contradicts the interests of other countries.

To convey their criticism of Germany, both Sikorski and Kaczynski resorted to the discursive strategy of perspectivation, which is particularly evident in phrases such as 'we are shocked' or 'we do understand'. Kaczynski did not mention Germany explicitly, but his allusion to it appears obvious in the light of the journalist's question. In spite of this reticence, Kaczynski's criticism was very harsh. His reasoning suggested that Germany's support of the Nord Stream pipeline had placed the country outside the framework of the European Union. This assessment stands in complete contradiction to German foreign policy makers' discourse Europeanising Nord Stream and German–Russian energy relations and epitomises the conflict between contemporary German and Polish discourses on the pipeline.

The narrative on European solidarity continued to play a role in Polish foreign policy makers' speeches on energy policy after the change of government in 2007. For instance, in an interview with *The Financial Times* in January 2010, Tusk (2010) defined Nord Stream as 'an example of lack of energy solidarity'. Moreover, in an article published in July 2010 in *The New York Times*, Sikorski (2010a) lamented that 'in areas like energy and military cooperation, some EU members act unilaterally'. However, references to the lack of European solidarity became less frequent and were framed within a more moderate rhetoric. Russia was no longer portrayed exclusively as a hostile country trying to disrupt Polish interests and European solidarity. For example, in January 2010 Tusk (2010) adopted an unusually positive tone to describe relations with Russia: 'While we [the Polish government] say that there is a need for maximum European solidarity in the area of energy security, we do not have any particular problems ourselves. Relations with Russia and with Gazprom are very correct'. Polish criticism of Nord Stream continued during Tusk's government also but it no longer focused on claims of betrayed European solidarity. Pragmatic arguments such as the economic cost of the pipeline became dominant.

Economics and pragmatism: Tusk's Poland and Nord Stream

Improving Poland's relations with Russia was one of Tusk's foreign policy aims after his election (*see* Chapter Three). Tusk attempted to pursue this objective by adopting a more pragmatic approach and rhetoric to address contentious issues in the relationship, including the Nord Stream question. His statements at the joint press conference with Putin in Gdansk in September 2009, during the commemoration of the seventieth anniversary of the outbreak of the Second World War, best summarise his change of rhetoric on Nord Stream: 'Concerning our position on Nord Stream, Poland is not suspicious on this issue. We do not suspect any evil political intentions [from Russia]. However, we evaluate this project sceptically from an economic and ecological point of view' (Tusk 2009).

Tusk rejected the argument that Russia made political use of energy, which had been a leitmotif in Polish leaders' speeches on Russia during Jaroslaw Kaczynski's government. Moreover, he did this on the occasion of a symbolic joint commemoration of a highly contentious historical event, on which Polish and Russian official memory narratives diverged (Ruchniewicz 2007; Siddi 2012). This contrasts strikingly with previous Polish discourses that used memory politics to discredit Nord Stream as a political project. Tusk's criticism of Nord Stream was voiced in more moderate terms than in previous discourses ('we evaluate this project sceptically') and, most importantly, it was grounded on economic issues. This line of argument is representative of Polish foreign policy makers' discourse on Nord Stream during Tusk's government. Economic advantage is the key topos of a discursive strategy that attempted to accommodate opposition to Nord Stream with a milder rhetoric, conducive to reconciliation with Russia.

The economic discourse against Nord Stream focused on the higher cost of laying an underwater pipeline rather than building a land connection. Tusk (2008a) argued that building an alternative pipeline via the Baltic countries and Poland was much cheaper. In an interview with *The Financial Times* in January 2010, he stated that he did not understand the 'economic rationale for a decision whose outcome is a much more expensive transit of gas than by the traditional land route' (Tusk 2010). The economic argument was reiterated in both Bronislaw Komorowski's and in Radoslaw Sikorski's remarks on Nord Stream in 2010 and 2011. In an interview with the European news channel *Euronews* shortly after his election as Polish president, Komorowski (2010) argued that 'the building of a more expensive pipeline via the Baltic [...] is the fruit of a decision that was taken too rapidly several years ago'. In November 2011, commenting on Nord Stream's inauguration, Sikorski (2011a) stated that the pipeline was 'a waste of money'. In spite of this criticism, neither Komorowski nor Sikorski portrayed Nord Stream as a major threat for Poland. In the same interviews quoted above, Sikorski argued that Poland's energy security was not affected by the pipeline because gas was not very important in the country's energy mix. Komorowski (2010) maintained that Poland should strengthen its ties with Russia and Germany 'without concentrating too heavily on the Baltic gas pipeline'.

As Sikorski's and Komorowski's reasoning highlights, economic rationalisations on Nord Stream enabled Polish leaders to downplay the actual importance of the pipeline for Poland. This approach supported the Polish government's policy of improving relations with Germany and Russia after 2007. Although Polish foreign policy makers remained critical of Nord Stream, they increasingly considered it as an old controversy that should not be allowed to disrupt present relations. This attitude was reflected, for instance, in Sikorski's statements during a joint interview with German Foreign Minister Westerwelle in November 2010. Asked whether Nord Stream was still a contentious issue in Polish–German relations, Sikorski (2010b) briefly argued that the controversy belonged to the past and suggested moving on to 'questions concerning the future'. In fact, the controversy would resurface five years later, when Germany advocated the expansion of Nord Stream's capacity (*see* Chapter Eight).

Environmental challenges and a norm-based partnership: Finnish discourses

In Finnish foreign-policy-making circles, the debate on Nord Stream was particularly lively between September 2005 and November 2009, when the Finnish authorities allowed the construction of the pipeline through Finland's exclusive economic zone in the Baltic Sea.[11] Nearly all the Finnish policy makers' speeches and statements on Nord Stream that were retrieved date back to this period. During this timeframe, Finland had two governments, both headed by Centre Party leader Matti Vanhanen. Social democrat Erkki Tuomioja was foreign minister under the first government (until April 2007), which was supported by a predominantly centre-left parliamentary coalition. Ilkka Kanerva (until April 2008) and later Alexander Stubb, both members of the centre-right National Coalition Party, were foreign ministers during Vanhanen's second government, which had a centre-right political orientation.

Tarja Halonen was President of Finland throughout the period when Nord Stream was a prominent topic in Finnish policy makers' discourses. Since the Finnish president is responsible for the conduct of foreign policy (together with the government)[12] and Halonen played an important role in the Finnish debate on Nord Stream, her speeches are also analysed. On the other hand, no references to Nord Stream were found in either the speeches of Halonen's successor Sauli Niinistö or in those of Prime Ministers Mari Kiviniemi and Jyrki Katainen, who were in office after Matti Vanhanen. This may be because Nord Stream lost prominence in the Finnish political debate after the country agreed to the construction of the pipeline in its exclusive economic zone.

---

11. 'Finnish Government grants consent for Nord Stream's offshore gas pipeline project', press release of the Finnish Ministry of Employment and the Economy, 5 November 2009, www.formin. finland.fi/public/default.aspx?contentid=179823&contentlan=2&culture=en-US (accessed 7 August 2016).

12. Article 93 of the Finnish constitution states that 'the foreign policy of Finland is directed by the President of the Republic in cooperation with the Government'. The full text of the constitution is available at www.finlex.fi/fi/laki/kaannokset/1999/en19990731.pdf (accessed 5 August 2016).

Table 4.3: Finnish foreign policy leaders, 2005–15

Prime Minister	Foreign Minister	President of the Republic
Matti Vanhanen (September 2005 – June 2010)	Erkki Tuomioja (September 2005 – April 2007)	Tarja Halonen (September 2005 – March 2012)
Mari Kiviniemi (June 2010 – June 2011)	Ilkka Kanerva (April 2007 – April 2008)	
Jyrki Katainen (June 2011 – June 2014)	Alexander Stubb (April 2008 – June 2011)[13]	
Alexander Stubb (June 2014 – May 2015)	Erkki Tuomioja (June 2011 – May 2015)	Sauli Niinistö (March 2012 – incumbent in 2015)
Juha Sipilä (May 2015 – incumbent in 2015)	Timo Soini (May 2015 – incumbent in 2015)	

Source: author's own compilation

Two key discourses emerged from Finnish policy makers' speeches on Nord Stream and energy relations with Russia. The first stressed that Finland and the EU should continue to foster energy relations with Russia because they needed Russian gas and Russia had proven to be a reliable supplier. Nord Stream was seen as a positive development for European energy security because, it was argued, more infrastructure was necessary to meet the EU's increasing energy demand. This discourse also had a strong normative focus, as it argued that energy relations with Russia should take place in accordance with a clear regulatory framework that was compatible with EU energy market rules.[14] The second discourse contended that, while a positive development for European energy security, Nord Stream also constituted an environmental challenge for Finland and other Baltic Sea countries. Within this discourse, Finnish policy makers claimed that Finland's support of the pipeline was conditional on respect of environmental standards.

The two dominant Finnish discourses on Nord Stream reflect Finnish historical perceptions of Russia both as an important economic partner and as Finland's security deficit (*see* Chapter Three). Russia's importance as an economic partner emerged from the first discourse, which portrayed it as a key energy provider.

---

13. Between June 2011 and June 2014, Stubb was Minister for European Affairs and Foreign Trade and continued to be influential in official Finnish foreign policy debates.

14. In this context, Finnish foreign policy makers often argued that EU–Russia energy relations should be based on the Energy Charter Treaty, an international agreement regulating cooperation in the energy sector. The EU and all its member states have signed and ratified the Treaty, see www.energycharter.org/fileadmin/DocumentsMedia/Legal/ECTC-en.pdf (accessed 7 August 2016). Russia signed but never ratified the agreement. In July 2009, the Russian government announced its withdrawal from the ECT (Westphal 2011: 2–3).

The perception of Russia as Finland's security deficit appeared in the second discourse; the 'security deficit' stemmed from the environmental risks concerning the construction of Nord Stream. Both discourses are present in speeches of policy makers of different political orientations. Hence, the texts under investigation suggest that political allegiance did not play an important role in shaping the Finnish foreign policy makers' stance towards energy relations with Russia.

Market and norms: Russia as a key energy partner

In most of the speeches under analysis, Finnish policy makers argued that the EU and Russia should cooperate in the energy field because they were interdependent. Cooperation should be based on clearly established norms, which would allow the formation of a united European energy market, including Russia. Economic advantage, legality and Europeanism are the topoi in this argumentative strategy. They connect the argument (the EU should engage Russia with a normative approach) to its logical conclusion that a norm-based cooperation will lead to mutual benefits and create a European energy market.

This discourse emerged clearly in Prime Minister Vanhanen's speech at the European Business Leaders Convention (a forum of top business leaders, experts and political decision makers) in Saint Petersburg in July 2006.[15] Vanhanen (2006) called Russia 'a strategic partner for the EU' and claimed that, in the energy field, 'Russia and the EU have complementary needs – the EU as a customer and Russia as supplier'. Moreover, he argued that EU–Russia energy cooperation should be developed in institutionalised frameworks (in particular the EU–Russia and G8 summits) and be based on international and European law.[16] According to Vanhanen, a norm-based cooperation with Russia and other EU partners would allow the creation of 'truly European energy markets. European not in the EU meaning, but pan-European including Norway, Russia, the Ukraine and other partners'.

Vanhanen thus substantiated his argument for cooperation with Russia through categorisation, by constructing European energy markets as an in-group of which Russia was a member. This inclusive discourse was grounded in economic considerations, which Vanhanen (2006) attempted to make more forceful through the use of perspectivation: 'I am convinced that market logic means that the EU will remain Russia's main energy customer and Russia the EU's main supplier. Demand and supply fit nicely, in geographical terms too'. Vanhanen's emphasis on market principles as the basis for EU–Russia cooperation was echoed in a speech made by Foreign Minister Tuomioja in May 2006. According to Tuomioja (2006), 'Finnish experiences of energy cooperation with Russia have been positive' and 'Russia has proved to be a reliable supplier' because Finland 'has always followed

---

15. A description of the Convention and its activities is available at www.eblc.org (accessed 6 August 2016).

16. First, he urged Russia to ratify the Energy Charter Treaty, then he stated: 'At EU level, we support the extension of internal market principles to our neighbouring countries'.

the market principles [...] in its energy relations with Russia'. He also stressed that 100 per cent of Finnish gas was imported from Russia and implied that this dependence did not constitute a problem because market rules were respected.

Tuomioja's emphasis on economic arguments may also be due to the context in which his remarks were made. The speech was made at a seminar co-organised by the embassies of the Visegrad Group countries (Poland, the Czech Republic, Slovakia, Hungary) in Helsinki. The leaders of some of these countries, most notably Poland, considered Russia's contemporary energy policy as an instrument to achieve geopolitical goals in East–Central European states that depended on Russian energy supplies (see earlier in this chapter on Polish discourses). Hence, Tuomioja's statements may have been aimed at conveying to the representatives of the Visegrad Group that positive energy cooperation was possible, in spite of energy dependence, if relations with Russia were based on market principles rather than on geopolitical arguments. According to Tuomioja, the market would also ensure that, in spite of the construction of Nord Stream, the Visegrad countries remained 'important transit routes for Russian energy supplies further to the West'.

Unsurprisingly, the argument in favour of fostering energy relations with Russia and basing them on market rules features prominently in speeches held before audiences that were likely to be more sympathetic to Russia and Nord Stream than the Visegrad countries. President Tarja Halonen's talk at the Federation of German Industry in June 2006 provides a good example.[17] Halonen (2006) argued that energy trade was beneficial for both buyers and sellers only if it was clearly regulated. According to her, EU–Russia energy dialogue had to be based on 'mutual interest and confidence'. In this context, she stated that she considered the Nord Stream pipeline 'an acceptable development', thereby suggesting that she had no reason to doubt the economic rationale of the project.[18]

Nord Stream's economic significance was emphasised also by Prime Minister Vanhanen in a speech made during a state visit to Japan in June 2008.[19] In his remarks, Vanhanen (2008a) positively characterised Russia as 'the most important energy supplier for the EU' and 'a reliable supplier of gas and electricity', using the discursive strategy of predication. If, occasionally, Russia had not managed to deliver the agreed quantities of gas, it was due to the lack of generating capacity and infrastructure. According to Vanhanen, Nord Stream contributed to addressing these deficiencies because it improved the infrastructure to transport Russian gas. Furthermore, he dismissed claims according to which the pipeline was a political project: 'The main question to be raised in this context is not whether energy might be used as a political weapon, but is there enough gas to be exported?'.

---

17. As argued earlier, German business interests played an important role in the Nord Stream project, as well as in other fields of German–Russian bilateral relations.

18. By contrast, Sikorski's analogy between Nord Stream and the Nazi–Soviet pact was made only three weeks before Halonen's speech.

19. The overall focus of the speech was on energy and environmental policies in the context of climate change, as well as on Russia as the common neighbour of Finland and Japan.

Vanhanen focused his assessment of Nord Stream and energy relations with Russia on economic and technical issues, such as Russia's export capacity. He believed that Russia had a genuine economic interest in the construction of Nord Stream and that its energy policy was the logical consequence of market structures: 'Russia is clearly interested in exporting more energy to Europe. The reason is simple: there is a buyer and there is a seller. Europe needs the energy, they need the money. This is what trade is all about' (Vanhanen 2008a). According to Vanhanen, energy trade with Russia should be secured through investments in energy production and transport, namely in projects such as Nord Stream.

The argument that the EU should engage Russia to satisfy its energy demand is reiterated in Foreign Minister Alexander Stubb's statements. In an article published on his personal website, Stubb (2009a) went as far as arguing that Nord Stream would not suffice to satisfy the EU's increasing energy demand and the implementation of other energy projects involving Russia would be necessary.[20] Echoing Vanhanen's argument, Stubb (2009b) claimed that Nord Stream was 'a commercial European energy security project' and that 'it gained a more political character than was probably intended'. According to Stubb, the European countries that opposed the project could have taken a different stance if more discussions and closer cooperation had taken place. Hence, he advocated further institutionalisation of EU energy relations with Russia in order to promote cooperation and dialogue.[21] This approach reflected the belief, recurrent in the speeches of the Finnish foreign policy makers under analysis, that a European energy market including Russia could be created through the establishment of adequate institutions and norms.

Nord Stream as an environmental challenge

Although Finnish foreign policy makers were generally favourable to the Nord Stream project, most of them emphasised the respect of environmental standards as a fundamental prerequisite for its implementation. As the argument went, Nord Stream was a contribution to European energy security, but it should not affect the Baltic Sea environment negatively, which was Finland's primary interest. As the pipeline was to be laid in Finland's exclusive economic zone and authorisation of the Finnish authorities was necessary for its construction, the debate on its environmental impact became prominent in the country. The stance of Finnish foreign policy makers on the issue is best summarised in the speech that President Tarja Halonen (2008a) gave in May 2008 at the Überseeclub in Hamburg, a German cultural and debating society.

---

20. In particular, Stubb mentioned the South Stream project, which was meant to export Russian gas to Europe via an offshore pipeline placed under the Black Sea and an onshore pipeline crossing the Balkans.

21. In particular, Stubb argued that the dialogue could take place within the EU's Baltic Sea Strategy, a policy framework launched in 2007 to promote cooperation in the Baltic region, and in regional forums such as the Baltic Sea States Summit.

Finland considers the project [Nord Stream] as a way of improving energy security in Europe. The pipeline in itself is a safe way of conveying gas, but we want – and indeed our legislation requires – that all environmental factors involved in the project will be carefully studied. When Finland decides on whether to allow the use of her sea areas, the decisions will be based on environmental factors.

Environmentalism and legality are the topoi that connect the argument (Nord Stream must respect environmental standards) to its logical conclusion (Finland will authorise the construction of Nord Stream only if it complies with its environmental legislation). Finnish policy is thus framed within a strong normative dimension: decisions concerning Nord Stream are contingent upon the respect of environmental norms during the construction of the pipeline.

Halonen's line of argument was reiterated in most other speeches under analysis in which Finnish policy makers referred to the Nord Stream project, irrespective of the audience to which they were addressed. In his remarks before the representatives of the Visegrad Group countries, Foreign Minister Tuomioja (2006) argued that Finland's interest was 'to ensure the fulfilment of environmental requirements'. In a speech at the Norwegian Nobel Institute, Tuomioja's successor Ilkka Kanerva (2008a) referred to Nord Stream within the context of an analysis of ecological threats in the Baltic Sea. He lamented that the Baltic was 'one of the most polluted seas' and had been 'transformed into an energy supply route'. He then stated that Finnish authorities would examine an environmental impact assessment before making decisions on Nord Stream. Along the same lines, Foreign Minister Stubb (2009a) claimed that Nord Stream was 'largely an environmental issue'.

Despite their reservations on the environmental impact of Nord Stream, Finnish foreign policy makers maintained a positive attitude towards both the project and energy cooperation with Russia. In fact, the controversy about the environmental impact of the pipeline ended in November 2009, when the Finnish authorities granted the authorisation to lay it in Finland's exclusive economic zone. Subsequently, references to the environmental impact of Nord Stream were framed in more positive terms. For instance, in a speech made in May 2010, Halonen (2010) suggested that the planning of Nord Stream was an example of good cooperation with Russia because 'its environmental impacts were investigated thoroughly before decisions concerning permits were made'.

Halonen's remark reflected the belief that Finland could best achieve its foreign policy objectives with Russia through dialogue and norm-based cooperation, particularly in such sensitive areas as environmental security. This belief emerged most clearly in Ilkka Kanerva's (2008a) speech at the Norwegian Nobel Institute, when he argued for the 'need to engage Russia in addressing global challenges and encourage full implementation of international commitments'. In the field of energy and environment, cooperation should lead to the 'sustainable utilisation of natural resources'. In this context, Kanerva claimed that 'for Finland, Russia represents both an opportunity and a challenge that are worth seizing', a statement that mirrors Finnish historical perceptions of Russia as both a partner and a threat.

Kanerva's remark also suggested that, if Finland did not seek cooperation, Russia might turn it into a strategic issue. Finnish foreign policy makers' statements on Nord Stream generally reflected this underlying logic. Russia tended to be referred to as a partner and was never openly criticised, an approach that was conducive to pragmatic engagement. As shown, the environmental controversy concerning Nord Stream was also eventually reframed into a narrative of a learning process with a positive outcome.

Conclusion

This case study exposed the diversity of national discourses on the Nord Stream project and energy relations with Russia, a highly relevant policy field for the EU and its member states. Most importantly, it showed that these discourses can be better understood through an analytical framework that focuses on national identity construction and Russia's role therein. German leaders' positive attitude to energy cooperation with Russia was explained within the context of the long-standing energy partnership between the two countries, which dated back to the Ostpolitik of the early 1970s and has become part of German foreign policy identity. On the other hand, Polish leaders' strong criticism of Nord Stream was set against the background of Poland's troubled historical relations with Russia and Germany, which influenced profoundly the Polish perceptions of both countries as foreign policy actors.

German discourses emphasised Russia's reliability as an energy partner and cited the history of German–Russian energy cooperation as evidence. They also stressed that, in the energy field, the EU and Russia were interdependent and had a mutual interest in cooperating. According to German leaders, the Nord Stream pipeline strengthened the partnership with Russia, contributed to European energy security and hence met the interests of the whole EU (rather than just German national interests). This discourse reflected the high relevance of the EU in German national identity. Furthermore, German policy makers argued that energy cooperation had positive repercussions for democracy and the human rights situation in Russia because it created favourable conditions for dialogue with the EU and hence for the implementation of these principles. This narrative mirrored the Ostpolitik tenet according to which economic cooperation had positive repercussions on Russia's domestic development.

Polish foreign policy makers' discourses were antithetical to German discourses in several respects. Like their German counterparts, Polish leaders also made reference to history in order to justify their stance on energy relations with Russia. However, in Polish discourses references to history were entirely negative and served the purpose of opposing energy cooperation. Russia was portrayed as the heir of Soviet Cold War policies, notably as an imperialist country that used its energy resources to pursue geopolitical objectives in East–Central Europe. Furthermore, Polish leaders took a diametrically opposite stance on the significance of Nord Stream for European energy security. Contrary to German policy makers, they argued that Nord Stream was a bilateral project that affected negatively the security of East–Central European EU members. Accordingly, the support of some EU countries for the pipeline showed the lack of solidarity within the EU.

The clash between German and Polish discourses on Nord Stream was particularly strong in the years 2005–7, when the far right Law and Justice party was in power in Poland. It lost impetus after 2007, following the election of centre-right leader Donald Tusk as Polish prime minister. Tusk adopted a more moderate discourse and a pragmatic approach to Poland's controversies with Germany and Russia. While the previous Polish government had made use of highly emotionally charged memory politics, Tusk focused his criticism of Nord Stream on economic arguments and simultaneously sought reconciliation with Germany and Russia.

Finnish leaders' discourses tended to be in line with those of German policy makers on issues such as the necessity to foster the energy partnership with Russia and Russia's reliability as an energy supplier. However, Finnish discourses put a stronger emphasis on norms (market rules, European and international law) as the basis of the EU's partnership with Russia. Moreover, Finnish leaders were more critical than their German and Polish counterparts on the question of the environmental impact of Nord Stream, which they considered a potential ecological threat. Finnish discourses on energy cooperation with Russia and Nord Stream reflected constructed images of Russia that are deeply rooted in Finnish identity. Consistently with its traditional image as Finland's key economic partner, Russia was portrayed as an essential energy supplier. On the other hand, long-standing Finnish fears of the security threat emanating from Russia emerged in the discourse on Nord Stream's environmental impact.

Finally, the chapter revealed considerable diversity in German, Polish and Finnish discourses on Nord Stream and energy relations with Russia. Divergences were particularly marked when Polish narratives emphasised Russia as a security threat, while German discourses simultaneously depicted it as a reliable partner. Following the departure from power of the Polish right in 2007, Polish official discourses became more moderate and more compatible with German narratives. Furthermore, after Finland granted environmental permits for the building of Nord Stream in its exclusive economic zone (November 2009), Finnish discourses ceased to present the pipeline as a potential threat. From 2010 onwards, Nord Stream no longer appeared as a major contentious issue across the three national discursive arenas under analysis. A large-scale clash in the EU discursive arena was thus avoided. However, the Nord Stream controversy would resurface in a much tenser scenario during 2015, following the decision of Gazprom and several Western European companies to expand the pipeline through the construction of Nord Stream-2 (*see* Chapter Seven).

Chapter Five

The August 2008 Russian–Georgian War

This chapter analyses German, Polish and Finnish foreign policy makers' discourses on Russia during the August 2008 Russian–Georgian war, which arguably marked the highest peak in tensions between Russia and the West in the first two post-Cold War decades. It shows how national identity and historically constructed conceptualisations of Russia as a security threat permeated different national readings of the crisis and of Russia's role in it. However, the chapter also reveals that national discourses during the August 2008 crisis were less discordant than those concerning Nord Stream in the previous two years (2005–7). The main events and actors and the broader background of contemporary European security are briefly introduced in the opening section, in order to contextualise the ensuing discourse analysis. The main national discourses are examined and compared in the following sections.

The August 2008 war: context and European response

In Europe and the United States, the five-day conflict between Georgia and Russia in August 2008 caused a vibrant debate about the nature of Russia's foreign policy. In the Western press, Russia was largely portrayed as an aggressive country with imperialist ambitions in its neighbourhood. Numerous journalists and academics spoke of a 'return to the Cold War' between Russia and the West (Heinrich and Tanaev 2009; Sakwa 2008: 593–5, 2012: 601–3). Within the European Union, the leaders of Estonia, Latvia, Lithuania, Poland and Sweden were particularly vocal in their criticism of Russian policies, whereas other countries (including Germany and Finland) took a more moderate stance (Lasas 2012). The causes, development and consequences of the August 2008 Russian–Georgian war have been analysed in depth in a large body of literature (Asmus 2010; Cornell and Star 2009; Forsberg and Seppo 2011; Jones 2013; Rich 2010; Sakwa 2012). A fact-finding mission appointed by the EU compiled a detailed, three-volume report on the conflict (IIFFMCG 2009). Drawing from these sources, the following paragraphs summarise very briefly the main phases of the conflict in order to outline the essential factual background and contextualise the ensuing discourse analysis.

The conflicts between Georgia and its separatist regions of Abkhazia and South Ossetia date back to the Russian Civil War (1917–22), when the newly independent Georgian state clashed with Ossetian and Abkhaz Bolsheviks. During the Soviet period, the two conflicts remained dormant, but re-escalated into armed hostilities during and in the years immediately following the dissolution of the USSR

(1991–4), resulting in the de facto independence of Abkhazia and South Ossetia from Georgia (Suny 1994; Zürcher 2007: 115–51). However, the independence of the two separatist entities was not recognised by any country. Russia played a key role in mediating a ceasefire and in the subsequent international peacekeeping missions, which were organised under the auspices of the Organisation for Security and Co-operation in Europe (OSCE) in South Ossetia, and the UN and the Commonwealth of Independent States (in Abkhazia). Nonetheless, conflict resolution efforts between 1994 and 2008 were not successful (IIFFMCG 2009: vol. 2, 74–118).

In January 2004, following the Rose Revolution, Mikheil Saakashvili was elected president of Georgia with a programme that included the return of Abkhazia and South Ossetia to Georgia as a key point. Relations between the new Georgian government and Russia quickly deteriorated as Saakashvili made clear that he would seek NATO and EU integration, demand the withdrawal of Russian troops from Soviet-era bases in Georgia and increase cooperation with the United States. Saakashvili also accused Russia of implementing policies that would lead to its annexation of Abkhazia and South Ossetia, such as the distribution of Russian passports and the payment of pensions to the local population. Between 2006 and the spring of 2008, incidents at the Abkhaz–Georgian and Ossetian–Georgian borders became more and more frequent, while tensions between Russia and Georgia steadily increased (see IIFFMCG 2009: vol. 2, 2–32, 200–8; March 2011: 195–6).

The wider geopolitical scenario contributed to exacerbating tensions. From the early 2000s onwards, Georgia acquired importance as a strategic transit country in the southern oil and gas corridor, a route that was not controlled by Russia and would allow the export of the abundant resources of the Caspian Sea basin to the EU. Russia considered the corridor a threat to its economic interests (German 2010: 98–101). Furthermore, in 2007 and early 2008 the Russian government became increasingly anxious about the prospect of Georgian NATO membership and US plans to deploy an anti-missile defence system in Eastern Europe, which Russian leaders considered a threat to their country's strategic deterrent (Mankoff 2012: 333–7). Russian concerns were emphasised in Putin's (2007) speech at the Munich security conference in February 2007.

In the months preceding the war, two international events greatly contributed to the escalation of tensions between Russia and the West. In February 2008, Kosovo declared its independence from Serbia, Russia's main partner in the Balkans. Kosovo's declaration of independence and its recognition by most EU and NATO member states irritated Russian leaders, who argued that it would constitute a precedent for separatist entities in other regions of the world (see Averre 2009: 586; Hamilton 2010: 207–8). Moreover, in April 2008 the leaders of NATO countries met in Bucharest to discuss *inter alia* the granting of a membership action plan to Georgia and Ukraine, a prospect that was strongly opposed by Russia. Due to strong German and French opposition, Georgia and Ukraine were not offered a membership action plan. Georgia's unresolved conflicts with Abkhazia and South Ossetia were one of the main arguments used by the opponents of its NATO accession. However, the prospect of Georgia's future NATO membership remained on the table and was strongly supported by both the United States and some East–Central European members of the alliance, including Poland (Blank 2009: 116).

Against this background, tensions in Abkhazia and South Ossetia escalated throughout the spring of 2008. Both Russia and Georgia increased their military presence and held military exercises near the conflict zone (IIFFMCG 2009: vol. 2, 47–8). On the night of 7–8 August, following several days of skirmishes and exchanges of fire along the Georgian–South Ossetian border, the Georgian army launched a full-scale attack on Tskhinvali, South Ossetia's capital. A few hours later, the Russian ground, air and naval forces became involved in the conflict (IIFFMCG 2009: vol. 2, 209–10). The intervention of Russian forces swiftly decided the outcome of the conflict. By 10 August, most Georgian troops had been expelled from South Ossetia, while the Russian army extended the theatre of operations to Abkhazia and mainland Georgia (IIFFMCG 2009: vol. 2, 211–14). An armistice was achieved on 12 August, when French president Nicolas Sarkozy (in his capacity as President of the European Council) convinced the parties to sign a ceasefire agreement. The agreement provided inter alia for the cessation of hostilities and the withdrawal of troops to the positions occupied prior to the conflict (see Forsberg and Seppo 2011; IIFFMCG 2009: vol. 3, 587–92).

However, the agreement did not end the political crisis. On 26 August 2008, Russia recognised the independence of Abkhazia and South Ossetia, a move that was harshly criticised by Georgia, the US and most European countries. NATO temporarily suspended talks with Russia in the NATO–Russia Council, and the EU postponed negotiations on a strategic partnership agreement with Russia (see Blank 2010: 189–91). Furthermore, some Russian troops delayed their withdrawal. In order to speed it up, an implementation agreement was signed in Moscow on 8 September 2008 (IIFFMCG 2009: vol. 3, 593–4). The document also provided for the deployment of a monitoring mission of the European Union (EUMM), which was established at the EU Council of foreign ministers on 15 September (IIFFMCG 2009: vol. 2, 219).

In spite of international conflict resolution efforts, particularly through numerous rounds of talks involving both the authorities of Georgia and of the two separatist republics, the post-conflict status quo has crystallised.[1] In the months following the war, Russia increased its economic and military presence in Abkhazia and South Ossetia (see Weitz 2009: 6–8). Following Russia's recognition of the two separatist entities, Georgia severed diplomatic relations with Moscow. Furthermore, in 2009 Russia vetoed the continuation of both the UN and the OSCE missions in Abkhazia and South Ossetia. As a result, after 2009 no international missions were present on the territory of Abkhazia and South Ossetia (IIFFMCG 2009: vol. 2, 441).[2]

---

1. The talks were held in Geneva and became known as the Geneva process.

2. The EUMM was not granted access to the South Ossetian and Abkhaz side of the border, which seriously hindered its monitoring of the post-war stabilisation process (IIFFMCG 2009: vol. 2, 441).

Russia's relations with the United States, NATO and the EU were negatively affected in the months following the war (Blank 2009). Within the EU, however, different positions emerged throughout the crisis of August 2008 and in the ensuing months. While the fighting was still taking place, Polish president Lech Kaczynski participated in a public demonstration held in Tbilisi in support of Georgia, together with the presidents of Ukraine, Estonia and Lithuania and the prime minister of Latvia. Conversely, German and French leaders took a much more cautious stance, which also allowed French president Sarkozy to mediate between the warring parties (see Sakwa 2012: 601). The Finnish government also took a moderate stance and sought a role as mediator through its OSCE chairmanship. Thus, in the three countries under analysis, the August 2008 war between Russia and Georgia was a central topic in foreign policy makers' speeches. The discourse analysis in the following subchapters focuses primarily on the period of the war and its immediate aftermath (August–October 2008). Some previous and later texts are also included in the study, in order to assess the nature of security discourses on Russia prior to the August 2008 crisis and its longer-term impact.

Partners in difficult times: German leaders' discourses

Chancellor Angela Merkel and Foreign Minister Frank-Walter Steinmeier commented extensively on the August 2008 crisis. Both Merkel and Steinmeier were very active throughout the crisis. Merkel travelled to Russia and Georgia and attended the extraordinary European Council held in Brussels on 1 September 2008 to discuss the EU's position on the conflict. Steinmeier discussed his views on the war and Russia in interviews with mainstream German newspapers and held relevant speeches in official contexts, including the UN General Assembly. He also travelled to Abkhazia and Georgia in late July 2008 and was the last high-ranking Western politician who attempted to mediate between the parties before the outbreak of war (IIFFMCG 2009: vol. 2, 59).

The investigation of German foreign policy makers' statements revealed three dominant discourses concerning the August 2008 war and contemporary security relations with Russia. The first discourse stressed Russia's importance as an international actor and as an essential partner for the EU on all key issues pertaining to European security. This discourse emerged in speeches held before, during and after the August 2008 war. It therefore reflected a broad, consolidated line of thought in German foreign policy making circles. On the other hand, the second discourse appeared mostly in speeches held during or immediately after the August 2008 war. It criticised some of Russia's political and military decisions during the crisis, such as the large-scale use of force and the recognition of Abkhazia and South Ossetia. However, this criticism was not particularly strong and was often accompanied by requests for further political consultations with Russia. The third discourse focused on Germany and the EU's role in the August 2008 crisis and their subsequent stance towards Russia. It praised the EU's mediation during the crisis and emphasised the need for a coherent and active EU foreign policy towards the conflict region and Russia.

No return to the Cold War: Russia as a strategic security partner

Within the context of increasing tensions between Russia and the West in late 2007 and early 2008, German leaders attempted to counter negative trends and sought dialogue with Moscow. The dominant German security discourse in this period stressed that Russia was a key player in the international arena and hence an indispensable partner for European security. German policy makers rejected the contemporary media discourse foreshadowing a new Cold War with Russia and portrayed comparisons between the Soviet Union and Russia as anachronisms. Political pragmatism and history are the topoi linking the argument (Russia is a key partner for European security and no longer a Cold War rival) to its logical conclusion that Germany, NATO and the EU should seek cooperation with Russia. This discourse reflects long-standing German perceptions of Russia as an essential factor in European security (Siddi 2016a). Negative memories of the Cold War, when Germany was politically divided and stood on the frontline of superpower confrontation, played an important role in the rejection of the Cold War discourse.

German leaders' preoccupation with halting the deterioration of relations with Russia emerged as early as March 2007, in a speech made by foreign minister Steinmeier a few weeks after Putin's (2007) critical remarks at the Munich security conference. Addressing the German parliament on the issue of the US anti-missile shield in Eastern Europe, Steinmeier (2007d) argued:

> In my opinion, the danger of a division of Europe and NATO, as well as Russia's lapse into old habits, would be a very high price to pay [for the deployment of the anti-missile shield]. German foreign policy aims to unite Europe, maintain the transatlantic partnership and the strategic partnership with Russia. A new Cold War between the USA and Russia, even if it is only fought with words, damages the interests of our country.

Steinmeier defined the partnership with Russia as 'strategic' and juxtaposed it to the partnership with the US, thereby implying that, for Germany, it was of no less importance. Through perspectivation (signalled by the phrase 'in my opinion'), he emphasised his opposition to confrontation with Russia and its negative effects on German interests. In the attempt to reconcile Germany's alliance with the US and the partnership with Russia, Steinmeier (2007d) proposed a 'shared system, or at least joint efforts in the field of missile defence'. Steinmeier's desire to find an agreement with Russia on controversial issues of European security also surfaced in his speech at the German parliament on the recognition of Kosovo's independence in February 2008, where he stated that 'We all would have wanted a solution […] that took Russia's position more into account' (2008b).

From mid-May 2008 until the outbreak of war in the South Caucasus, Steinmeier's statements on Russia were dominated by the launch of the German–Russian modernisation partnership, a policy initiative aimed at cooperation and promoting internal reforms in Russia (Spanger 2011: 655). After the election of apparently reform-oriented Dmitri Medvedev to the Russian presidency in March 2008, Steinmeier became the main advocate of the modernisation partnership. In a relevant speech held at the University of Yekaterinburg in May 2008, the German foreign minister argued:

> Russia is and remains an indispensable partner for Germany and the EU, also for the shaping of tomorrow's world. We need your country [Russia] as a partner for security and stability in Europe and beyond. We need each other for issues such as energy security, arms control or in the worldwide struggle against terrorism.

> (Steinmeier 2008c)

Through the discursive strategy of predication, Russia was described as 'an indispensable partner' in a vast range of key European and global security issues. As this extract shows, Steinmeier used the modernisation partnership to promote cooperation in security policy and reiterate Germany's consideration of Russia as an essential international partner. His views were echoed by Chancellor Angela Merkel, who recurrently portrayed Russia as a partner. Most significantly, she did so at the Bucharest NATO summit of April 2008, where relations with Moscow on the question of NATO membership for Georgia and Ukraine were a highly divisive issue among member states (Merkel 2008a).

During the August 2008 war and the ensuing crisis, the discourse on Russia as a key security partner was toned down but continued to be present in German leaders' speeches. On 15 August, while Russian troops were still operating on undisputed Georgian territory, Merkel and Medvedev concurred that dialogue with the US on the anti-missile shield should continue, despite the simultaneous US–Polish agreement to deploy the system without consulting Russia (Spiegel Online 2008). In late August, despite the tensions with Russia due to Moscow's unilateral recognition of Abkhazia and South Ossetia, Steinmeier (2008d) returned to the issue of the anti-missile shield and criticised the US–Polish agreement on the grounds that it was ill timed and could be misunderstood by Russia. In an interview with a mainstream German newspaper, *Welt am Sonntag*, the German foreign minister also spoke against suspending cooperation with Russia at the EU level and in the NATO–Russia Council (Steinmeier 2008e). As early as September 2008, Steinmeier returned fully to his pre-war discourse, stressing the need for a partnership with Russia on security issues. At the opening of a conference of German and EU diplomats and parliamentarians at the German ministry of foreign affairs, he emphasised the need for 'Russia's constructive contribution in the region [the South Caucasus], as a partner in shaping the European security and peace order and in tackling global challenges' (Steinmeier 2008f).

Steinmeier's statements in favour of cooperation with Russia were often accompanied by a resolute rejection of the contemporary media discourse on a new Cold War. In an interview with *Süddeutsche Zeitung* on 27 August 2008, the day after Russia's recognition of Abkhazia and South Ossetia, Steinmeier (2008d) stated:

I am appalled by those who, in the West and Russia, seem to wish a return to the cynical realities of the Cold War. I am disconcerted by the loss of historical memory about years that I remember very well and that saw the death of many. And I don't understand what leads some to make frivolous comparisons with historical situations such as Munich 1938 [the symbol of Western appeasement of Nazi Germany] or Sarajevo 1914 [the outbreak of the First World War]. It is clear that our conflicts are no longer guided by systemic differences and ideologies.

Steinmeier used the discursive strategy of perspectivation to convey his harsh personal criticism of a memory politics discourse that constructed similarities between the August 2008 crisis and some of the most tragic events of European history. During a conference at the German foreign ministry in September 2008, Steinmeier (2008f) argued (with the same emotionally charged rhetoric) that Cold War times were 'over once and for all. And therefore all the talk about the Cold War is just a rhetorical relict of past times'. Similarly, in a speech made in December 2008, Steinmeier (2008g) emphasised the differences between German and European security in 2008 and during the Cold War:

There are no longer soldiers patrolling borders in Central Europe, no simulation games involving the use of tactical nuclear weapons in the Fulda gap [in Central Germany] […] All those who inconsiderately talk of a new Cold War today seem to forget what the [Berlin] Wall and barbed wire, ideological rivalry and a nuclear arms race meant concretely.

The speech was made at an event held by the Heinz Schwarzkopf Foundation focusing on European politics for the thirty-seventh anniversary of Willy Brandt's Nobel Peace Prize speech.[3] The commemoration provided Steinmeier with the opportunity to praise Brandt's Ostpolitik and portray his approach to the Soviet Union as a model for cooperation with Russia. According to him, only a cooperative approach could lead to arms control and to the settlement of the frozen conflicts, which 'cannot be resolved without Russia's constructive contribution'. By the time Steinmeier made these remarks, Barack Obama had been elected president of the United States (in November 2008) and had announced a reformulation of US relations with Russia, based on a cooperative approach. Hence, Steinmeier's discourse on treating Russia as a partner was also in tune with the new policy line of the White House. This further encouraged him to advocate the resumption of dialogue with Russia in forums that had been suspended after the August 2008 war, notably the EU–Russia summits and the NATO–Russia Council.[4]

---

3. A description of the Heinz Schwarzkopf Foundation is available on its website at http://schwarzkopf-stiftung.de/en/about/ (accessed 8 August 2016).

4. In the speech at the Heinz Schwarzkopf Foundation, Steinmeier (2008g) praised Obama for his call to 'overcome Cold War thinking' and 'to build a partnership encompassing the whole [European] continent, including Russia'. He also called for the resumption of meetings in the NATO–Russia Council and for cooperation with Russia on numerous global security issues.

The military escalation of August 2008: mild criticism, no rash judgements

Although German leaders tended to see Russia predominantly as a security partner, a more critical discourse emerged during the August 2008 war. This discourse mildly criticised Russia's disproportionate use of force, the delay in the withdrawal of Russian troops after the ceasefire agreement and Moscow's unilateral recognition of Abkhazia and South Ossetia. However, Merkel and Steinmeier's criticism focused mostly on a few technical and legal issues and was not radical. In fact, they both advocated further talks with Russia to solve the crisis and were opposed to retaliatory measures that might lead to harsher confrontation. Furthermore, German leaders refused to put all the blame for the outbreak of war on Russia, which contrasted strikingly with the behaviour of their Polish and American counterparts and with the dominant Western media discourse (Heinrich and Tanaev 2009). In particular, Steinmeier's statements suggested that Georgians and South Ossetians shared responsibility for the crisis.

German leaders' stance towards Russia during August 2008 can be interpreted as a reflection of two essential constitutive elements of German national identity: the rejection of war as a means to solve disputes and the support of multilateralism and international law (*see* Chapter 3). Preference for multilateralism and long-standing German perceptions of Russia as a key partner in European security also help explain Merkel and Steinmeier's insistence on engaging Russia to achieve a negotiated solution of the crisis. Legality and political pragmatism are the topoi that link the key argument in this discourse (Russia's reaction to the crisis was disproportionate, but a solution can be found only through dialogue with Moscow) and its logical conclusion (talks with Russia have to continue).

The critical discourse on Russia was prominent in particular in the first public statements issued after the outbreak of war. On 15 August 2008, during a meeting with Russian President Dmitri Medvedev, Merkel defined Russia's military intervention as 'partly disproportional' and claimed that Georgia's territorial integrity was a precondition for conflict resolution (Spiegel Online 2008). During her visit to Tbilisi two days later, the Chancellor forcefully demanded the withdrawal of Russian troops from Georgian territory (Merkel 2008b). Merkel's arguments were echoed in a harsher tone in Steinmeier's (2008e) interview with *Welt am Sonntag* on 17 August.

> Georgia's territorial integrity remains the foundation of our [the EU's] policy [...] In our talks with the Russian side we have made very clear that, by bombing and sending troops to the core of Georgian territory, they have crossed a red line.

In the interview, Steinmeier referred to international norms and called for the withdrawal of Russian troops from Georgian territory. Russia's recognition of Abkhazia and South Ossetia on 26 August was perceived as another violation of international law. Merkel (2008c) defined Russia's recognition as 'completely unacceptable and contrary to international law'. The day after, in an interview with

Süddeutsche Zeitung, Steinmeier (2008d) called the Russian decision 'wrong', 'dangerous', 'very regrettable' and 'in no way acceptable'.

Despite these occasional peaks of tension, German discourses during the conflict were mostly balanced and never took an anti-Russian tone. Contrary to the dominant trend in the Western media, German leaders did not accuse Russia of starting the conflict. In his interview with *Welt am Sonntag,* Steinmeier (2008e) stated that the conflict had roots that reached far back into the past and that 'making a chronology of the escalation and blaming either side' was not his task. Moreover, he suggested that, by July 2008 (when he visited Abkhazia to mediate between the parties), conflict appeared inevitable.

> In Abkhazia I had to witness how uncompromising and irreconcilable the parties to the conflict were. For this reason, I did not delude myself about the explosiveness of the situation, even if it was not possible to predict that the outbreak of war would take place in South Ossetia.

Steinmeier attempted to make his claim about the likelihood of a military escalation more compelling through perspectivation, which is highlighted by the first-person narrative and the ensuing subjective description of the situation on the ground. By emphasising that the parties were 'uncompromising' and 'irreconcilable', Steinmeier also conveyed the idea that responsibility for the crisis was shared. This view was reiterated more clearly in his interview with *Süddeutsche Zeitung* on 27 August 2008.

> Attributions of responsibility are certainly not a key issue now, but we should base our assessments on the fact that the Georgian attack of Tskhinvali was preceded by days of mutual provocations between Georgians and South Ossetians.

> (Steinmeier 2008d)

In this passage, Steinmeier suggested that Georgians and South Ossetians shared responsibility for the outbreak of war, but he also implied that the Georgian attack on Tskhinvali was to blame for the start of full-scale military operations. Russians were neither accused of having started the war, nor of having played a role in the 'mutual provocations'. This interpretation of events was functional to alleviating tensions with Russia and returning to the negotiating table, which appeared as the main objective of German diplomacy during the August 2008 crisis. Even in the tensest phase of the crisis, Steinmeier (2008h) argued that 'a solution of the conflict is hardly possible without Russia. We must therefore keep all communication channels open […]'. In the statements made immediately after Russia's recognition of Abkhazia and South Ossetia, Merkel (2008c) continued to advocate talks with Medvedev, while Steinmeier (2008d) hoped for 'joint efforts [with Russian leaders] that will allow us to return to normality in our relationship'.

Negotiating with Russia: the EU as a successful mediator

Following the August 2008 crisis, German leaders argued that the EU had proved successful in crisis management and that, based on this positive experience, it should play a key role in improving relations with Russia and the Eastern neighbourhood. This discourse reflected German leaders' tendency to support EU policies and multilateralism, which is a well-established trait of Germany's foreign policy identity. Europeanism, meaning the commitment to EU values and policies, is the topos linking the key argument (the EU proved successful in negotiations with Russia and in crisis management in Georgia) with its logical conclusion (EU policies towards Russia and the Eastern neighbourhood should be aimed at improving relations).

In German leaders' speeches, the claim that the EU had been successful at mediating in the Russian–Georgian crisis appeared as early as mid-August 2008. In his interview with *Welt am Sonntag* on 17 August 2008, Steinmeier (2008e) argued:

> Europe can achieve something. The mediation of president Sarkozy and of his foreign minister Kouchner, supported by other EU states including Germany, has contributed to the cessation of hostilities [...] From the phone calls that I made after the outbreak of war, I know how difficult it was to stop the fighting. Therefore we should not underestimate the successful mediation of the French Council presidency and of the EU.

Through perspectivation, Steinmeier emphasised the significance of Sarkozy's mediation, which he framed as a joint EU effort, rather than as a success of the French President.[5] Further on in the interview, he underplayed internal divisions in the EU during the crisis and stressed the 'common positions' on which all member states converged, namely the support of Georgia's territorial integrity and the decision to contribute to stabilisation and humanitarian relief efforts. In his interview with *Süddeutsche Zeitung* on 27 August, Steinmeier (2008d) bluntly rejected the assertion that the EU was helpless and deeply divided over the crisis, calling such claims 'superficial' and 'unjustified'. His views on this issue were shared by Angela Merkel. Following the extraordinary European Council on 1 September 2008, Merkel (2008d) claimed that the EU had sent out 'a signal of unity and resoluteness' regarding the Caucasus crisis and described the EU-brokered six-point plan as 'an important document' on which to build future endeavours.

Based on these positive assessments of the EU's role in the crisis, both Merkel and Steinmeier advocated the enhancement of EU policies towards the

---

5. A debate exists on whether the achievements of Sarkozy's mediation should be attributed to his authority as French President, rather than to his simultaneous clout as President of the European Council. For instance, Whitman and Wolff (2010: 10) suggest that Sarkozy's achievements were largely due to his being 'accepted as equal' by Russian leaders on the basis of his national political role and to the support he received from the 'well-experienced and well-resourced [French] foreign office staff'.

conflict zone and Russia. In August 2008, shortly after the ceasefire agreement, Merkel (2008b) argued that there were 'good reasons to step up the EU's neighbourhood policy with Georgia'. A few days later, she claimed that the EU should do all it could to support Georgia through its 'policy of neighbourliness' (Merkel 2008c). On 8 September 2008, Steinmeier (2008f) argued that the EU was ready to take part in conflict management and monitoring operations. He also advocated the intensification of EU policies in the Eastern neighbourhood in order to create 'a European space of security, stability and prosperity'. In his speeches of late 2008, Steinmeier (2008g, 2008i) encouraged the formulation of the EU's Eastern Partnership, a policy framework that aimed to intensify relations with European post-Soviet countries. Furthermore, he argued that the EU should continue to engage Russia in order to negotiate a new Partnership and Cooperation Agreement and jointly build security and stability in Europe (Steinmeier 2008e, 2008g).

The long shadow of history challenging pragmatism: Polish discourses

Polish foreign policy leaders engaged differently in the debate concerning the Russian–Georgian war. President Lech Kaczynski was the most vocal in condemning Russia's policies. Prior to the August 2008 escalation, Kaczynski established a close relationship with the Georgian leadership and became one of the staunchest supporters of Georgia's integration in NATO and the EU. During the August 2008 war, Kaczynski travelled to Tbilisi and gave a deeply emotional speech attacking Russia during a rally in support of Saakashvili. He maintained the same stance after the conflict, travelling to Georgia and meeting Georgian leaders on several occasions in late 2008 and early 2009.[6] Radoslaw Sikorski and Donald Tusk also commented extensively on the August 2008 crisis. Moreover, on 20 August 2008, Sikorski signed an agreement with US Secretary of State Condoleeza Rice concerning the deployment of elements of the US anti-missile shield on Polish territory. As the document was signed during the Russian–Georgian crisis and contributed to worsening tensions with Russia, the debates on the anti-missile shield and the war in the Caucasus became intertwined (de Quetteville 2008).

The analysis of Polish leaders' statements highlights two dominant discourses. The first discourse appeared in Lech Kaczynski's speeches and emphasised Russia's alleged role as aggressor. Memory politics is central to this discourse, as Kaczynski described Russia's policies during the August 2008 crisis as a continuation of Tsarist and Soviet imperialism. In addition, he advocated greater NATO and EU involvement in the crisis and the adoption of a tougher stance against Russia. The second discourse was found in Tusk and Sikorski's speeches and can be understood better within the context of the Polish Government's attempts to improve relations with Russia after the autumn of 2007. This discourse

---

6. Official meetings between Kaczynski and Georgian leaders are reported on the Polish presidential website, http://www.president.pl/en/archive/news-archive/news-2009/ (accessed 9 August 2016).

was critical of Russia, but made a more moderate use of memory politics (mostly limited to a few statements by Sikorski in August 2008) and was framed in a less emotional rhetoric. It advocated a pragmatic approach to Russia and, particularly when the August 2008 crisis subsided, it highlighted improvements in Polish–Russian relations after the election of Tusk's government.

Lech Kaczynski: confronting the imperialist aggressor

Kaczynski's speeches during and after the August 2008 war were virulently anti-Russian. Kaczynski claimed that Russian political elites and foreign policy were inherently imperialistic and aggressive as a result of the country's history. In most of Kaczynski's speeches, the argument for Russia's culpability in the August 2008 crisis was based entirely on memory politics, notably the construction of parallels with Russia's imperial history. Occasionally, violations of international law were cited in order to support the argument. History and legality are the topoi connecting Kaczynski's main argument (Russia's imperialism and aggressiveness are to blame for the outbreak of the August 2008 war) with its logical conclusion that the EU and the United States should take a tougher stance against Russia.

The discourse propagated by Kaczynski reflected traditional Polish perceptions of Russia as an imperialist country, which became deeply engrained in Polish national identity as a result of the Tsarist occupation, the wars with the Soviet Union and Poland's inclusion in the Soviet sphere of influence during the Cold War. Kaczynski's occasional references to differences in values between Russia and the rest of Europe resonated with long-standing Polish discourses that describe Russia as oriental, less civilised and hence morally incompatible with European civilisation. Furthermore, his calls for EU and particularly NATO actions to confront Russia reflected the strong Euro-Atlantic dimension of post-communist Poland's foreign policy identity. On the other hand, Kaczynski's disappointment at the alleged failure of some EU member states to support Georgia can be understood within the context of the historical discourse on Poland's unreciprocated commitment to the Western cause (*see* Chapter 3).

The shared experience of historical conflict with Russia and a strong support for Georgia's NATO and EU integration were the foundations on which Kaczynski's partnership with Saakashvili was built before the August 2008 crisis. This emerged in a speech Kaczynski (2008a) made in early March 2008, during Saakashvili's official visit to Warsaw.

The Polish and the Georgian nations have a diverse history in the sense that the Georgian nation was in existence for a longer time. In a sense, our histories are similar, though, for both nations had to fight a tough fight for their independence. Both at one time fell victim to Russian imperialism. This happened more or less at the same time. Both rebelled. [...] And then, the time has come when independence could be once more regained, after years of struggle and vicissitudes, when in both countries the striving for freedom finally prevailed. And this has become a platform for very close cooperation.

In the speech, Russia was portrayed in unambiguously negative terms: imperialist, oppressive, opposing the 'striving for freedom' in Poland and Georgia. The construction of a common experience of 'falling victim to Russian imperialism', rebelling against it and finally regaining independence was considered so significant as to constitute 'a platform for very close cooperation' in the present. In the following sentences, Kaczynski (2008a) explained the concrete focus of this cooperation.

> I am confident that Georgia has entered the finishing straight as far as NATO membership is concerned. I also think that the EU perspective will open up soon. Be assured that in four weeks' time in Bucharest [...] you will be able to take advantage of our support. We are doing this in the name of the old maxim which was coined in the nineteenth century: 'For your freedom and for ours!'

Kaczynski clarified the rationale of his promise to support Georgia's NATO and EU integration with a nineteenth-century motto that Polish romantic nationalists used in their fight against the occupying Tsarist army. The historical parallel suggests that Kaczynski supported Saakashvili's bid for NATO and EU membership in order to protect both Poland's and Georgia's freedom from Russian imperialism. This logic was therefore based on the assumption that Russia still threatened Polish and Georgian independence. At the NATO summit in Bucharest (2–4 April 2008), Kaczynski upheld his pledge to support Georgia's application for NATO membership, in spite of strong German, French and Russian opposition. In an open letter published in *The Financial Times* a few days before the start of the summit, Kaczynski (2008b) went as far as claiming that leaving Georgia and Ukraine out of NATO 'might put at risk the construction of a stable European security system'.

As tensions in Georgia's separatist republics increased in the spring and early summer of 2008, Kaczynski continued to give unrelenting support to Saakashvili and held only Russia as responsible for the deterioration of the situation on the ground. In mid-July, he publicly appealed to Russia 'to refrain from measures which could exacerbate the tension and might imperil the achievement of an agreement' (Kaczynski 2008c). When the war started on 8 August, Kaczynski blamed Russia alone and openly sided with Saakashvili. In his speech at the political rally in Tbilisi on 12 August, Kaczynski (2008d) argued that the war in Georgia exposed Russia's desire to reconstruct the Soviet empire.

> It is the first instance in a long time that our neighbours from the North [...] have shown the face that we used to know all too well for centuries. Those neighbours believe that the nations surrounding them should be subordinated to them [...] The country I have in mind is Russia. That country believes that the old days of an empire that collapsed some twenty years ago are now about to return, that domination will be again the distinctive feature of the region.

Through perspectivation and the use of memory politics, Russia was portrayed as imperialist and aggressive. Kaczynski's condemnation of Russia was not limited to the decisions of its political elites, but concerned the country as a whole. Russia was personified (it had a 'face', it 'believes') and treated as a malevolent entity, poised to subjugate neighbouring nations.

Kaczynski used memory politics and references to Russia's imperial past in numerous other speeches concerning the August 2008 crisis. On 24 September 2008, in his address to the conference of the Foreign Policy Association in New York, Kaczynski (2008e) argued that Russia's desire to reconstruct its empire had never subsided.

> This imperial tendency started to revive slowly and in various forms [...] The fundamental reason, I believe, is something that is ingrained in the tradition of a given nation and state, in the tradition of relations between the rulers and the people; this is a question of paramount importance in Russia [...] My point is that the revival of the imperial tendency was a natural phenomenon in a sense, a natural striving of the Russian elite.

According to Kaczynski (2008e), Russia and its elites were inherently imperialist as a result of the country's history. Imperialism was 'ingrained' in Russian tradition, hence 'the revival of the imperial tendency' (of which Russia's war in Georgia was 'the best example', see Kaczynski 2008f) was 'a natural phenomenon'. He also emphasised the alleged peculiarity of Russian imperialism, which according to him was the result of 'national customs often very different from our European customs'. Through the categorisation of Russia as non-European and opposed to the West, Kaczynski (2008e) went as far as to frame the Russian–Georgian war in terms of a clash of civilisations: 'I can say that, in Georgia, Russia showed the face it wanted to show. It was not a coincidence. "We are powerful, and you are helpless". Who are the "you"? "You" stands for the West as a whole'.

Kaczynski believed that the Russian–Georgian war was only the first episode of a larger geopolitical clash between Russian imperialism and the West.

> What is the meaning of that [the violation of Georgia's territorial integrity] in geopolitical terms? Namely, for Europe, as well as for the United States, it is not Georgian territory – for Georgia merely serves as a pathway – but today definitely Azerbaijan, and tomorrow Kazakhstan perhaps, and the same is true of Turkmenistan [...]
>
> (Kaczynski 2008e)

For Kaczynski, taking a tougher stance and confronting Russia was the only way for the EU and NATO to stop this expected succession of crises. This emerged in his speech at the rally in Tbilisi on 12 August 2008, where he claimed that the purpose of his visit to Georgia was 'to make the world react even stronger [against Russian actions], the European Union and NATO in particular' (Kaczynski 2008d). Furthermore, in his address to the Foreign Policy Association conference, Kaczynski (2008e) argued that after the Russian–Georgian war 'NATO should return to defence objectives', namely focus on the military defence of its member states from foreign aggressors. In this context, he welcomed the signature of the agreement on the anti-missile shield between Poland and the United States as 'a major victory' of his foreign policy line. He also stated that, most likely, Georgia would not have been attacked by Russia if it had been granted a NATO membership action plan at the Bucharest summit in April 2008.

Within the discourse advocating a tougher stance towards Russia, Kaczynski often criticised EU and NATO countries that supported a more cooperative approach. In his remarks to the Foreign Policy Association, he lamented that some European states 'display an attitude vis-à-vis the existing threats that I would describe as extremely moderate; outright extremely soft'. In the speech made in Tbilisi in August 2008, Kaczynski's (2008d) criticism of these states echoed the Polish identity discourse on Poland's unreciprocated commitment to Western values.

> If the values that are to be the foundation of Europe are to have any practical significance at all, we can defy [we have to defy Russia]. If those values are to matter at all, we must be here; the whole of Europe must be present here. Among us, there are four NATO members [...] There is Mr President Sarkozy, who at present presides over the European Union. But there should be 27 of us here.

Besides Poland, the four NATO members which Kaczynski referred to included Lithuania, Latvia and Estonia, three former Soviet republics where past conflicts with Russia had influenced profoundly the construction of national memory and identity (Grigas 2013).

While parallels with Russia's imperial past and aggressive foreign policy provided the main rationale for Kaczynski's discourse, his criticism of Russian actions during the August 2008 crisis was occasionally substantiated with references to international law. In his statement condemning Russia's recognition of Abkhazia and South Ossetia, he argued that the 'unprecedented aggression by the Russian Federation against the independent Georgian state' was 'entirely incompatible with international law' and hence 'cannot fail to elicit a resolute response from the states of the free world' (Kaczynski 2008g). Similarly, in his speech before the UN General Assembly in September 2008, Kaczynski (2008h) condemned the Russian intervention in Georgia on the grounds that 'fundamental principles of international law, namely the inviolability of borders and territorial integrity, were infringed'. However, memory politics also played a role in these speeches, even if in a subtler way. Phrases such as 'the states of the free world' were borrowed from Western Cold War rhetoric and implied that Russia belonged to the 'unfree', 'undemocratic world', just like the Soviet Union during the Cold War (see Neumann 1998: 103). Similarly, in the speech at the UN General Assembly, Kaczynski (2008h) argued that Russia's intervention in Georgia was reminiscent of the power politics that characterised Europe until the Second World War and posed 'a problem for every country which struggles [...] with the superiority of its more powerful neighbours'.

Sikorski and Tusk: a rocky path to pragmatism in relations with Russia

The reactions of the Polish prime minister and the foreign minister to developments in Georgia in August 2008 differed significantly from Kaczynski's, in both tone and content. Although both Tusk and Sikorski were critical of Russia's actions, they developed a discourse that did not preclude dialogue with Moscow. This discourse can be understood within the context of Tusk's attempt to improve Poland's relations with Russia after his election in the autumn of 2007. It emphasised that, thanks to the pragmatic approach of his government, relations between Poland and Russia had improved in the months before the start of the Russian–Georgian war, particularly through trade. Assessments of the origins of the war were more balanced and the continuation of pragmatic engagement with Russia was advocated. Occasionally, this discourse coexisted with the use of memory politics and harsh criticism of Russia's foreign policy, notably in Sikorski's speeches. However, the core of the discourse stressed that, due to Russia's economic and political importance, Poland should continue its attempts to improve relations, while maintaining a critical attitude towards Russia's foreign policy decisions. Political pragmatism and economic convenience are the topoi linking the main argument (in spite of the war in Georgia, Russia is an important actor for Poland) to its logical conclusion (Poland should continue to engage Russia, while maintaining a critical stance). Within this discourse, the focus on engaging Russia reflected the government's efforts to forge a new foreign policy identity in which traditional Polish perceptions of Russia and Germany as Poland's historical enemies were downplayed. On the other hand, the positive potential of engagement and cooperation was emphasised. Criticism of Russian policies was based mostly on substantive arguments (violation of territorial integrity, disproportionate use of force), rather than on the construction of historical parallels.

Tusk's aversion to using memory politics emerged during his first official visit to Moscow. The visit took place in February 2008, only three months after his appointment as prime minister, and was a clear attempt to restart dialogue with the Kremlin after the period of frosty relations under the government of Jaroslaw Kaczynski. In an interview with the Russian newspaper *Novaya Gazeta*, Tusk (2008a) argued that he preferred not to focus on the history of Polish–Russian relations but rather to 'overcome its consequences'. In addition, he stated:

> It's important to solve the difficult issues of our [Poland and Russia's] neighbourhood in the spirit of truth, but without excessive and exaggerated emotions from both sides. History must not be used in the political struggle, as it causes more problems mainly.

Tusk's replies in the interview focused exclusively on current issues, which were analysed in pragmatic terms and with a clear intention of minimising contentious issues. Disputes over the price of Russian gas were described as the logical result of different market interests, hence 'No drama should be made out of it!'. Regarding the anti-missile shield, Tusk stated that Poland was 'not interested in anything that could be meant to be anti-Russian'. Furthermore, he stressed the improvement of relations with Russia during his first months in office, focusing particularly on substantive issues such as the resolution of trade disputes.

Tusk's discourse was echoed in Sikorski's statements in the spring of 2008. In an interview with the BBC television programme *Hardtalk*, Sikorski (2008a) claimed that Polish–Russian relations had improved during his time in office. He explained that Poland was 'dealing with Russia pragmatically, because it is an important country and a major trade partner; we [Poland] have 17 billions of trade with Russia'. Like Tusk, Sikorski emphasised that relations with Russia should be guided by pragmatism, rather than by historical controversies: 'We [Poland and Russia] are neighbours and there is plenty of history between us, but it is a pragmatic relationship'.

The outbreak of the August 2008 war constituted a major challenge for Tusk and Sikorski's discourse advocating a pragmatic relationship with Russia. The Russian military intervention in Georgia reawakened deep-seated fears of Russia among Polish public opinion. The fear of future Russian military operations against Poland increased, together with support for the deployment of the anti-missile shield and US troops on Polish territory, which had previously encountered much opposition due to the risk of undermining relations with Russia. Confronted with this change of attitude, Sikorski attempted to hold to the discourse emphasising pragmatism, but occasionally slipped into arguments that show the enduring relevance of memory politics and wariness of Russia in his foreign policy thinking. In an interview with the British newspaper *The Telegraph* on 20 August 2008, Sikorski (2008b) gave a much more balanced assessment of the war's origins than Kaczynski, claiming that 'Georgia had allowed itself to be provoked' and that the 'Russian response' (implying that Russia did not start the escalation) had been 'disproportionate'. He also stated that the Polish decision to announce the agreement on the deployment of the anti-missile shield during the Georgian crisis 'had nothing to do with [developments in] Georgia' and was not targeted against Russia. However, in the same interview Sikorski argued that Russian military operations in Georgia were 'reminiscent of things we hoped belonged to the past'. He also used memory politics, particularly references to the Nazi–Soviet invasion of Poland in 1939, to justify his demands for additional US military presence and weapons on Polish territory.

A similar combination of pragmatism and slips into memory politics can be detected in other speeches given by Sikorski in the months after the August 2008 war. In November 2008, during his talk at the Atlantic Council (a US-based think tank focusing on transatlantic issues) he argued:

Poland had difficult, sometimes very painful relations with Russia in the past, but we don't want confrontation with our neighbours. The government of Donald Tusk has restarted pragmatic dialogue with Russian authorities […]. I have already visited Moscow twice. Warsaw is the first NATO capital visited by the Russian foreign minister after the war in Georgia. We had good, frank discussions [...] In fact, Poland is the last country on earth that wants a return of the age of East–West confrontation [...] On the contrary, we would like to see Russia as a partner.

(Sikorski 2008c)

In these remarks, Sikorski reiterated the pragmatic foreign policy approach to Russia that Poland had developed before the August 2008 war. Russia was associated with a positive semantic field ('neighbour', 'partner') and portrayed as a country with which it was possible to have 'good, frank discussions'. Sikorski emphasised his commitment to improving relations with Russia through perspectivation, which highlighted both his personal involvement in the diplomatic efforts ('I have already visited Moscow twice') and his desire to build a partnership with Moscow ('we don't want confrontation', 'we would like to see Russia as a partner'). This approach is all the more remarkable if compared with Kaczynski's contemporary speeches, which advocated confrontation with Moscow by stirring traditional Polish fears of Russia. However, Sikorski made occasional use of memory politics also in his talk at the Atlantic Council, particularly when he compared Russia's justification for its intervention in Georgia with the rationale the Soviet Union had provided for its invasion of Poland in 1939. He also accused Russia of undermining European security and argued that NATO should improve its defence capabilities as a result of 'Russian tanks rolling into Georgia'.

Tusk disapproved of Russia's actions in Georgia, but his criticism concerned exclusively substantive, contemporary policy issues. For instance, in his interview with the German daily *Neue Osnabrücker Zeitung* in early September 2008, Tusk (2008b) focused primarily on questions concerning the EU's role in the crisis and the presence of Russian troops in Georgia. No significant use of memory politics was made. As the crisis subsided, Tusk reframed his criticism within a narrative arguing that relations with Russia might improve through a pragmatic approach, but only after a long and uneasy process. This narrative emerged clearly in an interview with *The Financial Times* in December 2008.

We showed a lot of good will and Russia also appeared interested in improving ties with Poland [...] My meetings with Putin and Medvedev showed [that we were heading in] a good direction. However, the crisis in the Caucasus definitely showed that this process will not be easy [...]

(Tusk 2008c)

In spite of the expected difficulties, Tusk (2008c) claimed that he saw Russia as 'a potentially positive partner for Poland and the EU' and defended his pragmatic approach to relations with Moscow, arguing that it corresponded to the expectations of Poland's EU partners.

I get the impression from European capitals that there is a clear expectation that Poland play the role of a leader in the positive change of European–Russian relations, and that is the policy we are trying to follow. We don't have any particular illusions about Russia and I think we see her rationally. I am one of the politicians who does not have an anti-Russian obsession. In Brussels and in many European capitals, this change in Warsaw's approach was treated very well, even with relief.

(Tusk 2008c)

Tusk argued that his reformulation of Poland's policy towards Russia would allow the country to be considered a leader in steering the EU's relations with Moscow. Remarkably, as is implied by his reasoning, this could only be achieved by developing a new foreign policy approach that downplayed long-standing Polish fears of Russia, which Tusk critically labelled as an 'anti-Russian obsession'.

Finnish discourses: Russia's comeback, challenge or a new partnership?

The August 2008 crisis took place during Finland's chairmanship of the OSCE. As the OSCE is the main pan-European security organisation, and both Russia and Georgia are members, Finnish foreign minister and OSCE chairman Alexander Stubb felt the urge to take the initiative and seek a mediated solution to the crisis.[7] He travelled to both Georgia and Russia and held negotiations with the leaders of both countries. Among Finland's top foreign policy makers, he was the most active contributor to the debate on the August 2008 crisis. His predecessor Ilkka Kanerva (in office until April 2008), Prime Minister Matti Vanhanen and President Tarja Halonen also participated in the public debate, but featured less prominently than Stubb in the media.

Two main discourses emerged from the analysis of Finnish foreign policy makers' statements on the Russian–Georgian war and contemporary security relations with Russia. The first discourse emphasised Russia's return to the role of key actor in European security. Russia's foreign policy was generally described as assertive and at times even militaristic, hence posing a challenge for Finland. The discourse stressed the necessity to engage Russia in order to defuse tensions. This narrative emerged also in texts preceding the outbreak of the Russian–Georgian war, but it became more prominent during the August 2008 crisis. The second discourse highlighted Russia's role as a partner for Finland and the EU. Before the outbreak of war, the second discourse coexisted with the first. It lost momentum during the August 2008 crisis but became dominant again in the final months of 2008, when top Finnish foreign policy makers responded positively to a

---

7.   As he wrote in an article published on his personal website in October 2008, 'Finland happens to hold the presidency of the Organisation for Security and Cooperation in Europe (OSCE). This meant that we had to be involved on the ground [during the August 2008 crisis]' (Stubb 2008a).

controversial Russian proposal to reform the European security system (Zagorski 2009).[8] In both discourses, neither Russia nor Georgia were explicitly blamed for the outbreak of the August 2008 war. Finnish leaders' speeches focused on supporting diplomatic efforts with both belligerents and on the need to alleviate the humanitarian crisis, without delving into the contentious debate concerning responsibilities for the conflict.

Russia's assertiveness and military comeback: engagement as the only option for Finland

The first of the two discourses introduced above emphasised Russia's military revival under Putin and the assertiveness of its foreign policy. Confronted with this scenario, Finnish foreign policy leaders claimed that there was no alternative to engagement and cooperation with Russia. Foreign ministers Ilkka Kanerva and Alexander Stubb were the main proponents of this discourse, which was dominant from the early months of 2008 until the end of August 2008. Danger, notably the perception of a potential threat emanating from Russia, and political pragmatism are the topoi linking the main argument (Russia's foreign policy is assertive and constitutes a challenge for Finland) to its conclusion (Finland should engage with Russia). This discourse can be interpreted and understood through the prism of Finnish national identity, in which Russia has been constructed both as the source of Finland's main security deficit and as an unavoidable actor in the security field.

The narrative highlighting the assertiveness of Russia's foreign policy was already present in speeches made in the months preceding the outbreak of the Russian–Georgian war. In February 2008, in his remarks at the Woodrow Wilson International Center (a think tank based in Washington), Kanerva (2008b) argued:

> Today, Russia is much more active in foreign policy and seeks to position itself as a superpower – not only regionally but more globally, too. Moscow is pursuing its interests with determination and Russia's military posture has become more active in our region also.

The statement that Russia's military posture had become more active in Finland's neighbourhood also reflected a perception of danger for Finnish security, to which Kanerva responded by advocating cooperation with Russia.

> Even if it is difficult at times, I do not see any other possibility than trying to engage Russia in dialogue and cooperation [...] Russia's contribution is needed in combating terrorism and arms proliferation in many regional conflicts as well as in fighting climate change.

---

8.   Briefly, the Russian proposal advocated a new legally binding security treaty enhancing the role of the UN Security Council (where Russia has veto power) in European security issues. For more details, see Zagorski 2009.

Through the use of perspectivation ('I do not see any other possibility'), Kanerva presented cooperation with Russia as the only possible policy option for Finland. Significantly, he referred to the resolution of regional conflicts as one of the key areas in which Russia's contribution was needed. As emerges from a statement issued two days after his speech in Washington, Kanerva (2008c) considered the frozen conflicts in Georgia a priority for Finland's OSCE Chairmanship. As concrete evidence for this, he also paid a diplomatic visit to the area in late February 2008 (Ministry for Foreign Affairs of Finland 2008a). Hence, Finnish foreign policy towards the Abkhaz and South Ossetian conflicts already appeared well delineated before the escalation of August 2008; mediation and cooperation with Russia were its key tenets.

This policy line remained substantially unchanged after Kanerva was replaced by Stubb as Finland's foreign minister. During the August 2008 crisis, Stubb sought a solution to the crisis through dialogue with Russia. He took a more critical attitude only at the peak of the crisis, when Moscow delayed the withdrawal of its troops from the conflict zone and recognised the independence of South Ossetia and Abkhazia. On 25 August 2008, on the occasion of an address to top Finnish diplomats, Stubb (2008b) argued:

Victorious war strengthened Russia's position as superpower. Nationalistic and protectionist superpower thinking has characterised its external relations even before this. But its superiority is not solely based on size and energy anymore. Today, Russia has both the will and capacity to deploy its armed forces as a foreign policy instrument. Another significant change is the doctrine of protection of expatriate Russians, developed to justify the conduct of aggressive policy. It is impossible to think that these factors would not be taken fully into account in Finland.

The semantic field associated with Russia (nationalistic, protectionist, superiority in size and energy, willing and capable to deploy its armed forces as a foreign policy instrument, aggressive) constructed the image of a menacing country that based its foreign policy conduct on realpolitik. Stubb's claim that Finland should take into account the aggressive shift in Russia's foreign policy resonated with the Finnish historical narrative portraying Russia as Finland's main security deficit.

The tensest moment in Finnish–Russian relations during the Georgian crisis was reached on 26 August, when Stubb (2008c) issued a statement condemning Russia's recognition of Abkhazia and South Ossetia and arguing that 'the international community cannot accept unilaterally established buffer zones'. Thereafter, tensions subsided and Stubb returned to a more cooperative rhetoric. In fact, even at the height of the crisis the Finnish foreign minister did not abandon the discourse stressing the need for cooperation with Russia. In the address to Finnish diplomats quoted above, Stubb also argued that Russia did not pose a military threat to Finland. This statement appears in contradiction with his remarks concerning Russia's aggressive foreign policy, but it can be understood as a reflection of the belief, deeply rooted in post-1945 Finnish foreign policy identity, that Finland has no alternative to engaging Russia (*see* Chapter 3). Hence, Stubb avoided a discourse that might lead to confrontation between Finland and Russia and sought to take the debate to the EU level, most notably by arguing that Finland could 'restrain the nationalist and nation-state oriented trend only by being active in the EU' (Stubb 2008b). This approach was also compatible with the traditional Finnish preference for multilateralism in addressing international crises and the pro-European orientation of Finnish foreign policy.

The press release issued by the Finnish government's Communications Unit on 29 August, shortly before the extraordinary European Council on the crisis in Georgia, clearly shows in what direction Finland intended to steer EU policy towards Russia. After restating Finnish support for Georgia's territorial integrity, the communiqué declared that Finland did not support any sanctions against Russia and that sanctions 'would trigger a vicious circle of counter-measures that would be hard to break' (Ministry for Foreign Affairs of Finland 2008b). Therefore, at EU level also Finland rejected hostile confrontation with Russia and advocated dialogue as the best policy to solve the crisis.

Leaving the war behind: good neighbourly relations and strategic partnership

Following the government's communiqué on 29 August, the Finnish stance towards Russia was softened and a discourse stressing good neighbourly relations and strategic partnership became dominant. This discourse already existed before the crisis and can be detected especially in Prime Minister Matti Vanhanen and President Tarja Halonen's speeches. It lost prominence temporarily during the August 2008 war, but it did not disappear. Arguably, its enduring influence may have been one of the reasons why Finnish foreign policy makers focused on alleviating the humanitarian crisis and defusing tensions throughout the month, thereby paving the way for the resumption of friendly relations with Russia. Strategic advantage, meant as the benefits from cooperating with a key security actor, is the topos linking the main argument (Russia is a neighbour and a strategic partner) to its conclusion (Finland should pursue a co-operative relationship and be open to Russia's policy initiatives). This discourse reflected the post-1945 conceptualisation of Russia as a key partner in Finnish foreign policy identity.

Before the outbreak of the August 2008 war, the narrative describing Russia as a peaceful neighbour emerged, for instance in Vanhanen's (2008b) remarks at a seminar organised by the Finnish Centre Party on the topic of foreign and security policy.

> Above all, Russia signifies for us a neighbour, a neighbour, and a neighbour. Russia has changed fundamentally in terms of its societal systems since the Cold War era. Finland has a great interest in Russia remaining stable and co-operative [...] From Finland's perspective, certain conclusions can be made. Russia does not pose a military threat to Finland.

Vanhanen's description suggested that Russia was radically different from the Soviet Union and no longer posed an ideological and military challenge to Finland. Consequently, it was simply a 'neighbour', with no threatening intentions, and Finland had 'a great interest' in cooperating to ensure that it remained so. Within this context, the triple emphasis on the word 'neighbour' takes a positive connotation and conveys the idea that post-Soviet Russia deserved special attention in Finnish foreign policy due to its extensive border with Finland.

The stance of Finnish foreign policy makers during the August 2008 crisis can be interpreted as a reflection both of this narrative and of the discourse arguing for cooperation with Russia as the only option for Finland. Foreign Minister Stubb fostered diplomatic channels with Moscow, focused on negotiations and on de-escalating the crisis, an approach that is reminiscent of Finland's Cold-War role as a mediator between Russia and the West (*see* Chapter 3). Accordingly, Stubb (2008d) claimed to be 'in constant contact with [his] colleagues in the European Union and the United States', while at the same time he held talks with Russian foreign minister Sergei Lavrov (Stubb 2008e). On 12 August, as soon as the Russian army decided to halt operations in Georgia, Stubb (2008e) issued a statement to 'welcome president Medvedev's decision', which implied that he was still treating Russia as a partner, in spite of tensions due to its disproportionate use of force.

In the first month after the communiqué of 29 August, Finnish leaders' statements on the Russian–Georgian war primarily emphasised Finland's role in mediating and providing humanitarian relief. In Halonen's (2008b) words, 'Finland focused on achieving a ceasefire, ensuring the delivery of humanitarian aid and promoting respect for international law'. Similarly, in his speech at the UN Security Council in late September, Stubb (2008f) stressed his efforts 'to promote the implementation of a ceasefire agreement and the humanitarian efforts in the region'. The question of responsibility for the outbreak of war, which as seen played a prominent role in the speeches of German and Polish leaders, was never addressed. This omission served the purpose of avoiding further tensions and focusing on post-conflict developments.

In the following months, Finnish leaders responded in a remarkably positive way to Medvedev's controversial proposals to reform the European security architecture and described Russia as a strategic partner. In a speech at the London School of Economics in November 2008, Stubb (2008g) argued that, 'against the backdrop of the war in Georgia, the financial crisis and the election of Barack Obama', the world was 'witnessing the embryo of a post-American, multipolar world', thereby drawing conclusions that resonated with Russian leaders' contemporary analyses.[9] While most European and North American leaders reacted sceptically to Russia's

---

9. See, for instance, Medvedev's claim in an interview with the three main Russian TV channels: 'The world should be multi-polar. Unipolarity is unacceptable, domination is impermissible. We cannot accept a world order in which all decisions are taken by one country, even such a serious and authoritative country as the United States of America. This kind of world is unstable and fraught with conflict' (cited in Reynolds 2008).

calls for a debate on a new European security structure, Stubb welcomed them, with the proviso that existing institutions remained in place (see Lo 2009). In her address to the OSCE ministerial council on 4 December 2008, Halonen (2008c) went even further in meeting Medvedev's plea.

> The participants of this OSCE ministerial council should use the opportunity to […] share views on the future of security in Europe. The Presidents of the Russian Federation and France have already contributed to this debate. I hope that it will be continued in an open and constructive atmosphere. We should not assume that current practices of cooperation will continue forever unchanged.

The last sentence of this passage suggested openness to Russia's proposals to reform the existing European security system and sounded an invitation to the other OSCE member states to take a flexible stance on the issue. Halonen's approach to the topic reflected the tendency in post-1945 Finnish foreign policy to respond positively to Russia's foreign policy initiatives and act as a mediator with NATO countries.

By December 2008, the Russian–Georgian war no longer appeared as a source of tension in Finnish discourses about Russia. In an interview with the Finnish Journal of Foreign Affairs *Ulkopolitiikka*, Stubb (2008h) argued that the war had 'strengthened the unity of Europe', while Russia was defined as 'a strategic partner for the EU'. According to the Finnish foreign minister, the 'big challenge' was 'to transform the partnership into a functional relationship'. Hence, once the August 2008 crisis had subsided, Stubb returned to the deep-rooted Finnish identity narrative portraying Russia as both a partner and a challenge that could be turned into an opportunity, if Finland engaged it with appropriate policies.

Conclusion

This case study highlighted the relevance of historically constructed images of Russia as a security threat in national foreign policy discourses about the August 2008 crisis. In particular, it explored the extent to which Russia's Tsarist and Soviet imperial past provided the key for national leaders' interpretations of current events. References to Tsarist and Soviet imperialism were most prominent in Polish discourses, notably in those of president Lech Kaczynski. Kaczynski's statements were deeply fraught with memory politics and portrayed Russia's foreign policy in 2008 as a continuation of Soviet foreign policy. Conversely, German foreign minister Frank-Walter Steinmeier rejected the use of memory politics to blame Russia for the crisis in Georgia. Steinmeier made historical references only in order to emphasise the differences between East–West relations during the Cold War and tensions with Russia in August 2008. On the other hand, Finnish foreign policy makers never openly referred to Russia's past to interpret the war in Georgia. Nonetheless, their behaviour during the crisis was also influenced by deep-rooted national perceptions of Russia and of Finland's role as bridge builder in relations between Moscow and the West.

German discourses emphasised Russia's central role in European security and the consequent need of treating Russia as a partner. Negative memories of the Cold War, when Germany was divided and stood on the frontline of superpower rivalry, informed German leaders' rejection of confrontation with Russia. A German narrative criticising Russia's actions during the August 2008 crisis did emerge, but it focused mostly on technical and legal issues (the withdrawal of Russian troops after the ceasefire and the disproportionality of Russia's military intervention). Rather than a deep-rooted anti-Russian attitude, this discourse reflected elements of post-1945 German national identity such as the rejection of war as a means to solve disputes and the support of multilateralism and international law. These aspects of German identity also contribute to understanding Merkel and Steinmeier's discourse praising EU mediation during the crisis and advocating further EU engagement in relations with Russia.

Polish discourses revealed a marked dichotomy between top government officials and the presidency. The discourse advanced by Prime Minister Tusk and Foreign Minister Sikorski was critical of Russia's actions in Georgia but also emphasised the necessity of continuing to engage the Kremlin, reflecting the government's attempt to construct a new foreign policy approach towards Russia after 2007. Occasionally, Sikorski's speeches slipped into memory politics and comparisons with Russia's Soviet past. However, for the most part this discourse was pragmatic and not fundamentally irreconcilable with dominant German official narratives. Conversely, Lech Kaczynski's discourse was profoundly hostile towards Russia, which was portrayed as aggressive and intolerant of European values. This narrative reflected long-standing Polish perceptions of Russia as an imperialist country, morally incompatible with European civilisation. Kaczynski also accused other EU countries of being too conciliatory with Russia and of leaving him alone with a few other East–Central European countries to defend European values. This discourse resonated with the Polish identity narrative on Poland's unreciprocated commitment to the Western cause.

Competing discourses on Russia also existed in Finland throughout the Georgian crisis. Here, however, different narratives reflected traditionally ambivalent Finnish perceptions of Russia. At the peak of the crisis, in August 2008, the dominant discourse stressed the growing assertiveness and militarism of Russia's foreign policy and argued for the necessity to engage Russia in order to defuse tensions. This narrative can be understood through the prism of Finnish national identity, in which Russia was simultaneously constructed as a security challenge and as an indispensable partner for Finland. While this discourse appears wary of Russia's foreign policy posture, the narrative that became dominant in the weeks following the August 2008 military escalation supported cooperation with Moscow. Most strikingly, it argued for openness in the Western response to Russia's controversial proposal of reforming the European security system. Similarly to the German discourses, it portrayed Russia as a strategic partner.

Ultimately, the empirical analysis in this chapter reiterated the relevance of national identity and historically constructed images of Russia to foreign policy makers' discourses. Divergences in the conceptualisation of Russia in German, Polish and Finnish identity were reflected in the different stances that each country took during the August 2008 crisis. Kaczynski's discourse stood out from all the others because it relied on profoundly anti-Russian perceptions and memory politics that are specific to Polish identity. However, pragmatism and the support for a multilateral solution of the conflict were common traits across other national narratives. Compared with discourses on Nord Stream in 2005–7 (prior to the events discussed in this chapter), national narratives on Russia during the 2008 Russian–Georgian war were less discordant. Therefore, Chapters Four and Five have shown that, despite some discordant voices (notably Lech Kaczynski's), after 2007 the three countries under consideration seemed to be in the process of converging towards a pragmatic stance vis-à-vis Russia. Briefly, this stance advocated dialogue and cooperation as a way of shaping the relationship and of addressing the challenges stemming from Russia's increasing assertiveness as an international actor. This stance was widely supported at the EU level and resulted in a period (from the end of 2008 until early 2014) of relative calm in relations with Russia (see Forsberg and Haukkala 2016).

Chapter Six

Post-electoral Protests in Russia, 2011–12

Introduction

This chapter focuses on German, Polish and Finnish foreign policy makers' discourses on the post-electoral protests in Russia in December 2011 and in 2012. As opposed to the previous two chapters, which analysed discourses on Russia as an international actor, this case study examines narratives about domestic developments in Russia. This focus allows an investigation of the dichotomy between historical constructions of Russia as an authoritarian country that violates democratic principles and human rights and as an economic partner. The analysis attempts to establish which characterisation of Russia was dominant in 2011 and 2012, namely at a time when Russia was becoming both more authoritarian and increasingly important for the EU in economic and commercial terms. It is argued that the two historical narratives competed for dominance, but the one portraying Russia as a partner eventually prevailed in official discourses in all countries under analysis. The analysis starts with a brief survey of the street protests in Russia in 2011 and 2012, which contextualises the ensuing discourse analysis. The following sections analyse the discourses of German, Polish and Finnish foreign policy leaders. The concluding section reviews the main findings and compares national narratives.

Street protests in Russian cities, December 2011 – May 2012

The mass protests that took place in Russian cities between December 2011 and May 2012 were among the largest the country has experienced since the disintegration of the Soviet Union. As Russia was recovering from the 2008 economic crisis at a relatively swift pace, the demonstrations were largely unexpected. They started immediately after the national parliamentary elections of 4 December 2011, which were won by Vladimir Putin and Dmitri Medvedev's United Russia party, amid accusations of electoral fraud. United Russia received over 49 per cent of the votes, a drop of approximately 15 per cent compared with the party's 2007 election result, but still sufficient to ensure a majority of seats in parliament (Gill 2012: 449).

As Graeme Robertson (2013) and Lilia Shevtsova (2012) have argued, the protests may have been sparked by electoral fraud, but had much deeper causes and were a continuation of longer-term trends.[1] Frustration with the corruption

---

[1]. During 2009 and 2010, the number of protests and demonstrations in Russia grew steadily. It is, however, important to note that these protests focused mostly on local issues (the protection of a forest, the dismissal of a regional official, a local construction project), rather than on the Russian political system as a whole (Evans 2012).

of state officials, lack of opportunities for social mobility for younger Russians and disillusionment with politics had accumulated over the previous years. President Dmitri Medvedev's discourse on modernisation nurtured expectations of liberal reforms among the urban middle class, which were disappointed when his mandate drew to an end without any significant change (Gel'man 2013; Hahn 2012). Although the Russian economy had largely recovered by 2011, the 2008 crisis may have contributed to the discontent of the middle class by bequeathing to it a growing sense of political impotence and uncertainty about the future (Chaisty and Whitefield 2012: 202–4; Volkov 2012: 55). This discontent could not be channelled through established opposition parties, which were perceived as part of the Kremlin's corrupt system of power (see March 2012). Furthermore, Medvedev's continuous stress on the need to modernise the economy may have involuntarily conveyed the idea that the country was failing to recover from the 2008 financial crisis (Robinson 2013).

Other shorter-term factors also played a role. After 2010, the new mayor of Moscow Sergei Sobyanin proved more liberal than his predecessor on the issue of approving opposition protests, which allowed an increasing concentration of demonstrations in the Russian capital (Hahn 2012: 488; Robertson 2013: 18). Furthermore, in September 2011 Russian president Medvedev announced that he had already agreed a long time before with then Prime Minister Vladimir Putin that the latter should return to the presidency in 2012. (Putin had already served two terms as president between 2000 and 2008.) In return, Putin promised to support Medvedev's bid for the position of prime minister if their party United Russia won the December 2011 parliamentary elections. Together with the accusations of electoral fraud in December, the announcement of this pre-arranged swap of posts and the prospect of Putin's return to the presidency until 2018, or even 2024,[2] acted as the main catalysts for the post-election mass protests in Moscow and other Russian cities (Shevtsova 2012: 212; Volkov 2012: 55–7).

The protesters were mostly well educated, young or middle-aged and belonged to the middle class. They obtained information on political events primarily from the internet, a fact that differentiated them from the majority of Russians, who relied mostly on televised news (Volkov 2012: 57–60). They also used social media to organise and coordinate protest marches and rallies (see Bode and Makarychev 2013). Their ideological background was very diverse, ranging from liberalism to communism and nationalism (Koesel and Bunce 2012: 411–12). The demonstrations that they organised after the 2011 parliamentary elections were different from previous ones in post-Soviet Russia in several respects. Contrary to previous local protests, demonstrators were able to forge new ties among existing extra-parliamentary opposition groups (Greene 2013: 41). As a result, demonstrations became larger and focused on broader issues of national politics, with the declared aim of influencing them (Robertson 2013: 18). Protesters

---

2. In 2008, an amendment to the Russian constitution extended the presidential term to six years starting from the 2012 mandate. With the possibility of being re-elected once, Putin could potentially stay in power until 2024 (Shiraev 2013: 95).

demanded inter alia new parliamentary elections, easier rules for the registration of opposition parties and the dismissal of Central Election Commission head Vladimir Churov.

The first demonstration took place in Moscow on 5 December 2011, the day after the parliamentary elections. The protest was unsanctioned and involved approximately 8,000 people, mostly activists from civil society organisations and extra-parliamentary political parties, including street opposition leaders Boris Nemtsov and Alexei Navalny. Subsequent protests were much larger. On 10 December, a demonstration held in Moscow's Bolotnaya Square drew around 50–60,000 people. Two weeks later, on 24 December, over 100,000 protesters gathered on Sakharov Avenue. Smaller demonstrations were held in early 2012, throughout the campaign for the presidential elections in March. Prominent non-governmental organisations such as Golos and Memorial and the banned People's Freedom Party took part, together with other smaller civil society movements. They demanded free and fair presidential elections and harshly criticised United Russia's candidate Vladimir Putin (Greene 2013; Hahn 2012; Robertson 2013).

Between December and March, the Russian authorities responded to the protests with a 'mixture of repression plus half-hearted measures to redress grievances' (Volkov 2012: 56). Some reforms were announced, including easier rules for the electoral registration of political parties and the reinstatement of popular elections for regional governors (Gel'man 2013: 7). At first, Putin stated that the demonstrations were orchestrated from abroad, portrayed the street opposition as 'unpatriotic' and 'anti-Russian' and argued that protests would hinder Russia's economic recovery. However, as demonstrations continued, he reframed his rhetoric and claimed that he was pleased with the protests because they highlighted the strength of Russian democracy and civil society (Koesel and Bunce 2012: 415–16).

Until March 2012, Putin and his supporters focused primarily on achieving an absolute majority and winning the presidential elections in the first round. As the street opposition did not field a candidate, its actions appeared unlikely to have any concrete impact on the campaign.[3] Despite the lack of real challengers, United Russia launched a more aggressive media campaign than the one for the previous parliamentary elections, attacking opposition leaders and emphasising the negative consequences of social unrest on the country's economy (Gel'man 2013: 8). Moreover, it organised large pro-Putin rallies to show that he enjoyed overwhelming support among Russians (Smyth et al. 2013). Together with new instances of electoral fraud, the lack of any strong alternative candidate and

---

3. Billionaire businessman Mikhail Prokhorov was the only non-systemic candidate for the presidential election. According to leading Russian polling institutions such as VTsIOM and Public Opinion Fund, he never seemed to have had a chance to beat Putin. See VTsIOM, 'Elektoralny reiting politikov' [Politicians' electoral ratings], May 2012, www.wciom.ru/news/ratings/elektoralnyj_rejting_politikov/ (accessed 1 June 2014) and Public Opinion Fund, 'Presidentskye vyibory 2012. Elektoralny reiting' [Presidential elections 2012. Electoral ratings], 19 January 2012, www.bd.fom.ru/pdf/d02pv12.pdf (accessed 1 June 2014).

his genuine popularity among the electorate, these measures ensured Putin's re-election in the first round with over 63 per cent of the votes (Gel'man 2013: 3).

Following the presidential election, the authorities' strategy to deal with street protests became more repressive. Furthermore, demonstrations drew smaller crowds, showing that social media provided an insufficient base for permanent political mobilisation (Gel'man 2013: 8–9). As Gordon Hahn (2012: 497–503) noted, scarcer participation may have also been due to the growing belief that, with adequate organisation, the street opposition could acquire political power through the regular electoral process. In March 2012, opposition candidates won mayoral elections in several large provincial capitals, including Tolyatti, Yaroslavl and Oryol. On 2 May 2012, a law relaxing requirements for the electoral registration of political parties entered into force, making it easier for the extra-parliamentary opposition to be able to run in future elections. The authorities combined this concession with harsher measures against new demonstrations. On 6 May 2012, on the eve of Putin's inauguration to the presidency, the police crushed unsanctioned protests with the use of force and the arrest of over 250 people (Elder 2012). After Putin's return to power, the extra-parliamentary opposition underwent a process of internal reorganisation to create a more solid and coherent political base, which culminated in the election of a coordinating council in October 2012. Demonstrations continued during the summer and autumn of 2012, but on a smaller scale and in a context of increasing repression (Robertson 2013: 21–2).

Democracy or partnership? German leaders' conflicting discourses

The post-electoral protests in Russia were a prominent topic in the German political debate throughout 2012. From mid-2008, German–Russian bilateral relations focused on the development of a modernisation partnership, including economic, technological and legal cooperation. From the German perspective, the partnership was to serve Germany's economic interests, contribute to the modernisation of the Russian economy and strengthen the rule of law in Russia (Auswärtiges Amt 2014). By the autumn of 2011, however, the partnership had seemingly failed to produce tangible results regarding the rule of law. Within this context, German policy makers considered the December 2011 and March 2012 elections as important factors to assess the strength of the rule of law in Russia and the Russian political leadership's willingness to modernise the country (Gotkowska 2010; Meister 2012).

While the elections and the ensuing demonstrations took place in Russia, two dominant and conflicting discourses developed among German foreign policy makers. One was very critical of Russia's political system, the authorities' handling of post-electoral demonstrations and the overall running of the country's economy and society. From the autumn of 2011, this discourse featured prominently in the speeches of some officials at the German foreign ministry, most particularly in those of Andreas Schockenhoff and Markus Löning. At the federal foreign office, Schockenhoff was responsible for German–Russian civil society cooperation, while Löning was commissioner for human rights policy and humanitarian aid.

Both played a significant role in German official discourses on events in Russia in 2011 and 2012 through interviews with the mainstream media, press releases and public appeals to the Russian leadership. Therefore, their statements are included in this analysis.

The other discourse appeared in particular in Chancellor Angela Merkel's and Foreign Minister Guido Westerwelle's speeches and was considerably less critical towards Russia. Merkel and Westerwelle described the protests in Russian cities as a positive development and expressed disapproval of some of the Kremlin's measures to curb demonstrations and restrict civil freedoms. However, they consistently reiterated their commitment to building a strategic partnership with Russia, regardless of the outcome of its parliamentary and presidential elections. They also argued that their occasional criticism of Russia's internal affairs was no obstacle for bilateral dialogue and economic cooperation.

Democracy, human rights and Russia's failed modernisation

Russia's failure to modernise and the repressive policies implemented by the Russian ruling elite during the 2011 and 2012 elections were the dominant themes of Schockenhoff and Löning's speeches. According to them, Russia had consistently violated democratic principles and human rights, namely core German and European values. Hence, they argued that Germany should take a more critical stance towards Russia (including the application of sanctions) and support the cause of Russian street demonstrators. Legality and humanitarianism are the topoi linking the key argument (Russia violated democratic principles and human rights) to its conclusion (Germany should take policy countermeasures and support the Russian opposition). Schockenhoff and Löning's emphasis on human rights and democracy can be understood through the prominent role which these principles have played in identity construction and foreign policy discourses in post-1945 Federal Germany. In German foreign policy discourses, individual freedoms and democracy have long been described as core elements of the German state and as major constituents of its foreign policy.[4] Furthermore, Schockenhoff and Löning's arguments resonate with German historical narratives describing Russia as a backward and corrupt country (*see* Chapter Three).

Schockenhoff expressed his concerns about political developments in Russia shortly after Medvedev and Putin announced their intention to swap their posts. In October 2011, while speaking at a conference on Russia at the Heinrich Böll Foundation in Berlin, Schockenhoff (2011a) questioned whether the country's modernisation would be possible after Putin's return to the presidency.

---

4.   In the speeches under analysis, this concept was best summarised by German State Secretary Cornelia Pieper (2012) in her statements at the opening of an exhibition on German and Russian history in Moscow in June 2012: 'The free and democratic constitutional order is the core element of our state and guarantees individual freedoms and rights. These shape our actions and thinking and are the precept for Germany's value oriented domestic and foreign policy'.

I am worried about internal developments in the country [Russia] [...] Above all, I am worried because the Russian middle class does not see its interests represented in the political system [...] In my opinion, the main problem is the lack of consensus in Russia on the need to modernize the country. On the contrary, among the elites and in society there is a consensus for the preservation of the status quo, so against modernisation!

Through perspectivation (signalled by the phrases 'I am worried', 'it seems to me' and by the use of exclamation marks), Schockenhoff clearly positioned himself against the Russian elites' political line. He also claimed that his only hopes for Russia's modernisation were based on the 'revitalisation [...] of particular parts of the Russian civil society', namely those that were ready to become engaged in civil campaigns to address the country's problems.

These themes were developed further in his interview with the German daily *Der Tagesspiegel* on 27 November 2011, a week before the Russian parliamentary elections. Schockenhoff (2011b) drew a bleak picture of the Russian political system and, quoting prominent Russian scholars, described it as 'neo-feudal power system', 'tyranny of incompetence', 'blatantly inefficient' and degrading. Within this context, he claimed, 'the most important chance [for Russia's modernisation]' was to be found in 'the increasing activeness of Russia's civil society'. He therefore concluded that

Germany and the EU need these citizens as partners for the modernisation partnership! [...] In the future, it is therefore essential to get civil actors, NGOs, independent initiatives and experts much more involved in all fields of the modernisation partnership with Russia!

The mass protests following the parliamentary elections consolidated Schockenhoff's belief in the political potential of Russian civil society. On 15 December 2011, speaking to the lower house of the German federal parliament, he argued that the demonstrations had changed both Russia and Western perceptions of Russia.

The protests were a victory over the fear of the Kremlin. They were above all a victory over the political apathy that had paralysed Russian society in the last years. They have revealed a new generation, a changed society, many young people, activists and a growing middle class. For me, these are the new Russians – democratically-minded, active, engaged, well-informed [...] These people are the most important force in favour of reforms and the most important modernisation partner of the Russian state and hence an important partner for us.

(Schockenhoff 2011c)

Through predication, Schockenhoff described the demonstrations as a momentous triumph for Russian civil society and emphasised the importance of protesters for Russia's future. The semantic field associated with the demonstrations ('victory over fear', 'victory over political apathy') and demonstrators ('a new generation', 'young', 'active', 'engaged', 'well-informed') is unambiguously positive, which is functional to Schockenhoff's declared aim to get Russian civil society more involved in the German–Russian modernisation partnership. By contrast, in the same speech, the Russian political establishment is described as 'leading to apathy, cynicism and to a dangerous estrangement between power and society'.

Schockenhoff's criticism of the Russian political system was echoed by Löning in an interview with the German daily *Die Welt* on 20 December 2011. Löning (2011) denounced 'many violations of human rights, the infringement of basic democratic principles and the near absence of the rule of law'. Furthermore, he appealed to the Russian authorities to respect the freedoms of opinion and assembly and not to 'beat up or arrest demonstrators just because they have different opinions from the Russian government'. Most importantly, he urged the European Union to take a more critical stance in defence of democracy and human rights in Russia.

> The Russian parliamentary elections [on 4 December 2011] were criticised, but we Europeans should express our opinion much more clearly [...] Human rights are the core values of the European Union. If we do not defend them, we betray our own values and the credibility of European foreign policy will go to the dogs.

Löning's statement reflects the relevance of human rights and the European Union in German foreign policy discourses. Through perspectivation and the use of direct, idiomatic expressions, he conveyed the message that the credibility of the EU's foreign policy depended on the Union's response to contemporary events in Russia. Accordingly, he argued that the EU should prioritise values over economic interests and 'clearly demand from Russian political leaders respect for the rule of law'. He also advocated the application of sanctions on Russian public officials who were responsible for human rights violations.

As the March 2012 presidential elections in Russia approached, Schockenhoff and Löning expressed their concerns about the conditions under which they would take place. Schockenhoff (2012a, 2012b) criticised the harassment of independent election monitors and the fact that no one had been held responsible for the ballot-rigging that occurred during the December 2011 parliamentary elections. Löning (2012a, 2012b, 2012c) denounced the further restrictions on civil freedoms and violations of human rights that took place, both before the elections and in the ensuing months. Following Putin's return to the presidency in May 2012, Schockenhoff overtly condemned political developments in Russia. In an interview with *Der Tagesspiegel* in August 2012, he argued:

> The Russian leadership does not offer any dialogue to society. Putin relies on repression and confrontation [...] Russia lags behind in all international

rankings, regardless of whether they concern fighting corruption, competition or demographic development. Putin sees his own [Russia's] population not as a partner, but as a threat to the state.

(Schockenhoff 2012c)

Schockenhoff's harsh critique of Russia reflected a clear prevalence of the normative dimension of Germany's foreign policy identity in his discourse. If Schockenhoff's stance had become dominant within the German foreign ministry, we could have expected a serious deterioration in German–Russian relations by the end of 2012, as the Russian authorities continued their repressive policies. However, a different discourse became prominent in German foreign policy circles after March 2012, toning down Schockenhoff's and Löning's criticism and arguing for partnership with Russia.

Strategic partnership and friendly criticism

An analysis of the German foreign ministry's and the federal chancellor's electronic archives suggests that Angela Merkel and Guido Westerwelle played a marginal role in the German public debate about developments in Russia between the fall of 2011 and February 2012. After the March 2012 presidential elections, their official statements about Russia's internal affairs became more frequent and constructed a distinct German official discourse. This narrative criticised the Russian authorities' handling of the presidential elections and the subsequent crackdown on street opposition and civil freedoms. However, Merkel and Westerwelle's criticism was much milder than Schockenhoff and Löning's. Most importantly, Merkel and Westerwelle argued strongly in favour of continuing dialogue with the Russian authorities and developing a strategic partnership, based on shared economic and security interests. According to them, criticism and partnership were not mutually exclusive, as reciprocal trust and friendship were necessary while discussing difficult issues.

In this argumentative strategy, economic advantage and security are the topoi linking the key argument (Russia is an essential economic and security partner for Germany) to its logical conclusion (Germany should continue to develop a strategic partnership with Russia). The discourse reflected long-standing German perceptions of Russia as an economic and security partner. It also appeared as a logical continuation of the basic principle of German Ostpolitik, namely the idea that economic cooperation may have positive effects on Russia's internal affairs (*see* Chapter Three). Considerations about the violations of human rights and democratic principles played a role in this discourse, but they were largely overshadowed by the prominence of arguments in favour of economic and security cooperation.

As argued, until February 2012 Merkel and Westerwelle's statements on Russia largely ignored the issue of electoral fraud. The irregularities that took place during the December 2011 parliamentary elections and the ensuing mass demonstrations were mentioned only briefly in a few statements. For instance, at the OSCE ministerial council of 6 December 2011, Westerwelle (2011) declared:

> We have noted with concern the reports by the OSCE election observers on the recent parliamentary elections in Russia. These reports show that the Russian Federation still has some way to go before it completely meets all OSCE standards [...] We encourage the Russian Federation to take this path now, particularly with an eye to the next elections due in Russia.

In the light of the serious violations of democratic principles which the international press revealed immediately after the elections (Elder 2011), Westerwelle's statement appears remarkably mild. The German foreign minister ignored the calls of the Russian opposition for a repetition of the vote and merely 'encouraged' Russia to respect democratic standards at the next elections. Merkel (2012d) only made a brief reference to events in Russia at the New Year reception for German diplomats, expressing her hopes that the Russian presidential elections would 'take place well, democratically' and anticipating that German–Russian cooperation would 'remain a focal point' for her government after the elections also.

Willingness to cooperate with the Kremlin became a central theme in Merkel and Westerwelle's statements after February 2012, when internal developments in Russia began to feature more prominently in their speeches. This emerges clearly from Westerwelle's (2012a) interview with the mainstream German newspaper *Welt am Sonntag* on 4 March 2012, the day when presidential elections were held in Russia.

> We would like to continue the modernisation partnership with Russia, which is urgently necessary, including the dialogue on the rule of law. Russia is a nation with a rich culture [*Kulturnation*] and a large part of it is in Europe. European security can only be achieved with Russia, not against it. I am committed to keep Russia as a strategic partner for Germany and Europe.

In the interview, Westerwelle associated Russia with a positive semantic field through predication, notably by calling it 'a nation with a rich culture'. Moreover, using the discursive strategy of categorisation, he constructed Russia as part of a European in-group on the argument that a 'large part of it is in Europe' and that 'European security can only be achieved with Russia'. This use of predication and categorisation was useful to substantiate Westerwelle's desire to continue the strategic partnership with Russia on the grounds that it played an indispensable role for Europe.

On the other hand, Westerwelle appeared keen to avoid comments on the street protests in Russia. When specifically asked for his opinion on the topic, he described the demonstrations as 'interesting and a positive sign', but refused to comment on the violent clashes between protesters and the Russian authorities. His subsequent criticism of 'worrying developments' concerning press freedom and homophobia in Russia was toned down by the assertion that 'economic, political and social progress' was also taking place (Westerwelle 2012a). In his next newspaper interview, held with the German daily *Passauer Neue Presse* on 10 March 2012, Westerwelle (2012b) clearly explained Germany's foreign policy line towards Russia following Putin's re-election.

> We believe president Putin's announcement that all evidence of electoral fraud will be investigated [...] We have a strategic interest in the partnership with Russia. We want to expand this partnership further. But this does not mean that we will not express any criticism.

Remarkably, Westerwelle trusted Putin's promises about investigating electoral irregularities, despite the fact that the irregularities had benefitted Putin himself and had been executed by a state apparatus that Putin largely controlled. As the passage shows, expanding the existing partnership with Russia was in Germany's 'strategic interest' and hence its main priority. On the other hand, Westerwelle's pledge to maintain a critical stance towards Russia appears weak, as it was constructed with a double negation ('does not mean', 'we will not express') and was not accompanied by any actual criticism in the interview.

Westerwelle's discourse was embraced by Merkel, which in practice meant that throughout the spring of 2012 both of Germany's top foreign policy makers emphasised achievements in economic relations and only made mild statements about democracy and human rights in Russia. This emerged, for instance, at Merkel's joint press conference with Putin in Berlin, on 1 June 2012. The German chancellor first praised the 'very intense, good and friendly relations with Russia', with particular emphasis on 'economic cooperation' (Merkel 2012a). Her comments on Russia's internal affairs were limited to the claim that:

> We [Germany] have a strong interest in the continued development of democratic plurality in Russia. Because, as far as I can tell from my experience, this is the only way a strong civil society can form and support the development of a country.

Using perspectivation (signalled by the phrase 'as far as I can tell from my experience'), Merkel alluded to her personal experience as a former citizen of the German Democratic Republic in order to stress the importance of civil society in democratic transitions. However, by referring to her experience in East Germany, she also avoided addressing directly the situation in Russia. Moreover, the phrase 'continued development of democratic plurality' suggests that democratic plurality was already developing in Russia, a remarkably optimistic assessment in the light of two recent flawed elections.

The few times when Merkel and Westerwelle discussed the violation of democratic principles and fundamental freedoms in Russia, they both strongly emphasised that criticism and occasional disagreement was not intended to disrupt the German–Russian strategic partnership. For instance, in his November 2012 interview with the *Frankfurter Allgemeine Zeitung*, Westerwelle (2012c) claimed that German and Russian leaders had 'differences of opinion' on some of Russia's recent internal developments, but remained 'honest friends and strategic partners'. Similarly, speaking at a German–Russian civil society forum in November 2012, Merkel (2012e) argued that Germans and Russians should listen to each other's arguments 'as partners and friends', including when discussing issues on which they disagreed. Furthermore, disagreements were downplayed and portrayed as a normal feature of bilateral relations: 'Sometimes people disagree, it is necessary to have arguments. As we say in Germany, this happens in the best families' (Merkel 2012e).

Pragmatism and reconciliation before values: Polish leaders' discourses

The analysis of Polish top foreign policy makers' public statements in 2011 and 2012 revealed that they were reluctant to comment on contemporary domestic developments in Russia. In this period, the main focus of their diplomacy towards Russia was on promoting trade and seeking reconciliation by tackling contentious issues in bilateral relations. During 2011, Poland and Russia negotiated the establishment of a special visa-free regime for their citizens residing in the Russian enclave of Kaliningrad and the adjoining Polish territories. The agreement was signed by the Russian and Polish foreign ministers in Moscow in December 2011 and was hailed as a step towards the lifting of all visa requirements between the European Union and Russia (Bridge 2011). Much attention was devoted to the process of historical reconciliation, a highly sensitive issue in both Poland and Russia (see De Lazari 2011). The Polish–Russian Working Group for Difficult Matters, an official forum bringing together academics from both countries, advanced projects that were conducive to a shared interpretation of contentious events in the history of Polish–Russian relations. The Polish foreign ministry strongly supported these efforts and reported the achievements of the Group's meetings in press releases on the ministerial website (Poland's Ministry of Foreign Affairs 2012a). Reflecting the atmosphere of cultural reconciliation, the head of the Russian Orthodox Church Patriarch Kirill paid a historic visit to Poland in August 2012 (BBC News 2012).

Throughout 2011 and 2012, Polish diplomacy tackled several bilateral disputes, most notably the investigation of the plane crash in which president Lech Kaczynski died in April 2010 and the return of the plane's wreck to Poland. Tensions and disagreements persisted on the matter, but they did not prevent progress in other areas of bilateral relations. Most importantly, in November 2012 the Polish state-controlled energy company PGNiG successfully negotiated a reduction in the price of gas purchased from the Russian state company Gazprom (Marson 2012). The wider context of Polish diplomatic efforts to improve relations with Russia in 2011 and 2012 helps understand why Polish foreign policy leaders refrained from commenting on electoral manipulations and on the repression of mass protests in Russia. The discourse advocating a pragmatic approach to relations with Russia, which was constructed in governmental circles after the election of Donald Tusk in 2007, shaped the statements of Polish Foreign Minister Radoslaw Sikorski. Conversely, long-standing Polish perceptions of Russia as an undemocratic and corrupt country played a lesser role in official discourses.

Sympathy with demonstrators, but other priorities

Foreign Minister Sikorski was the only Polish foreign policy leader who made regular statements regarding the mass protests in Russia, mostly on occasions in which journalists specifically asked him to comment on the events. When addressing the issue, Sikorski's main line of argument consisted of expressing sympathy towards the demonstrators. However, these expressions of sympathy were not accompanied by any criticism of the Russian authorities. Conversely, Sikorski argued that Putin enjoyed large support in Russia. Furthermore, he juxtaposed his interpretation of events to claims that Poland needed to pursue reconciliation and cooperation with the Kremlin regardless of domestic developments in Russia. Political and economic advantage are the topoi linking this argumentative strategy to its logical conclusion: reconciliation and economic cooperation took priority over value-driven support of civil society and democratic change in Russia.

In the months preceding the outbreak of mass protests in Russian cities, Sikorski maintained an ambiguous stance in his assessments of domestic developments in Russia. In a speech made at Harvard University in February 2011, he argued that Poland was 'dedicated to good relations with Russia', but criticised its system of government.

> Democracy, markets and respect for the rights of the individual – these define relations between Europe and America. Russia, along with many other former Soviet republics, still does not accept those values. Moscow hankers after something rather different: 'managed democracy'. Which is fine – if you are one of the managers.

> (Sikorski 2011b)

Through the discursive strategy of categorisation, Sikorski constructed Russia as alien to Europe and the United States due to its disregard of democratic principles and human rights. This description of Russia appeared in continuity with traditional Polish perceptions of the country as oriental, undemocratic and corrupt (*see* Chapter Three).

However, a few weeks later Sikorski described domestic developments in Russia in more positive terms. In his speech before the lower house of the Polish parliament (*Sejm*), he claimed: 'Those who believe that one way of thinking reigns in Russia are mistaken [...] Many Russians, including top leaders, are becoming aware of the need to curb corruption, modernise the economy and enhance the rule of law and democracy' (Sikorski 2011c). Furthermore, on this occasion Sikorski argued that Russia could choose 'the democratic path leading to integration with the West', thereby blurring the boundaries of the categorisation that he constructed in his speech at Harvard. Admittedly, he also stated that part of the Russian leadership 'continue[d] to long for superpower glory and heavy-handed rule' and that he did not know 'which way Russia [would] go'. However, he unambiguously argued that Poland needed to cooperate with the Kremlin 'no matter how Russia is ruled' because it was an 'important neighbour'.

While the December 2011 elections in Russia approached, this pragmatic stance prevailed in Polish foreign policy circles. This emerges clearly in Polish President Bronislaw Komorowski's (2011) letter to the EU–Russia civil society forum that took place in Warsaw on 1 December 2011. In spite of the forum's primary focus on issues such as the promotion of democracy and the rule of law,[5] Komorowski made no reference to the violation of democratic principles that took place in Russia during the electoral campaign. Instead, he advocated 'normalisation' and 'rapprochement' in Polish–Russian relations. Using the discursive strategy of predication, he positively described Russia as 'our [Poland's] neighbour' and as an actor that would 'always play one of the key roles on the European scene'. Accordingly, he argued, improving Polish–Russian relations was 'an investment in the European future'.

Despite the numerous denunciations of irregularities in the December elections and the beginning of mass protests in Russia, the rhetoric of Polish foreign policy leaders did not change. On 14 December, ten days after the elections and the beginning of street protests, Sikorski paid an official visit to Moscow and signed the agreement establishing a visa-free regime for the Russian enclave of Kaliningrad and the adjoining Polish territories. At the joint press conference with the Russian Foreign Minister Sergey Lavrov, Sikorski (2011d) praised Russia as Poland's 'supportive neighbour' and did not make any reference to the mass protests that were taking place in many Russian cities. Only when specifically asked by a journalist from the Polish magazine *Polska Times* did Sikorski (2011e) comment on the demonstrations.

At this time we are observing a reinvigoration of civil society in Russia. This makes us happy, because so far it has been said that Russians are passive and it turns out this is not true. We have our Polish experiences in this area. Poland is a country that fought for freedom, won it and that is why we sympathise with those who want to democratise their countries.

Sikorski's statement reflected the national identity narrative about Polish heroism and fight for freedom in the nineteenth and twentieth centuries (*see* Chapter Three). He constructed a historical parallel between the struggle of Polish patriots and that of Russian demonstrators, thereby exposing his empathy for the latter. However, Sikorski's support was limited to expressions of happiness and

---

5. See Mission Statement of the EU–Russia Civil Society Forum, www.eu-russia-csf.org/index.ph p?id=38&L=1%2F%2FcHash%3D6c950f1b162a24d79b8d1ae85d29bf07 (accessed 11 August 2016).

sympathy. Most importantly, the Polish foreign minister failed to criticise the Russian authorities' handling of the elections and of the subsequent protests.

In January and February 2012, as the Russian presidential elections approached and street protests continued, Polish foreign policy leaders continued to avoid commenting on Russia's domestic developments. For this period, only a statement by Sikorski (2012a) vaguely expressing support for Russia's 'democratic aspirations' was retrieved. On 7 March 2012, following Putin's victory in the elections, Komorowski (2012) congratulated the newly elected Russian president and advocated 'cooperation and dialogue' with Russia. On the same day, Sikorski briefly referred to the Russian election during a joint press conference with US Secretary of State Hilary Clinton. Despite numerous reports of electoral fraud and the repression of demonstrations in Russian cities (*The Guardian* 2012), he made no negative comments. He merely defined Russia as 'an important neighbour of Poland' and stood by Clinton while she argued that the Russian presidential election had 'a clear winner', namely Putin (Sikorski 2012b).

Sikorski (2012c) returned to the topic of the Russian presidential elections and mass protests during an interview with the French daily *Le Monde* in late March, in response to a question on the lawfulness of Putin's election.

> The prime minister [Putin] has demonstrated that he has strong support among the population, but at the same time we see the awakening of civil society. I have sympathy for these Russians who do not want to move to London or Paris, but wish it were the same in Russia. This will give Vladimir Putin the chance to keep his promises, particularly those of his first mandate, when he spoke of Russia's modernisation, of the fight against corruption and of entrepreneurship.

In addition to reiterating some of the claims made in previous interviews (such as expressing sympathy towards Russian demonstrators), Sikorski highlighted that Putin enjoyed strong support in Russia. Furthermore, the Polish foreign minister portrayed the street protests as an opportunity for Putin to carry out reforms and, in the same interview, he categorised Russia as 'a potential member of the West'.[6] Sikorski's rhetoric revealed the intent of his government to seek pragmatic cooperation with the new Russian president.

This intent was formulated most clearly in Sikorski's annual address to the *Sejm* on the priorities of Poland's foreign policy, on 29 March 2012. The Polish foreign minister argued that his government would 'continue to work towards Polish–Russian reconciliation' and that in 2012 the reconciliation would 'take on a spiritual dimension' thanks to the first ever visit of the Patriarch of Moscow to Poland (Sikorski 2012e). The press releases of the Polish foreign ministry during the following months show that the policy of reconciliation and cooperation with Russia was pursued consistently, focusing in particular on the resolution of

---

6. Also in late March, Sikorski (2012d) expressed similar views in a speech made at the Paris office of the European Council on Foreign Relations, a London-based think tank focusing on the European Union's foreign policy.

historical contentions, the visit of the Moscow Patriarch and the implementation of the visa-free regime between the Kaliningrad enclave and the bordering Polish region (Poland's Ministry of Foreign Affairs 2012a and 2012b).

In the last months of 2012, Sikorski's interviews continued to reflect the Polish government's pragmatic approach to its relations with Russia. In an interview with the BBC programme *Hardtalk*, he argued that Poland was 'working to reconcile with Russia' and had an important 'commercial relationship' with it (Sikorski 2012f). Questioned on whether Poland's approach implied turning a blind eye to Russia's domestic developments, Sikorski deliberately refused to comment on the issue, claiming that trade had 'nothing to do' with Russia's domestic developments. Furthermore, in an interview with the French television channel France24, he claimed that Poland's relations with Russia were 'steadily improving' and that Putin was 'in the lead in improving relations with Poland' (Sikorski 2012g). Sikorski's last statements of 2012 on Polish–Russian relations epitomised the rhetoric of pragmatism and reconciliation that permeated Polish discourses throughout the period under analysis in this chapter. At a joint press conference with his Russian counterpart Sergey Lavrov, the Polish foreign minister expressed 'satisfaction with the progress made in Polish–Russian relations in both the economic and socio-cultural context', highlighting the achievements of the preceding year (Sikorski 2012h). No comment was made on the electoral process and the handling of mass demonstrations in Russia during the previous months.

Overshadowed by trade: the Russian demonstrations in Finnish official discourses

Throughout 2011 and 2012, Finland's relations with Russia focused primarily on trade, investments in the Arctic region and the facilitation of cross-border mobility for Finnish and Russian citizens. Commercial relations were the most salient issue. Russia's application to join the World Trade Organization (WTO) was accepted on 16 December 2011, after eighteen years of negotiations, and took place formally on 22 August 2012 (WTO 2011, 2012). As Russia was Finland's main commercial partner, its WTO accession had a strong positive impact on bilateral relations. From the Finnish perspective, it established legal guarantees on trade and future investments in the Russian market.[7] Furthermore, Finnish leaders fostered cooperation with Russia over the exploration of Arctic mineral resources, which in their view offered the prospect of large long-term profits for Finnish companies. In particular, they encouraged Finnish investments in Arctic Russia and promoted the export of relevant Finnish technology and expertise. In order to further enhance bilateral relations, Finnish authorities attempted to facilitate the mobility of Russian and Finnish citizens across the border, particularly through the opening of new visa application centres and the issuing of a large number of visas to Russian citizens (see Tuomioja 2012a).

---

7. For data on Finnish–Russian trade, see www.tulli.fi/en/finnish_customs/statistics/ (accessed 11 August 2016).

Among Finnish foreign policy makers, Russia's accession to the WTO and growing bilateral contacts strengthened the deep-rooted conviction that Russia was an essential partner for Finland. This context helps understand why Finnish leaders refrained from comments on the violation of democratic principles and human rights that characterised the 2011 and 2012 elections in Russia. During this period, their statements on Russia focused almost exclusively on economic cooperation. A more critical discourse emerged only in the spring and summer of 2012, urging the Russian authorities to strengthen the rule of law and respect human rights. However, this discourse did not supplant the one on economic cooperation, which remained dominant until the end of 2012.

Values matter, but economics more

In most of the statements retrieved for this analysis, Finnish foreign policy makers portrayed Russia as a fundamental economic partner for Finland. The increasing violations of democratic principles and civil unrest in Russia did not affect this discourse significantly. According to the main argument in this narrative, Russia was becoming increasingly important for Finland as a result of its WTO accession and economic growth. Hence, Finland had to seek cooperation and intensify commercial relations. Economic advantage is the topos in this argumentative strategy. Russia's democratisation and modernisation were considered as desirable developments, but by no means as fundamental preconditions for cooperation. This foreign policy stance reflected Finland's traditional pragmatic approach towards Russia, which shaped its bilateral relations with the Soviet Union during the Cold War and became a key constituent of Finnish foreign policy identity (*see* Chapter Three).

In December 2011, while mass protests were spreading to numerous Russian cities, Finnish leaders rejoiced about Russia's WTO accession. Speaking at a seminar on the future of Europe in the Finnish city of Turku, Prime Minister Jyrki Katainen (2011) argued that 'both Russia and its trading partners like us benefit hugely from Russia's integration into the global, rule-based system of trade relations'. A few days later, Alexander Stubb (2011) (then minister for European affairs and foreign trade) claimed that trade with Russia 'headed towards a new era' and invited Finnish companies to make investments in the country.[8]

Finnish policy makers did not comment on the electoral manipulations and mass protests that were taking place in Russia during the same period. This stance was also maintained in forums where civil society and electoral issues were normally discussed. This emerges, for instance, from Foreign Minister Erkki Tuomioja's (2011) December 2011 speech at the ministerial council of the OSCE, the organisation which inter alia monitors and reports on elections in most European countries, including Russia. By the time the speech was held, OSCE reports about electoral manipulations had become available and spurred critical

---

8.   Alexander Stubb was foreign minister until June 2011, when he moved to the position of minister for European affairs and foreign trade.

remarks on Russia by other participants in the ministerial conference, including German Foreign Minister Westerwelle (2011). Nevertheless, Tuomioja abstained from commenting on the topic. Similarly, President Tarja Halonen did not discuss internal developments in Russia during her last official visit to Moscow, on 17 and 18 January 2012 (President of Finland 2012).

The discourse advocating economic cooperation with Russia also remained dominant after the election of Sauli Niinistö, who succeeded Halonen as president of Finland in March 2012. In his inauguration speech, Niinistö (2012a) argued that 'the values important to us [Finns] are fairness, strengthening sustainable development and supporting democracy, human rights and the rule of law'. Nevertheless, his remarks on Russia reflected the pre-eminence of economic pragmatism over normative considerations.

> Our relationship to Russia remains at the centre of our foreign policy. Both our bilateral relations with Russia and the evolving co-operation between the EU and Russia are important for us. Human and commercial interaction is increasing, and it is important to develop an operating environment as predictable as possible.

Developing a positive 'operating environment' for trade with Russia remained Finland's chief preoccupation under the new president. In Niinistö's (2012b, 2012c) speeches, Russia was constructed as a fundamental partner and defined as 'extremely important for Finland', 'our greatest single trading partner' and 'at the centre of our foreign policy'. Until the spring of 2012, this stance did not leave much room for criticism.

Nordic identity: dealing with an authoritarian partner

A partial change in Finnish official discourse took place in the spring and summer of 2012, when the country's foreign policy leaders started to voice their concerns about authoritarian developments in Russia. Most likely, the emergence of a more critical discourse was linked to the increasing repressiveness of Russian official policies after Putin's re-election in March 2012. Finnish leaders felt they could no longer ignore Russia's growing authoritarianism, which stood in clear contradiction of the values and norms they cherished in public statements (see Niinistö 2012a, 2012c).

While taking a more critical stance towards internal developments in Russia, Finnish policy makers continued to foster economic cooperation. In order to justify this posture, Finnish leaders made instrumental use of the country's Nordic identity. They argued that Finland was a Nordic society, based on values such as the rule of law, democracy, openness and equal opportunity (Niinistö 2012c). This provided them with moral ground to criticise domestic developments in Russia. At the same time, however, they argued that Russian society was fundamentally different from Nordic societies and had to be accepted for what it was. This approach, together with the narrative portraying Russia as a fundamental economic partner, allowed Finnish leaders to reconcile criticism with support for a strong commercial relationship. Pragmatism and economic advantage are the topoi linking this argumentative strategy to its policy implications.

The discourse criticising internal developments in Russia emerged progressively during the spring of 2012. Its inception can be detected, for instance, in a speech made by foreign minister Tuomioja (2012b) in Helsinki on 12 April 2012, at a seminar concerning security in Northern Europe.

> For Europe and the Nordic area, developments in Russia are an important factor. It is of crucial importance that the situation in Russia remains stable and the democratic reform process continues along with strengthening the rule of law. Without this, Russia's leaders cannot expect to achieve their goal of modernisation.

Tuomioja's statement was somewhat ambiguous, as it argued for both stability and for democratic change. However, if compared with previous statements, it reveals that the state of democracy and the rule of law were acquiring a more important role in Finnish official discourse on Russia.

By the late summer of 2012, the critical discourse about authoritarian developments in Russia had become more clearly delineated. On 20 August 2012, Niinistö (2012d) expressed his concerns during a talk to Finnish ambassadors. After discussing post-Soviet Russia's economic achievements, he argued:

> Even in the eyes of the Russians themselves, Russia has not yet become everything that was perhaps hoped for. The reactions of the civil society show signs of frustration, disappointment and protest [...] We should not avoid voicing problems relating to the rule of law, democracy or human rights in Russia.

Finnish leaders followed this policy line during the visit of Russian Foreign Minister Sergei Lavrov to Finland in August 2012. Tuomioja expressed his concerns about the tightening of laws on the freedom of speech in Russia, while Niinistö and Katainen discussed the state of civil society in the country (Ministry for Foreign Affairs of Finland 2012). This was a remarkable shift from the official discourse in the previous months. However, as argued, the new narrative did not replace, but rather coexisted and was reconciled with, the discourse focusing on economic cooperation. In the talk to Finnish ambassadors referred to above, Niinistö (2012d) also claimed:

> As for us Finns, we must always take Russia for what she is. This is often easier said than done, as Russian society needs to be viewed through different lenses from those we use for Nordic society. Russia will remain important for Finland. Our strengths lie in our relations, which are functional at all levels, and in our ability to launch initiatives and create fruitful cooperation with Russia. Our economic contacts have grown to become extremely significant.

Niinistö argued that any criticism of Russia had to take into account its different societal development and its economic importance for Finland. Most importantly, in spite of increasing concerns about its domestic developments, the image of Russia as a key partner remained dominant in his discourse. In official statements made in the last months of 2012, Niinistö (2012e) and the other Finnish foreign policy leaders (see Stubb 2012) continued to portray Russia as one of the most attractive markets for Finnish companies, as well as a friendly neighbour offering significant opportunities for cooperation in the Arctic region.

Conclusion

This chapter highlighted the prevalence of economic interests over normative considerations in German, Polish and Finnish discourses on Russia during the street protests that took place in Russian cities in late 2011 and in 2012. As the protests occurred at a time when trade relations between the European Union and Russia were rapidly improving, they provided an invaluable opportunity to research the discursive interaction between economics and norms in policy makers' narratives about Russia. As shown in Chapter Three, parallel national discourses about Russia as both an economic partner and an authoritarian state had coexisted and clashed for a long time, each becoming dominant in different periods and social contexts.

German discourses best reflected the tension between economic interests and normative concerns. Between December 2011 and February 2012, low ranking foreign ministry officials focusing on civil society and human rights in Russia shaped the dominant German discourse. This narrative reflected the democratic and humanitarian component of German foreign policy identity. It was very critical of authoritarian developments in Russia and advocated a normative approach for German and EU foreign policy, including targeted sanctions towards Russian officials that were considered responsible for electoral mismanagement and human rights violations. From March 2012, this narrative became increasingly challenged by a milder, more pragmatic stance, which was advocated by Chancellor Angela Merkel and Foreign Minister Guido Westerwelle. Their discourse attempted to reconcile the normative component of German foreign policy identity with long-standing German perceptions of Russia as an economic partner. Merkel and Westerwelle argued that cooperation with Russia and criticism of its internal affairs were not mutually exclusive. Practically, however, this discourse put greater emphasis on economic interests, thereby implicitly rejecting the normative foreign policy approach advocated by the competing narrative. Due to Merkel and Westerwelle's higher position in the hierarchy of government and greater access to national media, their discourse became dominant after March 2012.

As with their German counterparts, Polish leaders emphasised economic and political cooperation far more than the respect of democratic standards. In 2011 and 2012, the Polish debate on Russia focused primarily on reconciliation and the resolution of practical issues in bilateral relations, such as the renegotiation of the price of Russian gas and the investigation of the crash of the presidential plane in which Lech Kaczynski died near Smolensk in April 2010. Polish leaders opted for a cooperative and pragmatic approach towards Russia. This reflected the substantial shift in Polish foreign policy identity under Tusk's government, which was discussed in Chapter Three. Within this context, little room was left for critical remarks on elections and street demonstrations. Foreign Minister Sikorski was the only Polish leader who regularly commented on domestic developments in Russia, mostly when journalists specifically asked him to do so. On these occasions, he expressed sympathy for Russian demonstrators and, drawing on a dominant Polish identity discourse, argued that Polish patriots had also had to fight for democracy in the past. However, these statements were not followed by criticism of Russian policies and authorities. Sikorski emphasised that Putin's popularity remained very high and that Poland would continue to pursue cooperation and historical reconciliation with the Russian establishment.

Finnish foreign policy leaders also prioritised trade and cooperation with Russia. As Russia was Finland's main trade partner, its accession to the World Trade Organization in August 2012 had positive effects on bilateral relations. Until the spring of 2012, Finnish leaders refrained from making critical comments on domestic developments in Russia. This foreign policy stance appeared as a continuation of Finland's long-standing cooperative approach towards both the Soviet Union and post-Soviet Russia. In the spring and summer of 2012, Finnish foreign policy leaders constructed a more critical discourse. Most likely, the new narrative emerged as a reaction to the increasing repressiveness of Russian policies after Putin's re-election, which stood in clear contradiction to the democratic and humanitarian values advocated by Finnish leaders. However, this narrative did not supersede the one on partnership and economic cooperation. It was relativised by the argument that Russian society was based on different values from those of Nordic societies such as Finland. Furthermore, Finnish leaders continued to claim that Russia would remain an important partner for Finland, regardless of its internal developments.

Therefore, narratives stressing economic cooperation emerged as dominant in all national discursive arenas under analysis. At official level, constructions of Russia as a partner proved stronger than those portraying it as a challenge for EU norms and values. From a comparative perspective, national discourses on Russia in 2011 and 2012 revealed a greater degree of convergence than in the two previous case studies. Economic and political pragmatism was becoming the common denominator of national narratives on Russia. While this approach appeared hard to reconcile with the normative and value-based tenets of EU external action, it temporarily resulted in increased coherence among national discourses on Russia within the EU. However, the growing authoritarianism of Russian domestic policies and, most significantly, Russia's destabilisation of Ukraine made this pragmatic and cooperative rhetoric untenable by the spring of 2014.

Chapter Seven

Russia in the Ukraine Crisis: Again a Threatening Other?

Introduction

This chapter analyses national leaders' discourses on Russia during the crisis in Ukraine in 2014 and 2015. It shows that the crisis led to a clear change in German, Finnish and Polish narratives. Previous discourses portraying Russia as an economic partner lost relevance and debates became focused on legal and security issues. Constructions of Russia as a security threat swiftly reacquired prominence, especially in Polish official discourse. In the period ranging from Moscow's annexation of Crimea to the signature of the Minsk-2 agreement, the national narratives under investigation converged towards the unanimous condemnation of Russia's use of force and violations of international law. However, differences began to arise between the German and Finnish narratives, on the one hand, and the Polish one, on the other, during the course of 2015. The chapter contends that these divergences reflect the enduring relevance of conflicting national identities and constructions of Russia within the EU.

The Ukraine conflict and the crisis in EU–Russia relations

The confrontation between the EU and Russia following Moscow's annexation of Crimea can be viewed as the culmination of a crisis that had been simmering for years (see Forsberg and Haukkala 2016: 33). As Chapter Six has shown, Russia's domestic developments in 2011–12 highlighted that the country was becoming increasingly authoritarian. The negative trend continued in the following period, as new repressive measures were introduced. Most notably, these involved the adoption of the 'foreign agent' law (essentially a crackdown on non-governmental organisations that received funds from abroad) and the 'anti-gay propaganda' law, which discriminated against sexual minorities. This legislation was accompanied by an increasingly conservative official rhetoric, which praised traditional values and portrayed EU countries as morally corrupt (Gel'man 2016; Wilkinson 2014).

However, it was on foreign policy issues that disagreements between the EU and Russia escalated into a full-blown crisis. Following his re-election to president of Russia, Vladimir Putin accelerated plans to re-establish Moscow's influence in the post-Soviet space, in particular through the implementation of the Eurasian Economic Union (EEU). From the Russian perspective, Ukraine's membership was key to the success of the project. However, Kiev was simultaneously pursuing a path towards greater integration with the EU, which included the prospective conclusion of an Association Agreement (AA) at the EU's Eastern Partnership summit in Vilnius in November 2013. The Russian leadership considered the AA incompatible with Ukraine's integration in Russia-led structures. Prior to the Vilnius summit, using a combination of economic offers and thinly veiled threats, Putin convinced Ukrainian president Viktor Yanukovych to postpone the signing of the AA with the EU (Forsberg and Haukkala 2016: 35–6; Sakwa 2015: 50–80).

Yanukovych's decision led to large-scale popular protests in Ukraine. The demonstrators assembled in the central square of Maidan Nezalezhnosti in Kiev, and their movement became known as 'Euromaidan'. Several EU leaders expressed sympathy with the demonstrators and some, including German Foreign Minister Guido Westerwelle, paid sympathetic visits to them in Maidan Square. Nevertheless, Yanukovych attempted to dislodge and silence the protestors. In January and February 2014, the confrontation between demonstrators and the government became violent. Following several days of intense clashes and a failed attempt of the foreign ministers of Germany, France and Poland to mediate the crisis, the Yanukovych regime dissolved on 21 February (Yanukovych himself left Kiev and fled to Russia) and the demonstrators claimed control of governmental buildings. A new government was formed under the leadership of opposition politician Arseniy Yatsenyuk, while Oleksandr Turchynov became acting president. The situation in the country remained unstable, and on 1 March thousands of people in the eastern and southern regions protested against the new political order (see Sakwa 2015: 81–99; Wilson 2014: 86–98).

On 27 February, Russian special forces without insignia took over government buildings in Crimea and cut off the peninsula from the rest of Ukraine, while pro-Russian political forces took control of the Crimean parliament. By 2 March, Russian troops controlled the whole of Crimea. Following a swiftly organised referendum that was not recognised internationally, the new local authorities declared the independence of Crimea on 17 March and requested the Russian government to incorporate the breakaway republic into the Russian Federation. The request was accepted by the Russian side and Crimea was annexed to Russia within a few days. The vast majority of the international community did not recognise Russia's annexation of Crimea. The European Council (2014) condemned Russian actions in Crimea at an extraordinary meeting on 6 March. From March 2014, the EU progressively imposed sanctions on Russia in response to the annexation of Crimea and the destabilisation of Ukraine. Initially, these included diplomatic measures (i.e. the cancellation of bilateral summits and the exclusion of Russia from the G8), the freezing of assets, travel restrictions against individuals who were considered responsible for Russian actions in Ukraine (excluding Putin) and restrictions on economic relations with Crimea. The sanctions were expanded significantly in July and September 2014, targeting whole sectors of the Russian economy and limiting Russian access to EU capital markets, arms and energy-related technologies (European Council 2016). Russia responded by imposing sanctions on a number of Western politicians and a ban on the import of food and agricultural products from the EU, US, Norway, Canada and Australia.

In April 2014, the crisis escalated again in the Donbass, resulting in the occupation of government buildings by pro-Russian militants and the proclamation of the Donetsk and Luhansk People's Republics. The uprising led to the military intervention of the Ukrainian armed forces, which was countered by local rebels, volunteers from Russia and, increasingly, members of the Russian armed forces. The fighting in the Donetsk and Luhansk regions intensified throughout the spring and summer of 2014, causing thousands of casualties and hundreds of thousands of refugees (Sakwa 2015: 148–82; Wilson 2014: 118–43). Moreover, on 17 July 2014, the Malaysian Airlines flight 17 was shot down over the conflict zone, most probably by pro-Russian insurgents, resulting in the death of 298 people. The tragedy had a strong impact in the EU (most passengers were of Dutch nationality) and led the EU to impose sectoral sanctions on Russia, which had presumably supplied the pro-Russian fighters with modern anti-aircraft missile systems.

A ceasefire was agreed at peace talks in Minsk on 5 September 2014 with the mediation of the OSCE, but it was breached repeatedly by both sides. After a period of relative calm in December 2014, the fighting escalated again in January and February 2015. After rejecting US proposals to supply arms to the Ukrainian government, German Chancellor Angela Merkel and French President Francois Hollande took the initiative to negotiate a peace plan in Minsk on 11–12 February (Gordon *et al.* 2015). The peace talks resulted in the Minsk-2 agreement, including a ceasefire, the pull-out of heavy weapons (both under OSCE monitoring), the holding of elections in the Donetsk and Luhansk regions according to Ukrainian law and a constitutional reform in Ukraine that would grant special status to both regions (*The Telegraph* 2015). The fighting abated and, although minor violations and occasional shelling continued to occur, the ceasefire mostly held in the following months. However, by the end of 2015 the conflict appeared to have been deadlocked, rather than resolved (Burridge 2016). Neither the elections in the Donbas and Luhansk regions, nor the Ukrainian constitutional reform had taken place as specified by the Minsk-2 agreement.

Thus, the conflict in Ukraine remained a major source of confrontation between the EU and Russia, with both sides extending reciprocally imposed sanctions into 2015 and 2016. In late 2014 and early 2015, the Russian economy was hit severely by the combined effect of the sanctions and, most significantly, the fall in the oil price. Despite the crisis in EU–Russia relations, the German and French political leaders continued to support peace negotiations. Since June 2014, the negotiations have taken place in the 'Normandy format', including the leaders of Ukraine, Russia, France and Germany. After the February 2014 negotiations in Kiev, Polish leaders have been excluded and Poland ceased to play a role as a mediator in the crisis.

In the second half of 2015, some modest (and divisive) steps towards the resumption of economic and diplomatic cooperation between Russia and some EU member states took place. Arguably, this was made possible by the lack of large-scale fighting in the Donbass and the simultaneous occurrence of other crises – notably the European refugee crisis, the Syrian civil war and the terrorist attacks in Europe – which shifted Western attention away from Ukraine. While upholding the EU sanctions, Germany has been one of the staunchest advocates of dialogue with Moscow (Siddi 2016a). In the summer and autumn of 2015, Berlin supported the construction of Nord Stream-2, an extension of the Nord Stream pipeline that would transport additional Russian gas to Germany via the Baltic Sea. The pipeline would circumvent East–Central European states and Ukraine, currently important transit countries for Russian gas deliveries to Western European markets. The project was criticised harshly by East–Central European EU members, including Poland (Gotev 2015). By the end of 2015, the question of the future EU approach to Russia appeared to be turning again into a divisive issue among EU member states.

The end of Ostpolitik? German leaders and the Ukraine crisis

Chancellor Angela Merkel and Foreign Minister Frank-Walter Steinmeier played a prominent role in the mediation of the Ukraine crisis. On 20 February 2014, Steinmeier flew to Kiev (together with his Polish and French counterparts, Radoslaw Sikorski and Laurent Fabius) to negotiate a deal that aimed at ending the clashes between the Ukrainian police and Euromaidan demonstrators. Throughout the crisis, the German foreign minister endeavoured to keep communication channels with Russia open. Angela Merkel coordinated the European response to Russia's annexation of Crimea and destabilisation of Eastern Ukraine. The EU's policy of condemning violations of international law, sanctioning Russia and calling for a diplomatic resolution of the crisis was largely shaped by the German chancellor. Together with French President Francois Hollande, Merkel negotiated the Minsk-2 agreement in February 2015 and held regular consultations with the representatives of both Russia and Ukraine throughout the crisis. Therefore, Merkel and Steinmeier's statements were highly influential, and analysing them is essential in order to understand both Germany and the EU's stances vis-à-vis the conflict in Ukraine.

The main German official discourse – advocated by both Merkel and Steinmeier – focused on Russia's violations of international law resulting from the annexation of Crimea and the destabilisation of Eastern Ukraine. It emphasised the need to impose sanctions on Russia and their link to Moscow's support of the implementation of conflict resolution efforts. Simultaneously, it argued for holding negotiations with the Russian leadership in order to solve the conflict by peaceful means. This discourse was dominant throughout the period under investigation. A second narrative emerged progressively in the months after the Minsk-2 agreement. While reiterating the criticism of Russian violations of international law and the support of sanctions, it put greater emphasis on the positive results of diplomatic negotiations and the prospect of the eventual resumption of cooperation between the EU and Russia. This narrative acquired increasing prominence in the latter part of 2015, when the military confrontation in the Donbass de-escalated and the focus of European political debates shifted towards other scenarios (the Iranian nuclear deal, the refugee crisis and the Syrian civil war) where Russia could be seen as a potential partner.

Violations of international law and the return of history

German leaders' condemnations of Russian actions in Ukraine were based primarily on legal arguments, notably the unilateral redrawing of international borders and the violation of the 1994 Budapest memorandum guaranteeing Ukraine's territorial integrity. Legal arguments were accompanied by historical considerations highlighting that Russia's actions allegedly constituted the first change of European borders through force since the Second World War and reflected nineteenth- and twentieth-century geopolitical thinking. In this discourse, history and legality were the topoi linking the main argument (Russia's actions breached international law and were anachronistic) to its logical conclusion that Russia should return to the negotiating table and solve the crisis in accordance with international law. The discourse reflected several key tenets of German identity, namely the rejection of the use of force in international relations and the commitment to multilateralism and international norms (*see* Chapter Three). Germany's peaceful security culture led to both the condemnation of Russia's actions and the refusal to try to solve the crisis by military means (i.e. by supplying Ukraine with weapons), as advocated by some members of the US Congress and some European politicians (see Gordon *et al*. 2015).

In German official statements, the normative component of German identity prevailed over the traditional Ostpolitik cooperative approach to Russia. This contrasts starkly with the stance of German policy makers vis-à-vis Russian domestic developments in 2011 and 2012, when pragmatism and the quest for economic partnership had prevailed over normative considerations (*see* Chapter Six). As emerges from Merkel and Steinmeier's declarations on the Ukraine crisis, the deep shock provoked by Russia's annexation of Crimea had a profound impact on the agency of German policy makers, who relinquished the long-standing discourse portraying Russia as a partner. However, Ostpolitik thinking continued to influence the declared long-term objectives of German policy, which emphasised the inclusion of Russia in the European security architecture and the creation of a common commercial area from Lisbon to Vladivostok.

The dominant German discourse emerges clearly from Merkel and Steinmeier's statements in March 2014. Speaking in the German parliament on 13 March, Merkel (2014a) argued that 'Russia's actions in Ukraine undoubtedly represent a violation of fundamental principles of international law [...] in the heart of Europe, and it is vital that we do not simply return to business as usual'. Merkel's wish not to return to 'business as usual' with Russia highlights the departure from the cooperative approach that preceded the annexation of Crimea. Merkel put Russian actions in Ukraine in historical perspective by commemorating the 'recurring rounds of horrendous bloodshed' that had haunted Europe throughout the twentieth century and claiming that:

> First in Georgia back in 2008 and now in the heart of Europe, in Ukraine, we are witnessing a conflict about spheres of influence and territorial claims, such as those we know from the nineteenth and twentieth centuries but thought we had put behind us.

Merkel's criticism is conveyed through the choice of emphatic vocabulary ('horrendous bloodshed') and perspectivation. Remarkably, Merkel also reassessed Moscow's involvement in the August 2008 crisis more critically than in her contemporary statements (*see* Chapter Five), which highlights the tougher stance adopted by German leaders in 2014. Steinmeier's rhetoric largely echoed that of Merkel. In a speech at the German–Russian forum in Berlin, he criticised Russia for acting 'according to the geopolitical categories of the twentieth century' and the 'attempt to redraw borders seven decades after the end of the Second World War' (Steinmeier 2014a). Both German leaders argued that Russia should face EU sanctions until it changed its policies, which implied the abandonment of the trade-driven Ostpolitik approach.

Nonetheless, Ostpolitik thinking was not rejected altogether, but continued to permeate the German strategy for the long term. While Merkel announced that further sanctions would be imposed if Russia escalated the crisis, she simultaneously advocated 'working together with Russia to find ways to resolve outstanding conflicts in countries which are neighbours to us both' and potentially 'talking with Russia about a new economic agreement' (Merkel 2014a). Moreover, Steinmeier (2014a) stated:

> I remain deeply convinced that security in and for Europe can only be achieved jointly with, and not against, Russia. This still holds true, despite the current crisis. The aim of a common space, from Lisbon to Vladivostok, remains the right one.

This stance could be reconciled with efforts to stop the escalation of the crisis and solve it through negotiations, which were vocally supported by both German leaders.

> I for one could never forgive myself if we did not seek out and use every diplomatic tool at our disposal, for as long as possible, with a view to finding a solution.
>
> (Steinmeier 2014a)

> The conflict cannot be resolved by military means. I say to everyone who is worried and concerned: military action is not an option for us.
>
> (Merkel 2014a)

German leaders upheld this discourse throughout the Ukraine crisis, often using an emotional tone (signalled by perspectivation in these passages, i.e. 'I remain deeply convinced', 'I for one could never forgive myself') that emphasised both the gravity of the crisis and their personal involvement in solving it.

When the fighting escalated – most notably in the spring and summer of 2014 and in January 2015 – the discourse became more critical and its tone more sombre. For instance, this emerges from Steinmeier's (2014b) article in the *Frankfurter Allgemeine Zeitung* on 6 May 2014 and his speech in the German parliament (2014c) on 7 May 2014, where he argued that 'the situation in eastern and southern Ukraine [was] terrible' and there was not much time left to solve the crisis. After the downing of the MH17 flight, the rhetoric became harsher. German leaders, who had previously been wary of imposing economic sanctions on Russia (see Steinmeier 2014d), argued that the situation had 'changed radically' (Steinmeier 2014e) and economic sanctions had become 'unavoidable' (Merkel 2014b). However, neither Merkel nor Steinmeier ever questioned the diplomatic approach to solving the crisis. Following the MH17 tragedy, Steinmeier (2014f) argued: 'There may be some who advocate a military response to Russia's policy [...] I don't share this view, and neither, I believe, do the majority of people in Germany'. Similarly, in the tense weeks that preceded the signature of the Minsk-2 agreement, Merkel (2015b, 2015c) repeatedly stated that the crisis could not be resolved by military means. In the winter of 2014–15, the German chancellor strived to uphold the dialogue with Moscow by arguing that she wanted 'security in Europe with Russia and not against Russia' (2014c) and 'political cooperation with Russia' (2015a).

Throughout the crisis, German policy makers attempted to present their leading role in negotiations as consistent with the EU's position and stressed the need of having a united EU response to the crisis. Merkel (2014d) stated that 'Europe has decided that it will not let itself be divided, but that it will act together more strongly than ever before in order to defend its peace order and its values'. The pro-EU rhetoric was accompanied by frequent reassurances to Germany's Eastern European NATO allies. In March 2014, shortly after the annexation of Crimea, Steinmeier (2014g) argued that 'NATO members must be sure their allies will protect them. There is no reason to doubt this'. This rhetoric reflected the deep-rooted support for European integration and the transatlantic alliance in German foreign policy thinking. While reassuring Germany's allies of its commitment to the Western cause, this stance allowed German leaders to act as bridge builders and maintain dialogue with Moscow in order to seek a diplomatic solution to the crisis (see Steinmeier 2014h).

Back to Ostpolitik?

The signing of the Minsk-2 agreement in February 2015 and the de-escalation of the conflict in the subsequent months allowed German leaders to intensify their rhetoric advocating a diplomatic solution of the crisis and the future return to a more cooperative relationship with Russia. German official discourses highlighted the positive results of the Minsk negotiations and argued that both the sanctions and Russia's isolation would end if the agreement were implemented. In the latter part of 2015, Russia was increasingly portrayed as a potential partner in other contemporary crises (the Iranian nuclear programme, the Syrian civil war and the fight against international terrorism). Legality and multilateralism were the topoi in the German argumentative strategy, connecting it to its logical conclusion that relations with Russia would improve if Moscow worked towards the implementation of Minsk-2 and helped to solve other international crises. This discourse reflected the normative dimension of German foreign policy, as well as Ostpolitik thinking and deep-rooted constructions of Russia as a key actor in the international arena.

In the statement that followed the conclusion of the Minsk-2 agreement, Merkel (2015d) argued: 'There is a genuine chance of improvement. Germany and France, France and Germany have together demonstrated that we have made a contribution, including in alignment with Europe'. The defence of the Minsk-2 agreement (which was often criticised by Western advocates of a tougher stance towards Russia) became a constant feature of her subsequent speeches. She defined it as 'the way to achieve a peaceful solution' (Merkel 2015e) and 'a ray of hope' (Merkel 2015f). Merkel (2015g) clarified that 'there [was] a correlation between existing sanctions and the full implementation of the Minsk package'. In the following months, both Merkel (2015e) and Steinmeier (2015a) expressed their opposition to imposing new sanctions on Russia. Steinmeier (2015a) argued that sanctions were not 'an end in themselves', but were 'intended to generate readiness to negotiate and pave the way for military de-escalation and political settlement'. Hence, he concluded that 'Once this road has been chosen [...] there will be no reason to keep the sanctions at current levels'. This reasoning suggested that Steinmeier was keen on progressively removing sanctions on Russia while the provisions of Minsk-2 were being implemented.

The endurance of the Ostpolitik approach to Russia can be inferred from Steinmeier's (2015b) interview with *Handelsblatt* on 5 March 2015, in which he referred to Willy Brandt's foreign policy and argued that isolating Russia from the EU would not help solve the crisis. His interview with *Neue Westfälische* in November 2015 best illustrates the influence of Ostpolitik in Steinmeier's thinking.

> The policy of détente towards the Warsaw Pact functioned in the days of the inter-bloc confrontation [...] Today we are living in a world largely without ordered structures [...] But the basic idea of overcoming a lack of communication and maintaining ongoing contact, despite clashing views, is still apposite.

(Steinmeier 2015d)

In the months after the Minsk-2 agreement, the quest for dialogue and reconciliation shaped Steinmeier's diplomacy and rhetoric. In May 2015, he attended the commemorations of the seventieth anniversary of the end of the Second World War in Volgograd, together with his Russian counterpart Sergey Lavrov. At the commemoration, Steinmeier (2015c) praised the historical reconciliation between Russia and Germany and linked it to current events.

> I say as a German that the people of Stalingrad are heroes, not only because 70 years ago they forced a turnaround in the war with their blood. They are also heroes because to this day they remind us to work for peace!

Remarkably, Steinmeier went beyond a simple call for German–Russian reconciliation and endorsed the Russian memory narrative emphasising the heroism of Soviet soldiers (see Torbakov 2011). Merkel pursued a similar policy, as witnessed by her trip to Moscow to jointly commemorate the anniversary together with Putin. However, she maintained a more critical stance and, while calling for reconciliation, she reiterated her condemnation of Russian policies in Ukraine (Merkel 2015h).

Attempts at seeking reconciliation with Russia intensified in the summer months of 2015. At the G7 summit in Germany, Merkel (2015i) stated that Russia 'needed to be a partner' on stopping Iran's nuclear programme and ending the civil war in Syria. In an interview published in June 2015, while defending the EU's double-track policy of sanctions and negotiations with Russia, Steinmeier (2015a) argued:

> There can be no interest on our part in the G8 remaining the G7 in the long term. On the contrary, we urgently need Russia to help resolve entrenched conflicts in our European neighbourhood, such as those plaguing Syria, Iraq and Libya, as well as Iran's nuclear programme.

As the focus of political debates increasingly shifted towards other crises in the latter part of 2015, cooperation with Russia in these scenarios was seen as desirable in order to achieve a comprehensive relaxation of tensions between the West and Moscow. In her government statement of 15 October 2015, Merkel (2015j) argued for 'a process of political dialogue which also embraces Russia and other international and regional actors' to end the Syrian conflict. Reflecting the German long-standing commitment to both the transatlantic alliance and the policy of dialogue with Moscow, Steinmeier considered US–Russian cooperation in solving these crises as an essential step towards the improvement of relations, and strongly advocated it in his last interviews of 2015 (see Steinmeier 2015e).

'Ukraine's ambassador in Europe': Poland between pragmatism and confrontation

Poland was one of the most vocal critics of Russian actions in Ukraine within the EU. Polish diplomacy was very active throughout the crisis, but its role changed in the course of 2014. Initially, the Polish foreign minister was directly involved in mediating the crisis. In February 2014, Radoslaw Sikorski flew to Kiev – together with his German and French counterparts – in order to negotiate a compromise between Viktor Yanukovych's government and the Euromaidan demonstrators. However, subsequent negotiations took place in the 'Normandy format', including the leaders of Germany, France, Russia and Ukraine. The end of Poland's role as mediator in the Ukraine crisis roughly coincided with the change of leadership in Warsaw. After seven years in government, in September 2014 Donald Tusk and Radoslaw Sikorski were replaced, respectively, by Ewa Kopacz and Grzegorz Schetyna. Like their predecessors, Kopacz and Schetyna were members of the centre-right Civic Platform. However, their domestic position was constrained by controversies concerning prominent members of their party and the proximity of presidential and parliamentary elections in late spring and fall of 2015 (BBC News 2015a). Being new to the foreign policy arena, Kopacz and Schetyna also seemed to be less prominent in European debates than their experienced predecessors.[1] Nevertheless, they maintained a vocal and active stance vis-à-vis the Ukraine crisis throughout their mandate.

The dominant Polish official discourse on the crisis criticised Russia harshly for its violations of Ukraine's territorial integrity and advocated robust EU sanctions. It called for a united EU and NATO response, including a military build-up on Polish territory, and for solidarity with and support of Ukraine. However, it backed a diplomatic (rather than military) solution to the crisis and kept communication channels with Moscow open. This stance was formulated during Donald Tusk's government and was later endorsed by Kopacz and Schetyna. However, Kopacz and Schetyna's rhetoric towards Russia swiftly became more hawkish than that of their predecessors and did not change in the second half of 2015, despite the partial de-escalation of the conflict in the Donbass.

Sanctions and security: Tusk and Sikorski's response to the crisis

The Polish government's condemnation of Russian actions in Ukraine was based primarily on legal arguments. Although Tusk and Sikorski occasionally used historical analogies to interpret current developments, memory politics did not play an important role in their rhetoric. Calls for European and NATO solidarity towards Poland (which was allegedly exposed to potential Russian threats) were justified with pragmatic arguments, notably the increased Russian military activity and the risk of future disruptions in Russian energy supplies. Legality and security were the topoi in Tusk and Sikorski's argumentative strategy, conveying the message that Russia had to be sanctioned for its violations of international law, while NATO and the EU had to strengthen the military resilience and energy security of their Eastern flank. Support of Ukraine was a central corollary of this discourse. On the one hand, this stance resonated with long-standing Polish identity narratives of Russia as a security threat, while the call for EU and NATO solidarity emphasised Poland's identification with the Euro-Atlantic alliance (*see* Chapter Three). On the other hand, Tusk and Sikorski's pragmatic rhetoric and the decision to maintain communication channels with Moscow highlighted the endurance of the new foreign policy course adopted by Poland in its relations with Russia after 2007 (*see* Chapters Three and Four).

The dominant Polish official discourse is clearly illustrated in Sikorski's (2014a) interview with the *Washington Post* on 18 April 2014. He argued that events in Ukraine mattered to the West:

---

1. Donald Tusk went on to become President of the European Council in December 2014.

because, for the first time since the Second World War, one European country has annexed a province from another European country. And that matters because it is a rejection of our entire legal system and international norms and treaties that we have regarded as the foundation of peace.

Sikorski highlighted the significance of Russia's illegal actions in historical perspective and qualified Russia as 'a revisionist power', bent on 'preventing Ukraine from reforming and becoming successful'. In addition, he argued that the US 'should reassure allies in Central and Eastern Europe'. However, he did not support the idea of delivering weapons to Ukraine and specified that Poland was 'not feeling militarily threatened as yet' (2014b).

A similar combination of harsh rhetoric and cold pragmatism emerges from Tusk's statements. Following Russia's occupation of Crimea, he advocated a resolute response from the EU, the imposition of sanctions on Russia and deeper military cooperation with the US (Tusk 2014a, 2014b). Simultaneously, he defended his policy of 'building up good relations' with Russia and argued that the Polish stance towards Moscow should be 'rational' and 'reasonable' (Tusk 2014c). In a context of increasing tensions with Russia, Tusk's statement should be read as a call for a critical, but pragmatic approach. His proposal for an EU energy union, presented in April 2014, epitomises this stance (Tusk 2014d). The proposal originated in response to the EU's dependence on Russian gas and the risk of potential supply disruptions (Siddi 2016b). However, its rationale was justified primarily with economic arguments ('Russia's monopolistic position') rather than political ones. This line of argument, focusing on economics rather than historical conflict, appeared in continuity with the one adopted by Tusk's governments to oppose the Nord Stream project (*see* Chapter Four).

European unity and solidarity were recurrent themes in Tusk and Sikorski's comments on the Ukraine crisis. In his address to the Polish parliament on 5 March 2014, Tusk stated that 'Poland's aim [was] to maintain a uniform policy of the whole community of the West'. Similarly, Tusk's energy union proposal focused on 'mechanisms guaranteeing solidarity among [EU] member states' (2014d). For the Polish government, calls for European solidarity were functional to obtaining military and strategic support from EU and NATO partners. Furthermore, Polish leaders aimed at steering the unitary EU position towards a more critical stance vis-à-vis Russia. Tusk and Sikorski's statements reveal that Poland consistently advocated a hard line against Russia within the EU. For instance, this emerges from Tusk's (2014e) comments on the weakness of EU sanctions against Russia (suggesting that he was keen on strengthening them) and in Sikorski's (2014c) claim that 'if the EU had reacted more strongly to Russia's annexation of Crimea and adopted sanctions more quickly, as Poland advocated, the current conflict in Donetsk, Ukraine, would not have happened'.

Next to deep-seated fears of Russian imperialism, genuine identification with the Ukrainian cause contributes to explaining the Polish stance in the crisis. Sikorski (2014d) argued that 'the Ukrainians are our [Poland's] neighbours. They are fighting for the same things we did back in 1989 – for a country that is more democratic, less corrupt and is European'. Ukraine was seen as a 'new Poland', replicating the Polish struggle for emancipation from Moscow's sphere of influence in 1989, and as 'the only place on earth where people have sacrificed their lives for the ideas of European integration' (Tusk 2014a). This discourse resonated with Polish identity narratives of heroism, martyrdom and commitment to the Western cause (*see* Chapter Three). Ultimately, it highlighted Ukraine's European orientation and conveyed the message that that the West should support Kiev.

Kopacz and Schetyna: support of Ukraine as Poland's raison d'état

Initially, the change of government in Warsaw in September 2014 suggested a softening of Poland's stance towards Russia (see Sobczyk and Wasilewski 2014). In her first speech at the Polish parliament, Prime Minister Ewa Kopacz (2014) argued that Poland should not isolate itself within the EU by setting 'unrealistic goals' in the Ukraine crisis; hence, she would 'pursue a pragmatic policy towards what is happening in Ukraine'. However, the analysis of the speeches of Polish leaders in the following months showed that their criticism of Russia continued unabated and, in fact, was accompanied by a harsher rhetoric than in previous months. The argumentation strategy adopted by Kopacz and Schetyna was largely the same as Tusk and Sikorski's, focusing on international law, security and transatlantic solidarity. The main difference was that their support of Ukraine became more vocal and contemplated the provision of military aid. Moreover, references to history and the use of memory politics to attack Russia became more frequent.

The foreign policy of the new Polish government was outlined in Schetyna's speech in the Polish parliament on 6 November 2014. He argued that the post-Cold War order in Europe had been questioned by Russia and:

> threats that we were confronted with before 1989 re-emerged in Europe: the spectre of military aggression, the unpredictability of a great power, contempt for the rights of sovereign nations and the risk of division of the continent into spheres of influence.

(Schetyna 2014a)

According to Schetyna (2014a), Russia 'chose the language of aggression, driven by the idea of spheres of influence and giving primacy to force in developing international relations'. In Schetyna's narrative, Russia was personified as an aggressive Other, speaking the 'language of aggression'. Moreover, it was categorised as alien to Europe due to 'the rising tide of isolationism and anti-Western feelings and the negation of European values', which 'build a wall that divides Russia from Europe'. Consequently, the continuation of economic sanctions and the strengthening of the military alliance with the United States were presented as the only possible course of action for Poland (see also Schetyna 2015a).

Schetyna occasionally softened his rhetoric by claiming that Poland and Russia 'remain[ed] neighbours and economic partners' (Schetyna 2014a), and Polish leaders would 'try to reverse this [negative] trend and return to normal, good-neighbourly relations' (Schetyna 2015b). These statements highlighted the endurance of the pragmatic stance towards Russia initiated by Tusk and Sikorski in 2007; they were intended to keep communication channels open and address issues bilaterally. However, they were marginal in the broader picture of Polish discourses on Russia. On the whole, the rhetoric of Polish leaders remained hawkish even after the signature of the Minsk-2 agreement, when German discourses became more optimistic. Kopacz (2015a) continued to argue for stricter sanctions on Russia even when German leaders considered them 'unhelpful' (Steinmeier 2015a), while Schetyna (2015b) stated that a renewed escalation of military operations in the Donbass would lead Poland to step up support for Ukraine, 'including its defence'.

In the winter and spring of 2015, the Polish leaders expanded the discursive confrontation with Russia to the field of historical memory. In January 2015, on the seventieth anniversary of the Soviet liberation of the Auschwitz extermination camp, Schetyna argued that the camp had been freed by Ukrainian soldiers. The statement caused a diplomatic row with Russian officials, after which Schetyna corrected his claims and credited a multi-ethnic Soviet army for the liberation of the camp (Easton 2015). History-related disputes continued in the spring, during the commemorations for the seventieth anniversary of the end of the Second World War. The Polish leadership hosted a commemorative event in the Westerplatte peninsula, near Gdansk, where the Second World War had started. The event was organised as an alternative for leaders who intended to boycott victory day celebrations in Moscow, and was attended almost exclusively by representatives of East–Central European countries (BBC News 2015b). Polish President Bronislaw Komorowski made a speech in which he vehemently attacked Russia's policies in the Ukraine crisis. He described Russia as:

> the forces which bring back memories of the darkest chapters in twentieth century history, the ones which continue to think through the prism of spheres of influence, which strive to maintain their neighbourhood in the condition of the dependency of vassals, which do not respect civilised principles of law and of relations among nations.

(Komorowski 2015)

Komorowski's narrative contrasted strikingly with the spirit of historical reconciliation that had been promoted by Tusk's government in previous years, particularly through the establishment of a Polish–Russian Working Group for Difficult Matters (*see* Chapter Six).

During the Kopacz government, Polish official discourses also became more radical in their assessments of the significance of the crisis and the future of Ukraine. Schetyna argued that 'the struggle for Ukraine is the biggest challenge for the EU' (Schetyna 2015c) and that 'a sovereign, democratic, pro-European and prosperous Ukraine is an element of the Polish *raison d'état*' (Schetyna 2015b). Moreover, he asked all Polish political forces to take a united stance on Ukraine and avoid making it a contentious topic in the 2015 national elections (Schetyna 2015b). According to Polish leaders, domestic agreement on the issue would allow Poland to further Ukraine's cause internationally. This posture was highlighted by Kopacz's (2015b) statements during a visit to Kiev in January 2015:

> I want to assure our friends in Kiev that we are going to do whatever we can to maintain the uniform position of the European Union on the policy towards Russia [...] We want to be a good ambassador for Ukraine in the EU, and encourage our partners to support Ukraine.

Through perspectivation, Kopacz emphasised her personal commitment to representing Ukrainian interests within the EU and upholding the sanctions against Russia. Her claim that Poland would be 'a good ambassador for Ukraine in the EU' illustrated how, by 2015, Warsaw's policy had shifted away from its earlier attempts to play a role as a mediator in the crisis towards the pursuit of pro-Ukraine lobbying.

In November 2015, following the defeat of Civic Platform in the national elections, the Kopacz government was replaced by a new one entirely controlled by the traditionally russo- and germano-phobic Law and Justice party. It is too early to assess its foreign policy; however, based on the previous stint in power of the party (2005–7; *see* Chapters Three and Four) and its current rhetoric, the prospects for both Poland's pragmatic foreign policy towards Russia and for a coordinated stance with Germany, Finland and most other EU member states are not promising.

Finnish discourses: security threats and the quest for dialogue

The Ukraine crisis had a profound impact on Finnish security and foreign policy debates. Before the crisis, Russia was seen mostly as an economic partner, albeit at times a difficult one and with authoritarian tendencies (*see* Chapter Six). In 2013, Russia was Finland's main trade partner and only gas provider. Russian state company Rosatom was involved in the construction of a nuclear power plant on Finnish territory and was thereby acquiring an important stake in the strategic nuclear sector (Reuters 2013; Yle 2015a). Moreover, multilateral cooperation with Russia had grown over the years within several policy frameworks and institutional settings, ranging from the EU's Northern Dimension policy to the Arctic Council. Russia's armed intervention in the Ukraine crisis and its increased military activities in the Baltic region cast doubts on the nature of Finland's relationship with Moscow and its security posture. The possibility of abandoning military non-alignment and joining NATO was discussed at official level, even if a clear majority of Finns continued to oppose NATO membership (Yle 2015b). At the same time, Finland's foreign policy leaders focused on the organisation of the commemorations for the fortieth anniversary of the Helsinki Final Act, which took place in the Finnish capital in July 2015. The Helsinki Final Act had marked the high point of détente between the West and Soviet Russia and of Finland's policy of neutrality and international mediation during the Cold War.

Against this background, Finnish official discourses on the Ukraine crisis focused on two main aspects. On the one hand, they highlighted Russia's breaches of international law and collective security. While blaming Russia for the crisis and supporting EU sanctions, Finnish leaders argued that it could be resolved only through diplomacy and dialogue. On the other hand, they attempted to separate the Ukraine crisis from other issues and uphold cooperation with Russia in regional forums concerning the Arctic and the Baltic Sea. Finnish official policy and discourses did not change substantially after the parliamentary elections of 2015, which brought to power a partly new government coalition – including most notably the far-right Finns' Party, whose leader Timo Soini became foreign minister.

Russia's challenge to law and security and the need for negotiations

Finnish official reactions to Russia's annexation of Crimea focused on its legal and security implications. President Sauli Niinistö argued that it was 'clearly against Ukrainian and international law' (Niinistö 2014a) and 'subjected Europe's security system to intense pressure and damage' (Niinistö 2014b). He was echoed by Foreign Minister Erkki Tuomioja (2014a), who stated that the annexation was 'against the fundamental principles of sovereignty, territorial integrity, as well as many binding international agreements', and 'damaging for the long-term stability, security and prosperity of all [Council of Europe] member states and their people'. As a result of Russia's military actions, deep-rooted narratives depicting Russia as a security challenge for Finland became dominant. However, both Niinistö and Tuomioja consistently argued that the crisis could only be solved through diplomacy and dialogue and in accordance with OSCE principles. Legality and cooperative security were the topoi of their argumentation strategy.

The relevance of cooperative security and diplomacy in Finnish official discourse on the Ukraine crisis emerges clearly from a speech made by Tuomioja (2014b) in Helsinki on 2 June 2014.

> The Helsinki Final Act provided a framework for dialogue and was considered to be a historic breakthrough at the height of the Cold War. Although the world has changed tremendously since its adoption, the main principles contained in the Helsinki Final Act are still as universal and relevant today as they were at that time. [...] I am fully convinced that more mediation and dialogue, not less, is needed in today's world. This is most recently demonstrated by the crisis in

Ukraine. Dialogue, diplomatic efforts and renouncing the use of force are the only way to find a sustainable resolution to that crisis.

Tuomioja's approach to solving the Ukraine conflict and the crisis between Russia and the West was strongly influenced by his understanding of Cold War détente and the Helsinki Final Act, which Finnish policy makers widely regard as one of Finland's greatest diplomatic successes (Tiilikainen 1998: 153–6). Tuomioja considered the OSCE – the institution that represents the main heritage of the Helsinki Final Act – as essential to solving the Ukraine crisis. In a speech made in Vienna in May 2014, he argued that it was 'hard to imagine a lasting settlement [of] the current crisis without the OSCE and its principles taking the centre stage in Europe again', and that he 'could not think of a better and more relevant mechanism and platform' than the OSCE for discussions on renewing commitments to common security in Europe (Tuomioja 2014c).

As the only pan-European security organisation including both Western countries and Russia, the OSCE embodied the notion of cooperative security. By emphasising the role of the OSCE in the resolution of the Ukraine crisis, Finnish policy makers appeared to be playing their traditional role of 'bridge builders' between Russia and the West (*see* Chapter Three). However, it is important to note that, while emphasising the importance of mediation to solve the crisis, Finnish leaders unequivocally placed themselves in the Western and EU camp. In other words, Russia's violations of international law and use of force led Finnish leaders to restate that Finland had placed itself at the Western end of the East–West continuum which had characterised national identity debates in the past (see Browning 2008: 12; and *see* Chapter Three). A speech made by Prime Minister Alexander Stubb in Berlin in September 2014 illustrates this. After reviewing the history of EU–Russia relations and condemning Russian actions in Ukraine, Stubb (2014) stated:

I referred earlier to the year 1995, the most important year in our recent history. Becoming an EU member was long overdue and the most natural thing to happen. We are where we belong. This is also where we firmly place ourselves in the current situation. We are in the EU family, fully committed to our common cause.

Stubb's emphatic remark can only be understood with reference to Finland's Cold War neutrality and Finnish identity debates. It was a statement of belonging to Europe and the West, which Stubb (2014) associated with liberal democracy and the respect of international law. On the other hand, he argued that Russia had not yet embraced these values, thereby categorising the country as currently distinct from the European and Western communities in which Finland recognised itself.

Pragmatism and the isolation of the Ukraine crisis from other policy fields

According to Stubb, Russia's exclusion from the Western community was not definitive, nor did it mean that cooperation with Moscow was impossible. He argued that the Soviet period had ended relatively recently and that democratisation was still possible in the longer run. Until then, Russia and the West could co-exist and consider a strategic partnership as a long-term goal: 'I believe we can co-exist. We need not be alike to be good neighbours, or even strategic partners again. We should aim at that' (Stubb 2014). Moreover, Stubb contended that Russia's current estrangement from Europe did not preclude cooperation, particularly in the economic arena.

> Russia has turned inwards. Many think it is now also turning east and therefore drifting away from Europe. The extent of this turn remains to be seen and, frankly, I do not think such a turn is a negative thing only. In fact, I think it would be wise for Russia to finally make better use of being geographically so Asian. It would profit their economy – and therefore, indirectly, also ours. It certainly would not exclude co-operation with Europe.

> (Stubb 2014)

Stubb's statement reflected Finland's pragmatic approach to Moscow and the conceptualisation of Russia as an economic partner regardless of its domestic developments. The argument, according to which Russia was societally different from EU countries, but could still be a partner, echoed those made by Finnish leaders in 2012 in order to reconcile their criticism of Russia's increasing authoritarianism with the promotion of bilateral trade (see Niinistö 2012c and Chapter Six in this volume). Pragmatism and economic advantage are the topoi in this strategy of argumentation.

Stubb argued that business relations and people-to-people contacts would help solve the crisis between Russia and the European Union – a view that coincided with the key tenets of the German Ostpolitik towards Russia, as Stubb (2014) himself noted in his speech in Berlin.

> In fact, Finland and Germany have a very similar approach to the crisis. But let me make one point very clear. I think we all need to be intellectually mature enough to differentiate between three things in our approach to Russia and things Russian. Firstly, Moscow-level, very hawkish decision-making and its implications. Secondly, mutually beneficial, still functioning business relations and people-to-people contacts; at the end of the day they can be our best guarantee for peace. And thirdly, Russian-speaking minorities living in our own countries. Finland has a longer common border with Russia, 1300 kilometres, than the rest of the EU countries put together. This means that we have a very pragmatic and common-sense approach in all of our Russia policies, knowing we will be in this relationship 'in sickness and in health'.

Stubb's claim that business relations were one of the best guarantees for peace is all the more remarkable if we bear in mind that it was made only a few weeks after the EU had imposed sectoral sanctions on Russia. Stubb also reiterated the long-standing argument that Finland needed to have a pragmatic policy towards Russia because of their proximity and long, shared border. In the contemporary scenario, this meant distinguishing between Finland's position towards Russia in the Ukraine crisis and in other regional forums. While Finnish policy makers condemned Russian actions in Ukraine, they continued to advocate cooperation with Moscow on Baltic and Arctic issues.

This approach is highlighted repeatedly throughout 2014 and 2015. At a summit on the EU Strategy for the Baltic Sea Region, Tuomioja (2014d) argued that, despite the Ukraine crisis, 'it should not be in anyone's interest to allow the conflict to negatively affect our pragmatic cooperation in the Council of Baltic Sea states and other regional fora'. Similarly, at a seminar on EU policies towards the Arctic, he argued that it would 'not be in anyone's interest to let the [Ukraine] crisis bring new obstacles for the kind of pragmatic cooperation on environmental, social and economic issues which has benefited all the member states and the people living on the Arctic' (Tuomioja 2014e). Niinistö (2014c) reiterated this argument in a speech made in Reykjavik:

> Russia's actions [in Ukraine] have damaged international security and co-operation especially in Europe. However, I am convinced that we should keep the North and the Arctic Council on a road towards more – not less – co-operation. The Arctic Council is the only circumpolar organization that deals with the specific problems of this region. Should its work get paralysed everybody would lose. We don't want that.

Niinistö claimed that the continuation of cooperation in the Baltic and the Arctic was compatible with Finland's stance on the Ukraine crisis because it did not mean a return to 'business as usual'. At the same time, it prevented an unnecessary escalation of the crisis between the EU and Russia: 'Even if there is no return to normal, this does not mean that we should continue moving towards an abnormal situation' (Niinistö 2015). Furthermore, this posture allowed Finnish leaders to play a role as bridge builders between Russia and the EU on regional policies, for instance by asking Russia to accept the EU's application for observer status in the Arctic Council (Tuomioja 2015) and by encouraging EU–Russia cooperation within the Barents Euro-Arctic Council (Soini 2015).

Conclusion

The Ukraine crisis caused a sudden change in dominant discourses on Russia in the countries under investigation. Russia was no longer constructed as an economic and strategic partner. Conversely, it was widely seen as posing a challenge to the European legal and security order. German, Polish and Finnish official discourses converged towards the unanimous condemnation of Russia's violations of international law. This convergence reflected the shared stance of EU member states towards the Ukraine crisis, which allowed Brussels to deliver a coherent response to Russian actions in the form of sanctions. Contrary to what had happened after the August 2008 crisis in the Caucasus (*see* Chapter Five), EU–Russia relations did not recover swiftly. The EU maintained a firm stance on the crisis, while Russian leaders in turn reconceptualised the EU as a geopolitical competitor.

This chapter has showed how the shared response to Russian actions in Crimea and the Donbass was discursively constructed (and made possible) in three member states that were particularly active in shaping EU relations with Russia, both before and during the Ukraine crisis. In Germany, Russia's use of force in Ukraine was perceived as a major challenge to European security – and not simply as a disproportionate response to a regional crisis, as had been the view in August 2008. The use of force was at odds with the peaceful security culture that had become deeply entrenched in German identity since 1945. In these circumstances, the Ostpolitik discourse was temporarily marginalised. Germany's peaceful security culture also influenced the policy enacted in response to the crisis: economic sanctions were imposed on Russia, whereas the option of sending military equipment to Ukraine was discarded.

The Polish and Finnish initial response to the crisis largely mirrored the German perspective. The main difference was that, in Poland, the Tusk government adopted a harsher rhetoric vis-à-vis Russia and emphasised the need for strengthening NATO's military presence in Eastern Europe. This reflected the Euro-Atlantic orientation of Polish foreign policy and identity-based conceptualisations of Russia as imperialist and aggressive (and thus posing a threat to Poland), which became dominant in Polish public debates after the onset of the Ukraine crisis. On the other hand, Finnish discourses portrayed Russia as a security challenge, but maintained that negotiations and cooperative security (most notably through the OSCE) were the most adequate instruments to address the crisis. This stance was driven by Finland's military non-alignment and long-standing support for negotiated solutions to crises between Russia and the West. These differences did not prevent national leaders from agreeing on a common position in the Ukraine crisis, combining the support for a diplomatic solution with economic sanctions against Russia.

However, Polish narratives began to diverge from German and Finnish discourses on several issues in early 2015. Following the signing of the Minsk-2 agreement and the de-escalation of the conflict in the Donbass, German leaders saw their diplomatic efforts vindicated and pursued a broader relaxation of tensions with Russia. This included the continuation of historical reconciliation with Moscow, as shown by Merkel and Steinmeier's trips to Russia in May 2015, and the support of the Nord Stream-2 pipeline in the following months. Moreover, German leaders advocated cooperation with Russia in other policy and regional scenarios, most notably the Syrian crisis and the fight against terrorism. While Germany's continued support of EU sanctions meant that it was not back to 'business as usual' with Russia, these developments signalled that the tenets of Ostpolitik remained influential in German foreign policy thinking. German leaders continued to consider Russia as a fundamental interlocutor in the construction of a stable European security system. Finnish official discourses evolved along similar lines. Finnish leaders remained firm in their condemnation of Russian actions in Ukraine, but argued for upholding cooperation with Moscow in other regional scenarios, notably the Arctic and the Baltic Sea. Despite stronger threat perceptions, conceptualisations of Russia as a neighbour with whom dialogue and cooperation were indispensable remained dominant.

Polish official discourses developed differently. The new Polish government appointed in the fall of 2014 adopted a harsher rhetoric towards Russia, which contemplated both deeper economic sanctions and the provision of military aid to Ukraine. In a sudden departure from the policy of historical reconciliation previously pursued by the Tusk government, Foreign Minister Schetyna and President Komorowski appeared keen on confronting Russia in the field of memory politics. During 2015, Polish leaders portrayed themselves as ambassadors for Ukraine in the EU and stated that the integration of Ukraine in EU structures was part of Poland's *raison d'état*. Contrary to Germany and Finland's policies, dialogue with Russia was restricted to a minimum. From the Polish perspective, the Ukraine crisis remained far more important than any other regional scenario in which Russia could possibly become a cooperative partner.

These discursive differences highlight the fragility of the EU's posture vis-à-vis the Ukraine crisis. As this chapter has shown, different and deep-rooted constructions of Russia in national identities continue to act as centrifugal forces in the European discursive arena.

Chapter Eight

Conclusion: Towards a Shared Discourse on Russia?

This book examined the relationship between national identity and official discourses about Russia in three member states of the European Union. One of its key aims was to assess to what extent the 'othering' of Russia was still an important component of foreign policy discourses in the countries under analysis in the years 2005–15. Through a comparison of national narratives, the book also explored prospects for the emergence of a shared European discourse on Russia. The analysis showed that national identity and historically constructed images of Russia permeated foreign policy narratives, both in the national and the European discursive arena. Based on the outcome of this research, it is also possible to make some general remarks concerning the study of international relations.

National identities are a key factor of international politics. They play an essential role both in inter-state relations and within international organisations. Some scholars (see Delanty 1995; Habermas 2003) have described the EU as a post-national organisation, namely an entity where supranational structures are more important than nation states and national identity. However, this book has shown that the EU constitutes no exception: national identity deeply influences foreign policy debates in the EU discursive arena also. Hence, national identity is an essential construct that neither International Relations scholars nor their colleagues working in the sub-discipline of European Studies can ignore. Within the study of national identity, particular attention must be devoted to the politics of memory. Narratives about a country's past are fundamental components of national identity because they define the historical heritage of the nation and create a reciprocal sense of obligation among its members over time. Furthermore, the study of memory politics exposes the construction of a country's historical Others and their impact on national identity formation. It is therefore essential for an investigation of EU member states' relations with Russia, which is one of Europe's main historical Others.

The book focused on the role that national identities and memory politics play in foreign policy narratives. Divergent national foreign policy discourses were expected because Russia played different roles in identity construction in the EU member states under analysis. The case studies confirmed this expectation. However, the analysis also suggested that, from 2008 onwards, German, Polish and Finnish official discourses about Russia started to display several similarities. In order to explain this shift, the book argued that political elites favouring a pragmatic relationship with Russia became dominant in the three countries under analysis. Having won the contest for political leadership, these elites constructed foreign policy narratives drawing on national identity discourses that were functional to a pragmatic approach to Russia. Where such discourses were not available, as in the Polish case, the governing elite attempted to forge a new narrative and partly reshape the country's foreign policy identity.

Russia's violations of international law and military assertiveness during the Ukraine crisis posed a serious challenge to narratives focusing on pragmatism and economic partnership. National leaders condemned unanimously Russian breaches of international law, and the EU managed to formulate a united response to the crisis. However, the ensuing confrontation with Russia has reawakened historical constructions of the Russian Other in national discourses. As conceptualisations of the Russian Other differ in the national identities and foreign policy traditions of the countries under analysis, national narratives began to diverge again, particularly in the course of 2015. While this has not yet impeded a common EU stance towards Russia, it will most probably make the formulation of shared policies more contested and controversial in the future. The current disagreements between Germany and some East–Central European member states on the Nord Stream-2 project and the permanent stationing of NATO troops in Eastern Europe exemplify this issue.

The following sections revisit the main findings and arguments of this research, drawing conclusions on the prospects for the emergence of a shared discourse on Russia in the European Union.

National identity and foreign policy discourse: reassessing the research puzzle

The divided nature of EU foreign policy towards Russia provided the initial empirical stimulus for this work. In the last decade, Russia was a country of great economic and strategic importance for the EU. However, it was also one of the most controversial partners for European foreign policy makers. The statement of former EU trade commissioner Peter Mandelson (cited in Kagan 2008: 14) that no other country revealed the EU's internal differences as much as Russia epitomised the relevance of this conundrum for European foreign policy. As these differences followed national fault lines, an adequate understanding of the issue had to focus on the domestic, national level of analysis.

EU member states have a long history of differentiated and in some cases very controversial relations with Russia, which had an impact on national identity construction. The book theorised that divergent discourses on Russia within the EU could be explained by using national identity as an interpretive framework. In order to do this, the research relied primarily on social constructivist scholarship that conceptualises identity as a cognitive device, providing national leaders with an understanding of other countries' motives, interests and actions. As Richard Ned Lebow (2008a) and Jeffrey Checkel (2006) have argued, identities are malleable constructs that guide the formulation of national interests and foreign policy decisions. Conversely, identity is exogenous to neorealist and neoliberal theory. Neoliberal and neorealist scholars tend to consider identities as constant factors which do not influence agents and structures.

Social constructivists contend that identity is an important constituent of international relations which is shaped by the interaction with one or more significant Others. However, different schools of thought exist within constructivism on the role of Others in identity formation and the epistemological approach to studying the relationship between identity and foreign policy discourses. Alexander Wendt (1999) claimed that conflict with external Others is an essential element of national identity construction. In addition, he adopted a positivist approach to the study of international relations, theorising a causal relationship between identity and foreign policy. Wendt's epistemology was criticised by those scholars who claimed that identities are not logically bounded entities and cannot be used as explanatory categories in causal models due to their complexity (Zehfuss 2001). Richard Ned Lebow (2008a) argued that identity is not always constructed in opposition to an Other; identity formation also entails positive interaction with external actors and the assimilation of elements of foreign cultures. Furthermore, Ole Wæver (2002: 22) contended that Wendt's approach neglected material power and therefore failed to account for an essential factor of international politics.

The book attempted to refine the Wendtian approach by addressing this criticism and incorporating its most compelling observations into a revised theoretical model. In this respect, it also sought to answer Jeffrey Checkel's (2006) call to bridge rationalist and interpretive constructivist approaches. The relationship between national identity and foreign policy discourses was conceptualised as complex and mutually constitutive, rather than in terms of a unidirectional cause–effect correlation. National identity construction was studied within the domestic constituency and in the context of a country's relations with external actors, allowing for the eventuality of both positive and negative interaction. Furthermore, the theoretical model endogenised material power as a key element of international relations that acquires significance within particular political contexts and discursive constructions.

The formulation of an identity-based model for the study of European foreign policy discourses on Russia was the book's main theoretical contribution. The application of discourse-historical analysis and the adoption of a historicist approach to the study of foreign policy discourses were the key methodological innovations of this work. The discourse-historical approach, a variant of critical discourse analysis developed by Ruth Wodak (2002b), had previously been applied to examine media and institutional debates about immigration and identity politics (see Krzyzanowski 2010 and 2009; Oberhuber *et al.* 2005; Reisigl and Wodak 2001; Wodak 2009). This book provided the first application of the methodology to the study of official European discourses on Russia and their relationship with national identity.

Thanks to the interdisciplinary nature of the discourse–historical approach, it was possible to integrate the theoretical model of the book with an interpretive framework that was largely derived from the findings of historical scholarship. As argued, national identity construction takes place over a long time span. For most European nations, this process dates back from the nineteenth century or earlier (see Gellner 1983; Guibernau and Hutchinson 2004; Hobsbawm 1990; Smith 1996a). Therefore, the book contended that current discourses are best studied in a *longue durée* perspective. This approach proved very apt for the understanding of the historical dimension of foreign policy narratives.

In order to explain why a particular discourse acquired or lost dominance, the analysis focused on foreign policy leaders' agency, notably their pursuit of political and economic goals and their reactions to developments in international structures. For instance, it was claimed that, after 2007, Polish leaders developed a new discourse on Russia in order to pursue economic and political objectives. Moreover, it was argued that Finnish discourses on internal developments in Russia became more critical in response to the increasing repressiveness of the Kremlin's policies in the spring of 2012. These findings suggest that a more thorough analysis of agency can contribute to explaining change in constructivist and discourse analytical approaches. Furthermore, it would tackle one of the recurrent issues of social constructivist approaches, which have struggled to address adequately the problem of agency (see Knafo 2008: 13).

National identities and Russia's role as Other in historical perspective

The investigation of national identity construction and historical narratives about Russia revealed considerable differences among the three countries under analysis, which were mostly linked to distinct historical experiences. Controversial bilateral relations with Russia in the past left an enduring trace in German, Polish and Finnish identities. While in Germany and Finland, positive and negative narratives about Russia coexisted and alternately became dominant, mainstream Polish discourses were unambiguously negative throughout the country's modern history.

In Germany, narratives portraying Russia as authoritarian and corrupt existed side by side with those depicting it as an important economic and strategic partner. Criticism of Soviet and Russian authoritarianism in post-war (West) Germany can be seen as a reflection of the country's own history. Following the catastrophic outcome of Wilhelmine and Nazi authoritarianism, the Federal Republic of Germany restructured German identity around democratic principles and the respect of human rights. This led the country to adhere to international institutions that claimed to support these principles (notably NATO and the European Union) and opposed Soviet authoritarianism.

However, from the late 1960s the Federal Republic adopted a more cooperative approach towards the Soviet Union, which became enshrined in the concept of Ostpolitik. The Ostpolitik discourse advocated dialogue and partnership with the Soviet Union. It argued that the resulting rapprochement with Moscow would lead to positive domestic change in the Soviet Union. Ostpolitik was also seen as contributing to Germany's economic interests and preference for a multilateral approach to international relations. German narratives depicted Soviet Russia as a key actor in the international arena and a partner that had to be engaged in a multilateral context. The Ostpolitik discourse became dominant and was endorsed by all the main political parties in the Federal Republic.

By contrast, dominant Polish historical narratives consistently portrayed Russia as one of the main national threats. The image of Russia as Poland's main Other was functional to the construction of discourses on Polish heroism and martyrdom, which are central to Polish national identity. According to these narratives, Poland fought valiantly against Russian imperialism and authoritarianism for most of its modern history, thereby sacrificing itself for the defence of Western civilisation. However, Poland's commitment was not reciprocated by its Western allies, which (as the narrative goes) abandoned it to its fate during the Tsarist and Soviet occupations. Religious imagery drawing on the country's Catholic identity was used to bolster the discourse on martyrdom. Poland was described as 'the Christ of nations', sacrificing itself for the sake of the other European peoples.

The construction of Russia as oriental, undemocratic and corrupt also served the function of relativizing Poland's cultural distance from the West. Polish narratives stressed the superiority of Polish over Russian culture in order to claim that, in spite of its long political subjugation to Russia, Poland belonged to the West. In the foreign policy of post-communist Poland, this discourse translated into a strong Euro-Atlantic orientation and opposition to Russia. Only in the late 2000s did dominant official narratives partially change, allowing for the emergence of a discourse that portrayed Russia as a potential partner within a pragmatic foreign policy.

In Finnish historical narratives, dominant representations of Russia changed considerably over time. For most of the nineteenth century, Tsarist Russia was portrayed as a benevolent Other, which had allowed Finland to emancipate itself from Swedish rule and granted political autonomy within the structures of the empire. Positive perceptions faded out in the latter part of the century, when the Tsarist Empire attempted to russify ethnic Finns. Tensions between newly independent Finland and Soviet Russia intensified in the interwar period, reaching a peak during the military confrontation that lasted almost uninterruptedly from 1939 until 1944.

Post-war Finland largely reformulated its identity and foreign policy posture. Anti-Russian narratives were considered responsible for the escalation that had dragged the country into a disastrous war and were marginalised in official discourse. Soviet Russia was reconceptualised as an important partner. During the Cold War, the cooperative stance towards Moscow allowed Finland to retain independent political and economic structures and fulfil its self-perception as a bridge between East and West. Military neutrality, the practical outcome of Finland's positioning between East and West, became part of the country's national identity and remained an essential constituent of its international posture after the end of the Cold War. At the same time, Russian military might and economic influence continued to be sources of insecurity for the Finnish elite. After the fall of the Soviet Union, these preoccupations were voiced more openly in official discourse, showing that perceptions of Russia as a potential threat persisted in spite of economic and diplomatic cooperation.

Having reviewed national identity formation and historical narratives about Russia in the selected countries, the book assessed whether these constructions had an impact on official discourses on Russia in recent years. In order to do this, four case studies of high relevance for EU–Russia relations were investigated. The chapter concerning the Nord Stream pipeline focused on discourses about Russia's energy power and related European energy security issues. Perceptions of Russia as a security and military actor were investigated in the case studies on the August 2008 crisis in Georgia and the Ukraine crisis. The chapter on post-electoral mass demonstrations in Russian cities in 2011–12 allowed an assessment of whether the normative constituents of German, Polish and Finnish identity were reflected in official pronouncements concerning Russia.

A European cacophony: national discourses on Nord Stream

The analysis of official discourses on Nord Stream revealed considerable divergences across member states, particularly in the years 2005–7. The debate on the construction of the pipeline became highly politicised and Polish officials made extensive use of memory politics in order to justify their opposition to the project. German leaders also made selective references to the past in order to back their policy. Conflicting German, Polish and Finnish historical narratives about Russia re-emerged in official statements. In this context, national identity provided an excellent framework to interpret official discourses.

German leaders' positive attitude to energy cooperation with Russia was explained with reference to the Ostpolitik tradition. German officials cited the history of German–Russian cooperation in the energy field from the 1970s onwards to argue that Russia was a reliable partner. Their claims that energy cooperation would also have positive repercussions in other fields, particularly for the dialogue on human rights and democracy with Russia, reflected the Ostpolitik logic of 'change through rapprochement'. This approach predicated that Western cooperation with Moscow would eventually lead to political and social change in Russia. Furthermore, German leaders attempted to reconcile their stance towards Russia with Germany's pro-European identity by claiming that Russia and the EU were interdependent in the field of energy, hence the German–Russian energy partnership served broader EU interests.

Polish leaders had a diametrically opposed view of German–Russian energy cooperation. They argued that it was detrimental to Polish interests and allowed Russia to use its energy power as an instrument to coerce Poland. In addition, they formulated analogies with German–Soviet cooperation at the beginning of the Second World War, which had resulted in the destruction of the Polish state. The construction of Russia as a threatening, imperialist power in Polish identity played a central role in this discourse. Moreover, Berlin's stance on Nord Stream reawakened Polish identity narratives portraying Germany as a menacing Other. This provided evidence for the theoretical arguments made in this book about the complexity of the construction of the Other in national identity (*see* Chapter Two). Multiple Others, notably Russia and Germany, played a role in shaping Polish foreign policy discourses.

Polish leaders also claimed that Nord Stream negatively affected European energy security as a whole because, by cutting off several EU member states, it showed the lack of solidarity within the European Union. This argument mirrored the Polish identity narrative about Poland's unreciprocated commitment to the West. It was argued that, in the Nord Stream controversy, Germany had proven a disloyal partner for Poland and other East–Central European countries. Following Donald Tusk's rise to power in late 2007, the use of identity and historical narratives against Nord Stream became less prominent in Polish official discourse. However, Polish leaders upheld their opposition to the project, relying mostly on economic arguments.

Finnish discourses on Nord Stream reflected the dichotomous construction of Russia in Finnish identity as both an important economic partner and a potential security threat. On the one hand, Finnish leaders portrayed the pipeline as a positive development, arguing that the EU needed additional energy infrastructure and that Russia had already proven to be a reliable supplier. On the other hand, they emphasised the normative foundations for energy cooperation with Russia (notably the respect of market and EU rules) and the potential environmental threats deriving from the construction of the pipeline. Finnish leaders' final decision to allow the building of Nord Stream in Finnish territorial waters can be understood within the established Finnish foreign policy tradition of engaging Russia and pursuing norm-based cooperation.

Overall, discourses on Nord Stream varied depending on the ways in which Russia's energy power was conceptualised in national identity narratives. In Poland, it was constructed as an instrument for Russia's geopolitical and imperialist goals, hence dominant discourses were very critical. In Germany, and also to some extent in Finland, it was perceived as an opportunity for enhancing trade and EU–Russia relations as a whole. Therefore, the different perceptions of Russia's energy power confirmed the theoretical assumption that material power acquires significance only within specific discursive constructions (*see* Chapter Two; see Wæver 2002: 22) Furthermore, the case study exposed multiple and ambivalent representations of Russia, which is consistent with Iver Neumann's (1998) claim that Russia is a liminal case of European identity: depending on the circumstances and context, European discourses either externalise it as a threat or portray it as part of geographic, cultural and economic constructions of Europe.

From a broader theoretical perspective, this case study also showed that national identities can lead to discursive conflicts in the international arena. As argued in the theoretical section of this work, national identities play an important role in interest formation. Hence, if identities are radically different, countries will develop divergent foreign policy interests and priorities. This implies that, if EU member states want to forge a common foreign policy, national identities will have to be reconciled and at least partially reconstructed around shared values and discourses.

The rocky path towards a shared discourse: the August 2008 war

Divergences were found also among national discourses concerning the Russian–Georgian war of August 2008. As in the previous case study, German and Polish leaders provided different readings of events, drawing largely on dominant narratives in national memory and identity. However, most discourses across the three national case studies were not as conflictual and irreconcilable as those concerning Nord Stream. This is particularly significant if we take into account that the events in question (Russia's military intervention outside its borders, in another European state) were highly dramatic and could have produced more radical responses in countries where Russia was traditionally perceived as a security threat. Only the Polish president formulated a very critical, anti-Russian narrative, which, however, did not find resonance in other Polish, German and Finnish official discourses.

German leaders rejected confrontation with Moscow and dismissed arguments about the beginning of a new Cold War with Russia, which were widespread in the international media and official discourses during the August 2008 crisis. German collective memories of the Cold War, particularly the country's division and the possibility of nuclear war on German soil, influenced the stance of policy makers in Berlin. German criticism of Russia during the crisis was mild, focusing primarily on the disproportionate nature of Russian military intervention and on the need to seek a mediated solution to the crisis. This discourse was a reflection of fundamental constituents of post-1945 German national identity, such as the rejection of war as a means to solve disputes, the support of multilateralism and international law. Ultimately, however, German leaders were reluctant to abandon their long-standing, cooperative stance towards Russia. Despite the tensions caused by the military escalation, the Ostpolitik approach prevailed.

In Poland, official positions on the crisis were discordant. This was mostly due to the fact that the president of the republic and the government (which were supported by different political forces) pursued divergent domestic and foreign policy goals and used national identity narratives differently. Polish president Lech Kaczynski formulated a discourse that was profoundly hostile towards Russia and drew from Polish identity narratives portraying Russia as aggressive, imperialist and incompatible with Western civilisation. On the other hand, Donald Tusk's government combined criticism with the advocacy of continued engagement with Russia. The book made the claim that this approach was part of a broader policy of the new Polish government, which aimed at normalising relations with Moscow and marginalising traditional anti-Russian attitudes in official discourse. Thus, Polish leaders' statements about the August 2008 crisis demonstrated the complexity of the national foreign policy arena, where conflicting discourses coexist and compete for dominance.

The analysis of Finnish official statements highlighted two dominant discourses. In contrast to the Polish case, where the two main official narratives were prominent at the same time, each discourse gained dominance at different stages of the crisis. In the tense months before the outbreak of war and during the military conflict, perceptions of Russia as a security challenge prevailed. The second discourse became dominant in the post-war period and advocated a quick resumption of the partnership with Moscow. The two discourses mirrored the dichotomous construction of Russia in Finnish identity as both a potential security threat and an essential partner. The shift in dominance from one discourse to the other did not occur abruptly, neither were the two discourses completely discordant. At the peak of the crisis, Finnish leaders voiced concerns about the security threat emanating from Russia, but they simultaneously advocated engagement with Moscow as the best way to defuse tensions. A gradual transition from the first to the second discourse occurred as the crisis de-escalated, reflecting the malleability and adaptability of discursive constructions.

Hence, with the exception of Lech Kaczynski's discourse, the analysis of official narratives about the August 2008 war revealed some convergence across the three national arenas under investigation. Conflicting views still existed; the image of Russia as a potential security threat influenced Polish and (to a lesser extent) Finnish discourses, whereas it hardly played a role in German narratives. Moreover, German and Finnish leaders were keener than their Polish colleagues to resume cooperation with Russia when the crisis de-escalated. However, narratives advocating a pragmatic approach to Moscow were prominent across the three national discursive arenas. By emphasising constructions of Russia as an important security and commercial partner, national leaders conveyed the message that engagement was the best policy option. This also suggested that, in the three countries under analysis, narratives about economic and security cooperation helped to reconcile discourses on Russia.

Paving the way for a common stance: pragmatism and economics

The case study concerning discourses on mass protests in Russian cities in 2011 and 2012 exposed the growing focus on Russia as an economic partner in German, Polish and Finnish official narratives. As the events in question signalled an unambiguous authoritarian shift in Moscow, the re-emergence of historical narratives portraying Russia as undemocratic was to be expected. However, the analysis showed that these narratives were marginal in official discourse. Representations of Russia as a key commercial partner and the advocacy of a pragmatic approach to bilateral relations overshadowed the normative discourse.

A very critical discourse on the Russian establishment was prominent only among some German officials during the first months of the protests. It was propagated by second-in-rank representatives of the foreign ministry, who managed to influence the relevant domestic debate while Germany's top leaders appeared reluctant to comment on internal developments in Russia. As the Russian presidential election of March 2012 approached, Chancellor Merkel and Foreign Minister Westerwelle intervened more frequently in the debate, arguing that cooperation with Russia and criticism of its domestic developments were not mutually exclusive. This discourse attempted to reconcile the normative component of German identity with constructions of Russia as a key economic partner. Due to

Merkel and Westerwelle's greater political prominence and media visibility, their narrative quickly became dominant, which highlighted the discursive power of national leaders in foreign policy debates.

Polish discourses revealed that, four years into Tusk's mandate, Poland's new pragmatic approach to Russia had been consolidated in the country's foreign policy. Following Lech Kaczynski's sudden death and the election of the more moderate Bronislaw Komorowski to the presidency in 2010, the Russophobic far right no longer had any representatives in top foreign policy posts. This allowed Poland to formulate a more coherent official stance towards Russia. Throughout 2011 and 2012, Polish official statements about Russia focused on practical issues (i.e. trade, cross-border mobility of citizens) and reconciliation in bilateral relations. When asked to comment on the protests, Foreign Minister Sikorski expressed sympathy for the demonstrators. Otherwise, he continued to advocate cooperation with the Russian authorities.

The stance of Finnish leaders was similar to that of their German and Polish counterparts. As Russia was Finland's main trade partner, Finnish policy makers rejoiced when Moscow joined the World Trade Organization in mid-December 2011. Despite electoral fraud and mounting protests in Russian cities, economic considerations dominated Finnish official discourses on Russia throughout the following winter. A more critical narrative focusing on Russia's domestic developments emerged in the spring of 2012, as the Kremlin adopted harsher measures to curb the protests. However, this narrative did not preclude economic cooperation. Russia's democratic deficit was relativized through claims according to which Russian society was fundamentally different from Finland's and hence had to be judged from a different perspective. Together with the construction of Russia as a key partner for Finland, this logic was used to justify further economic cooperation despite Moscow's repressive policies.

Hence, the national discourses under analysis showed a high level of convergence. By stressing that Russia remained a key partner in spite of its domestic developments, national leaders implicitly established a scale of priorities in which economic interests ranked higher than normative considerations. As seen in Chapter Three, both narratives stressing the principles of democracy and human rights and constructions of Russia as an economic partner were rooted in the national identities under analysis – with the exception of Poland, where the discourse depicting Russia as a partner had emerged more recently. In the winter of 2011–12, against the broader context of Russia's increasing economic importance and integration in international economic structures, the narrative about economic partnership emerged as dominant. This substantiates the claim made earlier in this work that international structures influence the domestic contest among conflicting identity discourses.

National leaders also played a key role in this contest. As theorised in Chapter Two, they were not simply influenced by identity discourses, but actively contributed to determining the dominance of one over another. This case study showed that policy makers emphasise particular identity constructions in order to pursue their domestic and foreign policy goals (in this case, supporting cooperation with Moscow and the national industry that traded with Russia). It is significant that the leaders of three countries which traditionally had different stances towards Russia chose to emphasise the same construction, namely that of Russia as a partner. This suggests that economic and political pragmatism potentially provided the discursive foundation for a shared stance towards Russia within the European Union. However, Russia's military intervention in Ukraine in 2014 provoked a deep crisis between Moscow and the EU. Russia's violations of international law were perceived as much more serious than in 2008. Consequently, normative and security discourses largely supplanted economic ones.

Russia and the Ukraine crisis: again a threatening and divisive Other?

In the countries under analysis, dominant discourses condemned Russia's annexation of Crimea and destabilisation of Eastern Ukraine from a normative perspective. Moreover, Russian actions revived historical perceptions of the country as a security challenge, most notably in Poland. Discourses portraying Russia as an economic and strategic partner lost dominance. In 2014, EU leaders agreed on pursuing a peaceful solution to the Ukraine crisis, which combined negotiations with punitive measures against Russia. Agreement on this strategy is reflected in the contemporary German, Polish and Finnish narratives. It prompted a coherent EU response to the crisis in the form of diplomatic and economic sanctions against Russia.

On the surface, the consistent support of all EU member states for the sanctions suggests that the EU found a united position towards Moscow, and that national discourses could be reconciled by focusing on the construction of Russia as an antagonistic Other. However, this research has highlighted that the current unity is precarious. At a discursive level, national positions on Russia began to diverge in 2015. Both German and Finnish leaders highlighted the importance of upholding cooperation with Russia in several strategic policy fields. German officials argued for cooperation with Moscow in energy trade, the Syrian crisis and the fight against international terrorism. They also supported the process of historical reconciliation through joint commemorations with their Russian counterparts of the seventieth anniversary of the end of the Second World War. Finnish leaders argued that cooperation with Russia should continue in regional forums concerning the Baltic and the Arctic. Ultimately, the German and Finnish stance reflected the deeply engrained belief that Russia remains a fundamental interlocutor for the construction of a stable European security system, even if a difficult one. In Finland, maintaining a dialogue with Russia is also considered fundamental for national security, due to the long shared border and common environmental challenges.

Conversely, Polish discourses towards Russia have taken on a more confrontational stance during 2015. This is partly due to the departure from power of Donald Tusk and Radoslaw Sikorski, who had crafted a more balanced and pragmatic foreign policy approach to Moscow between 2007 and 2014. Tusk and Sikorski's foreign policy had marked a clear shift from traditional Polish views of

Russia as a threatening and imperialist Other. With the change of leadership, the previous approach has largely regained dominance. During 2015, Polish leaders portrayed themselves as spokespersons for Ukraine in the EU and contemplated the provision of military aid to Kiev. For Warsaw, the Ukraine crisis was of paramount importance; the security threat emanating from Russian actions there could not be alleviated through cooperation in other contexts.

Under these circumstances, future prospects for a shared stance towards Russia within the EU look difficult. Moscow's policies in Ukraine have reawakened constructions of Russia as an antagonistic Other in national identities. As these constructions and consolidated strategies to address the Russian Other differ in each national context, their policy outcomes are divisive. This study has shown that othering and antagonising Russia has not proved to be a cohesive factor for EU member states in the recent past. The controversial debates surrounding the construction of the Nord Stream pipelines epitomise this. Different and divisive historical narratives resurfaced, leading to contrasting assessments of the nature of the Russian Other.

However, this research also highlighted that EU member states are not merely at the mercy of identity-driven divisions. The agency of policy makers plays an essential role in determining which particular narrative becomes dominant. National leaders have the discursive power to marginalise the most polarising constituents of national identity. Indeed, during the Tusk government, the Polish leadership formulated a new, pragmatic discourse that temporarily marginalised pre-existing conceptualisations of Russia as a threatening Other. On the other hand, in 2014 German policy makers steered official debates in such a way that allowed normative discourses to gain dominance over economic ones. The results of this research suggest that national leaders were able to formulate a shared discursive stance vis-à-vis Russia when they adopted a pragmatic stance and normative discourses. Conversely, narratives based on national memory politics proved highly divisive.

Hence, the shared stance of EU member states could be preserved if they maintain a pragmatic and normative approach towards Russia, both in the Ukraine crisis and in other scenarios. Such an approach would also prevent the crystallisation of images of Russia as a threatening Other, which would fuel distrust and conflict in Europe. As this research has shown, the boundaries between Self and Other are fluid and positive interaction can occur. During the last decade, German, Polish and Finnish policy makers often portrayed Russia as a partner. Despite the current crisis, processes of historical reconciliation – most notably between Germany and Russia – and regional cooperation have continued. Thus, essentialising Russia as a negative Other would mean overlooking the complexities and fluidity of the Self/Other relationship.

References

Aalto, P. and Tynkkynen, N. (2008) 'The Nordic countries: engaging Russia, trading in energy or taming environmental threats?', in P. Aalto (ed.) *The EU–Russian Energy Dialogue*, Aldershot: Ashgate, pp. 119–43.

Aalto, P. and Westphal, K. (2008) 'Introduction', in P. Aalto (ed.) *The EU–Russian Energy Dialogue*, Aldershot: Ashgate, pp. 1–21.

Adler, E. (1992) 'The emergence of cooperation: national epistemic communities and the international evolution of the idea of nuclear arms control', *International Organization*, 46(1): 101–45.

—— (1997) 'Seizing the middle ground: constructivism in world politics', *European Journal of International Relations*, 3(3): 319–363.

Ahonen, P. (2011) 'Unity on trial: the Mauerschützenprozesse and the East–West rifts of unified Germany', in A. Fuchs, K. James-Chakraborty and L. Shortt (eds) *Debating German Cultural Identity since 1989*, Rochester, NY: Camden House, pp. 30–45.

Ahrens, A. and Weiss H. (2012) 'The image of Russia in the editorials of German newspapers (2001–2008)', in R. Krumm, H. Schröder and S. Medvedev (eds) *Constructing Identities in Europe: German and Russian perspectives*, Baden-Baden: Nomos, pp. 147–69.

Albert, R. (1995) 'Das Sowjetunion-Bild in der sozialliberalen Ostpolitik 1969–1975', *Tel Aviver Jahrbuch für Deutsche Geschichte*, 24: 299–326.

Allison, G. and Zelikow P. (1999) *Essence of Decision: Explaining the Cuban missile crisis*, New York: Longman.

Anderson, B. (1991) *Imagined Communities: Reflections on the origin and spread of nationalism*, London: Verso.

Arnold-de Simine, S. (ed.) (2005) *Memory Traces: 1989 and the question of German cultural identity*, Bern: Peter Lang.

Ash, T. G. (1993) *In Europe's Name: Germany and the divided continent*, London: Jonathan Cape.

—— (2002) *The Polish Revolution: Solidarity*, New Haven, CT: Yale University Press.

—— (2011) 'This tortured Polish–Russian story is something we can all learn from', *The Guardian*, 23 February. www.guardian.co.uk/commentisfree/2011/feb/23/tortured-polish-russian-story (accessed on 19 July 2016).

Asmus, R. (2010) *A Little War that Shook the World: Georgia, Russia and the future of the West*, Basingstoke: Palgrave Macmillan.

Assmann, A. (2006) *Der Lange Schatten der Vergangenheit: Erinnerungskultur und Geschichtspolitik*, Munich: C. H. Beck.

Auswärtiges Amt (2014) 'Partners in Europe'. www.auswaertiges-amt.de/EN/Aussenpolitik/RegionaleSchwerpunkte/Russland/Russland_node.html (accessed 10 August 2016).

Averre, D. (2009) 'From Pristina to Tskhinvali: the legacy of Operation Allied Force in Russia's relations with the West', *International Affairs*, 85(3): 575–91.

Balmaceda, M. (2012) 'Russia's central and eastern European energy transit corridor', in P. Aalto (ed.) *Russia's Energy Policies: National, interregional and global levels*, Cheltenham: Edward Elgar, pp. 136–55.

Banchoff, T. (1999) 'German identity and European integration', *European Journal of International Relations*, 5(3): 259–89.

Barnett, M. (1996) 'Identity and alliances in the Middle East', in P. Katzenstein (ed.) *The Culture of National Security: Norms and identity in world politics*, New York: Columbia University Press, pp. 400–50.

Bayley, P. and Williams, G. (2012) *European Identity: What the media say*, Oxford: Oxford University Press.

BBC News (2012) 'Russian patriarch Kirill makes historic visit to Poland', 16 August. www.bbc.com/news/world-europe-19281205 (accessed 11 August 2016).

—— (2015a) 'Poland leak scandal: three ministers and Speaker resign', 10 June. www.bbc.com/news/world-europe-33089659 (accessed 23 August 2016).

—— (2015b) 'Europe and US mark VE Day anniversary', 8 May. www.bbc.com/news/world-europe-32619704 (accessed 23 August 2016).

Bedani, G. and Huddock, B. (eds) (2000) *The Politics of Italian National Identity*, Cardiff: University of Wales Press.

Bell, D. (2006) 'Introduction: memory, trauma and world politics', in D. Bell (ed.) *Memory, Trauma and World Politics*, Basingstoke: Palgrave Macmillan, pp. 1–32.

Benner, E. (2001) 'Is there a core national doctrine?', *Nations and Nationalism*, 7(2): 155–74.

Berger, S. (1997) *The Search for Normality: National identity and historical consciousness in Germany since 1800*, Oxford: Berghahn.

Berger, T. (1996) 'Norms, identity and national security in Germany and Japan', in P. Katzenstein (ed.) *The Culture of National Security: Norms and identity in world politics*, New York: Columbia University Press, pp. 317–56.

—— (2002) 'The power of memory and memories of power: the cultural parameters of German foreign policy making since 1945', in J. Müller (ed.) *Memory and Power in Post-War Europe*, Cambridge: Cambridge University Press, pp. 76–99.

Bikont, A. (2012) *My z Jedwabnego*, Wolowiec: Wydawnictwo Czarne.

Bjola, C. and Kornprobst, M. (2007) 'Security communities and the habitus of restraint: Germany and the United States on Iraq', *Review of International Studies*, 33(2): 285–305.

Blaikie, N. (2010) *Designing Social Research*, Cambridge (MA): Polity Press.

Blank, S. (2009) 'From neglect to duress: the West and the Georgian crisis before the 2008 war', in S. Cornell and F. Starr (eds) *The Guns of August: Russia's war in Georgia*, London: M. E. Sharpe, pp. 104–21.

—— (2010) 'Crisis in the Caucasus: Russia, Georgia and the West', in P. Rich (ed.) *Crisis in the Caucasus: Russia, Georgia and the West*, London: Routledge, pp. 175–201.

Bode, N. and Makarychev, A. (2013) 'The new social media in Russia. Political blogging by the government and the opposition', *Problems of Post-Communism*, 60(2): 53–62.

Boyd, C. (1997) *Historia Patria: Politics, history, and national identity in Spain, 1875–1975*, Princeton, NJ: Princeton University Press.

Bridge, R. (2011) 'Visa-free travel gets a lift from Russia–Poland agreement', *Russia Today*, 14 December. http://rt.com/politics/russia-poland-moscow-visa-free-travel-katyn-767/ (accessed 11 August 2016).

Browning, C. (2003) 'The region-building approach revisited: the continued othering of Russia in discourses of region-building in the European North', *Geopolitics*, 8(1): 45–71.

—— (2007) 'Branding Nordicity: models, identity and the decline of exceptionalism', *Cooperation and Conflict*, 42(1): 27–51.

—— (2008) *Constructivism, Narrative and Foreign Policy Analysis*, Bern: Peter Lang.

Browning, C. and Lehti, M. (2007) 'Beyond East–West: marginality and national dignity in Finnish identity construction', *Nationalities Papers*, 35(4): 691–716.

Brubaker, R. (1996) 'Nationalizing states in the old "New Europe" – and the new', *Ethnic and Racial Studies*, 19(2): 411–37.

Bryman, A. (2008) *Social Research Methods*, Oxford: Oxford University Press.

Burridge, T. (2016) 'Ukraine conflict: daily reality of east's "frozen war"', *BBC News*, 15 April. www.bbc.com/news/world-europe-35990401 (accessed 15 August 2016).

Cadier, D. (2014) 'Eastern Partnership vs Eurasian Union? The EU–Russia competition in the shared neighbourhood and the Ukraine crisis', *Global Policy*, 5(Supplement 1): 76–85.

Campbell, D. (1998) *Writing Security: United States foreign policy and the politics of identity*, Minneapolis, MN: University of Minnesota Press.

Casier, T. (2011) 'The rise of energy to the top of the EU–Russia agenda: from interdependence to dependence?', *Geopolitics*, 16(3): 536–52.

Castle, S. (2006) 'Poles angry at pipeline pact', *The Independent*, 1 May, www.independent.co.uk/news/world/europe/poles-angry-at-pipeline-pact-6102171.html (accessed 18 July 2016).

Chaisty, P. and Whitefield, S. (2012) 'The effects of the global financial crisis on Russian political attitudes', *Post-Soviet Affairs*, 28(2): 187–208.

Checkel, J. (1998) 'The Constructivist turn in IR Theory', *World Politics*, 50(2), 324–48.

—— (2004) 'Social Constructivisms in global and European politics: a review essay', *Review of International Studies*, 30(2): 229–44.

—— (2006) 'Constructivism and EU politics', in K. E. Jorgensen, M. Pollack and B. Rosamond (eds) *Handbook of European Union Politics*, London: Sage, pp. 57–76.

—— (2008) 'Constructivism and foreign policy', in S. Smith, A. Hadfield and T. Dunne (eds) *Foreign Policies: Theories, actors, cases*, Oxford: Oxford University Press, pp. 71–82.

Checkel, J. and Katzenstein, P. (eds) (2009) *European Identity*, Cambridge: Cambridge University Press.

Cichocki, B. (2013) 'Poland', in M. David, J. Gower and H. Haukkala, (eds), *National Perspectives on Russia: European foreign policy in the making?* London: Routledge, 86–100.

Copsey, N. and Pomorska, K. (2014) 'The influence of newer member states in the European Union: the case of Poland and the Eastern Partnership', *Europe–Asia Studies*, 66(3): 421–43.

Cornell, S. and Starr, F. (eds) (2009) *The Guns of August: Russia's war in Georgia*, London: M. E. Sharpe.

Curry, J. L. (2008) 'Poland and the politics of God's playground', in S. L. Wolchik and J. L. Curry (eds) *Central and East European Politics*, Plymouth: Rowman and Littlefield, pp. 165–89.

Daniliouk, N. (2006) *Fremdbilder in der Sprache: Konstruktion, Konnotation, Evolution. Das Russlandbild der Jahre 1961, 1989 und 2003 in ausgewählten deutschen Printmedien*, Münster: Lit Verlag.

David, M., Gower J. and Haukkala, H. (2011) 'Introduction: the European Union and Russia', *Journal of Contemporary European Studies*, 19(2): 183–8.

—— (eds) (2013) *National Perspectives on Russia: European foreign policy in the making?*, London: Routledge.

David, M. and Romanova, T. (2015) 'Modernisation in EU–Russian relations: past, present, and future', *European Politics and Society*, 16(1): 1–10.

Davies, N. (1996) *Europe: A history*, Oxford: Oxford University Press.

Davis Cross, M. (2013) 'Rethinking epistemic communities twenty years later', *Review of International Studies*, 39: 137–60.

De Cilla, R., Reisigl M. and Wodak, R. (1999) 'The discursive construction of national identities', *Discourse and Society*, 10(2): 149–73.

De Custine, A. (1989) *Empire of the Czar: A journey through eternal Russia*, Auckland: Anchor Books.

Delanty, G. (1995) *Inventing Europe: Idea, identity, reality*, London: Palgrave Macmillan.

De Lazari, A. (2011) 'Polish–Russian difficult matters', *The Polish Quarterly of International Affairs*, 1: 72–82.

De Quetteville, H. (2008) 'Condoleezza Rice signs missile defence deal with Poland', *The Telegraph*, 20 August. www.telegraph.co.uk/news/worldnews/europe/poland/2590043/Condoleezza-Rice-signs-missile-defence-deal-with-Poland.html (accessed 9 August 2016).

Easton, A. (2015) 'Poland–Russia row sours Auschwitz commemoration', *BBC News*, 26 January. www.bbc.com/news/blogs-eu-30957027 (accessed 23 August 2016).

Eder, K. (2005) 'Remembering national memories together: the formation of a transnational identity in Europe', in W. Spohn and K. Eder (eds) *Collective Memory and European Identity*, Aldershot: Ashgate, pp. 197–220.

Elder, M. (2011) 'Vladimir Putin set to lose majority amid complaints of electoral violations', *The Guardian*, 4 December. www.theguardian. com/world/2011/dec/04/vladimir-putin-majority-complaints-violations (accessed 10 August 2016).

—— (2012) 'Vladimir Putin's return to presidency preceded by violent protests in Moscow', *The Guardian*, 6 May. www.theguardian.com/world/2012/ may/06/vladimir-putin-presidency-violent-protests-moscow (accessed 10 August 2016).

Emmott, R. (2016) 'EU to extend Russia sanctions, divided over next steps', 20 June, *Reuters*. www.reuters.com/article/us-ukraine-crisis-eu-sanctions-idUSKCN0Z61QE (accessed 17 July 2016).

Etzold, T. and Haukkala, H. (2011) 'Is there a Nordic Russia policy? Swedish, Finnish and Danish relations with Russia in the context of the European Union', *Journal of Contemporary European Studies*, 19(2): 249–60.

European Council (2014) 'Statement of the Heads of State or Government on Ukraine', 6 March. www.consilium.europa.eu/workarea/downloadAsset. aspx?id=15199 (accessed 15 August 2016).

—— (2016) 'EU restrictive measures in response to the crisis in Ukraine'. www. consilium.europa.eu/en/policies/sanctions/ukraine-crisis/ (accessed 15 August 2016).

Evans, A. B. (2012) 'Protests and civil society in Russia: the struggle for the Khimki forest', *Communist and Post-Communist Studies*, 45(3–4): 233–42.

Evans, R. (2003) 'Introduction. Redesigning the past: history in political transitions', *Journal of Contemporary History*, 38(1): 5–12.

Ewans, M. (ed.) (2004) *The Great Game: Britain and Russia in Central Asia*, London: Routledge.

Fedorowicz, K. (2007) 'National identity and national interest in Polish Eastern Policy, 1989–2004', *Nationalities Papers*, 35(3): 537–53.

Feklyunina, V. (2012) 'Russia's foreign policy towards Poland: seeking reconciliation? A social constructivist analysis', *International Politics*, 49(4): 434–48.

Forsberg, T. (ed.) (1995) *Contested Territory: Border disputes at the edge of the former Soviet empire*, Aldershot: Edward Elgar.

—— (2006) 'Finnish–Russian security relations: is Russia still seen as a threat?', in H. Smith (ed.) *The Two-Level Game: Russia's relations with Great Britain, Finland and the European Union*, Helsinki: Aleksanteri Institute, pp. 141–54.

Forsberg, T. and Seppo, A. (2011) 'The Russo–Georgian war and EU mediation', in R. Kanet (ed.) *Russian Foreign Policy in the 21st Century*, Basingstoke: Palgrave Macmillan, pp. 121–37.

Forsberg, T. and Haukkala, H. (2016) *The European Union and Russia*, Basingstoke: Palgrave Macmillan.

Fulbrook, M. (1995) *Anatomy of a Dictatorship: Inside the GDR 1949–1989*, Oxford: Oxford University Press.

—— (1999) *German National Identity after the Holocaust*, Malden, MA: Blackwell.

—— (2011) *Dissonant Lives: Generations and violence through the German dictatorships*, Oxford: Oxford University Press.

Gellner, E. (1983) *Nations and Nationalism*, Ithaca, NY: Cornell University Press.

Gellner, W. and Douglas, J. (eds) (2003) *The Berlin Republic: German unification and a decade of changes*, London: Frank Cass.

Gel'man, V. (2013) 'Cracks in the wall: challenges to electoral authoritarianism in Russia', *Problems of Post-Communism*, 60(2): 3–10.

—— (2016) 'The politics of fear: how Russia's rulers counter their rivals', *Russian Politics*, 1(1): 27–45.

German, T. (2010) 'Pipeline politics: Georgia and energy security', in P. Rich (ed.) *Crisis in the Caucasus: Russia, Georgia and the West*, London: Routledge, pp. 94–112.

Gildea, R. (2002a) 'Myth, memory and policy in France since 1945', in J. Müller (ed.) *Memory and Power in Post-War Europe*, Cambridge: Cambridge University Press, pp. 59–75.

—— (2002b) *France since 1945*, Oxford: Oxford University Press.

Giles, K. and Eskola, S. (2009) *Waking the Neighbour: Finland, NATO and Russia*, Shrivenham, Oxon: Defence Academy of the United Kingdom.

Gill, G. (2012) 'The decline of a dominant party and the destabilization of electoral authoritarianism', *Post-Soviet Affairs*, 28(4): 449–471.

Gillis, J. (1994) 'Memory and identity: the history of a relationship', in J. Gillis (ed.) *Commemorations: The politics of national identity*, Princeton, NJ: Princeton University Press, pp. 3–26.

Gordon, M. R., Smale, A. and Erlanger, S. (2015) 'Western nations split on arming Kiev forces', *The New York Times*, 7 February. www.nytimes.com/2015/02/08/world/europe/divisions-on-display-over-western-response-to-ukraine-at-security-conference.html?_r=0 (accessed 15 August 2016).

Gotev, G. (2015) 'Seven EU countries oppose Nord Stream', *Euractiv*, 30 November. www.euractiv.com/section/energy/news/seven-eu-countries-oppose-nord-stream/ (accessed 15 August 2016).

Gotkowska, J. (2010) 'The German–Russian modernisation partnership: failing to meet great expectations', *Eastweek*, 25, Warsaw: Centre for Eastern Studies, pp. 2–4.

Grass, G. (2002) *Im Krebsgang*, Göttingen: Steidl.

Greene, S. (2013) 'Beyond Bolotnaya: bridging old and new in Russia's election protest movement', *Problems of Post-Communism*, 60(2): 40–52.

Greenfeld, L. (1990) 'The formation of the Russian national identity: the role of status insecurity and ressentiment', *Comparative Studies in Society and History*, 32(3): 549–91.

Grigas, A. (2013) *The Politics of Energy and Memory Between the Baltic States and Russia*, Farnham, UK: Ashgate.

Gromyko, A. (2015) 'Russia–EU relations at a crossroads: preventing a new Cold War in a polycentric world', *Southeast European and Black Sea Studies*, 15(2): 141–9.

The Guardian (2012) 'Hundreds detained after Moscow anti-Putin protest', 5 March. www.theguardian.com/world/blog/2012/mar/05/russian-election-reaction-putin-live (accessed 11 August 2016).

Guibernau, M. (2004) 'Anthony D. Smith on nations and national identity: a critical assessment', *Nations and Nationalism*, 10(1/2): 125–41.

Guibernau, M. and Hutchinson, J. (2004) 'History and national destiny', *Nations and Nationalism*, 10(1/2): 1–8.

Haas, P. (1992) 'Introduction: epistemic communities and international policy coordination', *International Organization*, 46(1): 1–35.

—— (2004) 'When does power listen to truth? A constructivist approach to the policy process', *Journal of European Public Policy*, 11(4): 569–92.

Habermas, J. (2003) 'Toward a cosmopolitan Europe', *Journal of Democracy*, 14(4): 86–100.

Hahn, G. M. (2012) 'Perestroyka 2.0: toward non-revolutionary regime transformation in Russia?', *Post-Soviet Affairs*, 28(4): 472–515.

Halbwachs, M. (1992) *On Collective Memory*, Chicago: University of Chicago Press.

Haller, J. (1917) *Die russische Gefahr im deutschen Haus*, Stuttgart: Engelhorn.

Halonen, T. (2006) Speech at the conference of the Federation of German Industry, 20 June. www.eilen.fi/en/1409/ (accessed 8 August 2016).

—— (2008a) Speech at the Überseeclub in Hamburg, 8 May. www.eilen.fi/en/1247/?language=en (accessed 8 August 2008).

—— (2008b) Speech during her official visit to Italian President of the Republic Giorgio Napolitano, 9 September. www.presidentti.fi/halonen/Public/default83da-2.html?contentid=177686andnodeid=41417andcontentlan=2andculture=en-US (accessed 9 August 2016).

—— (2008c) Speech at the OSCE ministerial council, 4 December. http://formin.finland.fi/public/default.aspx?contentid=144318andcontentlan=2andculture=en-US (accessed 9 August 2016).

—— (2010) Speech at the Estonian parliament, 5 May. www.eilen.fi/en/1098/?language=en (accessed 8 August 2016).

Hamilton, R. (2010) 'The bear came through the tunnel: an analysis of Georgian planning and operations in the Russo–Georgian war and implications for US policy', in P. Rich (ed.) *Crisis in the Caucasus: Russia, Georgia and the West*, London: Routledge, pp. 202–34.

Hansen, L. (2006) *Security as Practice: Discourse analysis and the Bosnian war*, London: Routledge.

Harnisch, S. and Maull H. (eds) (2001) *Germany as a Civilian Power? The foreign policy of the Berlin Republic*, Manchester: Manchester University Press.

Haukkala, H. (2005) 'Clash of boundaries? The European Union and Russia in the Northern Dimension', in M. Lehti and D. J. Smith (eds) *Post-Cold War Identity Politics: Northern and Baltic experiences*, London: Frank Cass, pp. 273–96.

—— (2010a) *The EU–Russia Strategic Partnership: The limits of post-sovereignty in international relations*, London: Routledge.

—— (2015) 'From cooperative to contested Europe? The conflict in Ukraine as a culmination of a long-term crisis in EU–Russia relations', *Journal of Contemporary European Studies*, 23(1): 25–40.

Haukkala, H. and Ojanen, H. (2011) 'The Europeanization of Finnish foreign policy: pendulum swings in slow motion', in R. Wong and C. Hill (eds) *National and European Foreign Policies: towards Europeanization*, London: Routledge, pp. 149–66.

Hegel, G. W. F. (1999) 'The German constitution', in L. Dickey and H. B. Nisbet (eds) *Hegel: Political writings*, Cambridge: Cambridge University Press, pp. 6–101.

Heinrich, H. and Tanaev, K. (2009) 'Georgia and Russia: contradictory media coverage of the August war', *Caucasian Review of International Affairs*, 3(3): 244–60.

Herman, R. (1996) 'Identity, norms and national security: the Soviet foreign policy revolution and the end of the Cold War', in P. Katzenstein (ed.) *The Culture of National Security: Norms and identity in world politics*, New York: Columbia University Press, pp. 271–316.

Hermann, R., Risse, T. and Brewer, M. (eds) (2004) *Transnational Identities: Becoming European in the EU*, Oxford: Rowman and Littlefield.

Herf, J. (1997) *Divided Memory: The Nazi past in the two Germanys*, Cambridge, MA: Harvard University Press.

Hildermeier, M. (2003) 'Germany and the Soviet Union', in E. Mühle (ed.) *Germany and the European East in the Twentieth Century*, Oxford: Berg, pp. 29–44.

Hillgruber, A. (1986) *Zweierlei Untergang: Die Zerschlagung des Deutschen Reichs und das Ende des europäischen Judentums*, Berlin: Siedler.

Hobsbawm, E. (1990) *Nations and Nationalism since 1780: Programme, myth, reality*, Cambridge: Cambridge University Press.

Hobsbawm, E. and Kertzer, D. J. (1992) 'Ethnicity and nationalism in Europe today', *Anthropology Today*, 8(1): 3–8.

Hodgin, N. and Pearce, C. (2011) *The GDR Remembered: Representations of the East German state since 1989*, Rochester, NY: Camden House.

Högselius, P. (2013) *Red Gas: Russia and the origins of European energy dependence*, Basingstoke: Palgrave Macmillan.

Hopf, T. (1998) 'The promise of constructivism in international relations theory', *International Security*, 23(1): 171–200.

—— (2002) *Social Construction of International Politics: Identities and foreign policies, Moscow, 1955 and 1999*, Ithaca, NY: Cornell University Press.

Hunt, N. (2010) *Memory, War and Trauma*, Cambridge: Cambridge University Press.

Huntington, S. (1997) *The Clash of Civilizations and the Remaking of World Order*, New York: Simon and Schuster.

Huyssen, A. (2003) *Present Pasts: Urban palimpsests and the politics of memory*, Stanford, CA: Stanford University Press.

IIFFMCG (Independent International Fact-Finding Mission on the Conflict in Georgia) Report (2009), vol. 1. http://news.bbc.co.uk/2/shared/bsp/hi/pdfs/30_09_09_iiffmgc_report.pdf (accessed 24 August 2016).

Isnenghi, M. (ed.) (2010) *I Luoghi della Memoria: Simboli e miti dell'Italia unita*, Roma: Laterza.

James, H. (1989) *German Identity 1770–1990*, London: Weidenfeld and Nicolson.

Jarausch, K. (ed.) (1999) *Dictatorship as Experience: Towards a socio-cultural history of the GDR*, Oxford: Berghahn.

—— (2010) 'Nightmares or daydreams? A postscript on the Europeanisation of memories', in M. Pakier and B. Stråth (eds) *A European Memory? Contested histories and politics of remembrance*, Oxford: Berghahn, pp. 309–20.

Jarausch, K. and Geyer, M. (2003) *Shattered Past: Reconstructing German histories*, Princeton, NJ: Princeton University Press.

Jarausch, K. and Lindenberger, T. (eds) (2007) *Conflicted Memories: Europeanising contemporary histories*, Oxford: Berghahn.

Jepperson, R., Wendt, A. and Katzenstein, P. (1996) 'Norms, identity and culture in national security', in P. Katzenstein (ed.) *The Culture of National Security: Norms and identity in world politics*, New York: Columbia University Press, pp. 33–78.

Jervis, R. (1978) 'Cooperation under the security dilemma', *World Politics*, 30(2): 167–214.

Joenniemi, P. (2002) 'Finland in the New Europe: a Herderian or Hegelian project?', in L. Hansen and O. Wæver (eds) *European Integration and National Identity: The challenge of the Nordic states*, London: Routledge, pp. 182–213.

—— (2010) 'Finland: always a borderland?', in M. Hurd (ed.) *Bordering the Baltic: Scandinavian boundary-drawing processes, 1900–2000*, Berlin: Lit Verlag, pp. 41–68.

Johnston, A. I. (1999) 'Realism(s) and Chinese security policy in the post-Cold War period', in E. Kapstein and M. Mastanduno (eds) *Unipolar Politics: Realism and state strategies after the Cold War*, New York: Columbia University Press, pp. 261–318.

Jokela, J. (2010) *Europeanisation and Foreign Policy: State identity in Finland and Britain*, London: Routledge.

Jones, S. (2013) *War and Revolution in the Caucasus: Georgia ablaze*, New York: Routledge.

Judt, T. (1992) 'The past is another country: myth and memory in post-war Europe', *Daedalus*, 121(4): 83–118.

Kaczynski, J. (2006) Interview with Handelsblatt, 'Man darf nicht mit zweierlei Maß messen', 30 October. www.handelsblatt.com/politik/international/interview-mit-jaroslaw-kaczynski-man-darf-nicht-mit-zweierlei-mass-messen/2725710.html (accessed 7 August 2016).

Kaczynski, L. (2006a) Interview with Spiegel Online, 'We are very vigilant when it comes to the German–Russian relationship', 6 March. www.spiegel.

de/international/spiegel/spiegel-interview-with-poland-s-kaczynski-we-are-very-vigilant-when-it-comes-to-the-german-russian-relationship-a-404675.html (accessed 7 August 2016).

—— (2006b) Transcript of interview with *Financial Times*, 6 November, www.ft.com/cms/s/0/aca4ec46-6ceb-11db-9a4d-0000779e2340.html (accessed 7 August 2016).

—— (2008a) Poland supports Georgia's membership of NATO, 3 March. www.president.pl/en/archive/news-archive/news-2008/art,18,poland-supports-georgias-membership-of-nato.html (accessed 9 August 2016).

—— (2008b) 'NATO has a duty to embrace Ukraine and Georgia', *Financial Times*, 31 March. www.ft.com/cms/s/0/d7aa03ba-feba-11dc-9e04-000077b07658.html#axzz2akelFTBj (accessed 9 August 2016).

—— (2008c) Statement of the chancellery of the president of the Republic of Poland in connection with the situation in Georgia, 12 July. www.president.pl/en/archive/news-archive/news-2008/art,132,statement-of-the-chancellery-of-the-president-of-rp-in-connection-with-the-situation-in-georgia.html (accessed 9 August 2016).

—— (2008d) Speech in Tbilisi, 12 August. www.president.pl/en/archive/news-archive/news-2008/art,119,president-of-rp-sets-off-to-visit-georgia.html (accessed 9 August 2016).

—— (2008e) Speech at the conference of the Foreign Policy Association, 24 September. www.president.pl/en/archive/news-archive/news-2008/art,93,nato-is-an-exporter-of-stability-and-peace.html (accessed 9 August 2016).

—— (2008f) Statements at a press conference in Tbilisi, 23 November. http://www.president.pl/en/archive/news-archive/news-2008/art,163,the-president-of-the-republic-of-poland-visits-georgia.html (accessed 9 August 2016).

—— (2008g) Statement on Russia's recognition of Abkhazia and South Ossetia, 26 August. www.president.pl/en/archive/news-archive/news-2008/art,109,statement-by-president-of-rp.html (accessed 9 August 2009).

—— (2008h) Speech at the General Assembly of the United Nations, 23 September. www.president.pl/en/archive/news-archive/news-2008/art,95,63rd-session-of-the-un-general-assembly-in-new-york.html (accessed 9 August 2016).

Kagan, R. (2008) *The Return of History and the End of Dreams*, New York: Knopf.

Kamen, H. (2008) *Imagining Spain: Historical myth and national identity*, New Haven, CT: Yale University Press.

Kanerva, I. (2008a) Speech at the Norwegian Nobel Institute, 22 January. http://formin.finland.fi/public/default.aspx?contentid=108314 (accessed 18 July 2016).

—— (2008b) Speech at the Woodrow Wilson International Centre, 11 February. http://formin.finland.fi/public/default.aspx?contentid=115051andcontent lan=2andculture=en-US (accessed 9 August 2016).

—— (2008c) Statement at the United States Commission on Security and Cooperation in Europe, 13 February. http://formin.finland.fi/public/default.aspx?contentid=115012andcontentlan=2andculture=en-US (accessed 9 August 2016).

Katainen, J. (2011) Speech at the seminar on the future of Europe in Turku, 12 December. http://www.eilen.fi/se/949/ (accessed 11 August 2016).

Katzenstein, P. (ed.) (1996) *The Culture of National Security: Norms and identity in world politics*, New York: Columbia University Press.

Keith, N. (2006) *Britain, Soviet Russia and the Collapse of the Versailles order, 1919–1939*, Cambridge: Cambridge University Press.

Klessmann, C. (1999) 'Rethinking the second German dictatorship', in K. Jarausch (ed.) *Dictatorship as Experience: Towards a socio-cultural history of the GDR*, Oxford: Berghahn.

Kloth, H. M. (2006) 'Indirect Hitler comparison: Polish minister attacks Schröder and Merkel', *Spiegel Online*, 1 May. www.spiegel.de/international/indirect-hitler-comparison-polish-minister-attacks-schroeder-and-merkel-a-413969.html (accessed 7 August 2016).

Knafo, S. (2008) 'Critical approaches and the problem of social construction: reassessing the legacy of the agent/structure debate in IR', Working Paper No. 3, Brighton: University of Sussex.

Knopp, G. (2003) *Der Aufstand: 17. Juni 1953*, Gütersloh: Hoffmann und Campe.

Knowlton, J. and Cates, T. (eds) (1993) *Forever in the Shadow of Hitler? Original documents of the Historikerstreit, the controversy concerning the singularity of the Holocaust*, London: Humanities Press International.

Kocka, J. (1996) 'Crisis of unification: how Germany changes', in M. Mertes, S. Muller and H. A. Winkler (eds) *In Search of Germany*, New Brunswick: Transaction Publishers, pp. 191–210.

Koczanowicz, L. (1997) 'Memory of politics and politics of memory: Reflections on the construction of the past in post-totalitarian Poland', *Studies in East European Thought*, 49(4), pp. 259–70.

Komorowski, B. (2010) Interview with Euronews, 31 August. www.euronews.com/2010/08/31/komorowski-seeks-greater-eu-involvement-for-poland/ (accessed 7 August 2016).

—— (2011) Letter to the EU–Russia civil society forum, 1 December.

—— (2012) Press release of the Polish Presidency, 7 March.

—— (2015) Address at the Westerplatte Commemoration Ceremony, 8 May. www.president.pl/en/president-komorowski/news/art,830,address-at-the-westerplatte-commemoration-ceremony.html (accessed 21 July 2016).

König, H. (2008) 'Erinnern und vergessen. Vom Nutzen und Nachteil für die Politik', *Osteuropa*, 6: 27–40.

Koesel, K. and Bunce, V. (2012) 'Putin, popular protests and political trajectories in Russia: a comparative perspective', *Post-Soviet Affairs*, 28(4): 403–23.

Kopacz, E. (2014) Speech at the Sejm, 1 October. www.premier.gov.pl/en/policy-statement-by-prime-minister-ewa-kopacz-stenographic-record.html (accessed 23 August 2016).

—— (2015a) Press conference, 25 June. www.premier.gov.pl/en/news/news/prime-minister-kopacz-on-deployment-of-us-weapons-in-poland-it-strengthens-natos-eastern.html (accessed 23 August 2016).

—— (2015b) Press conference with Arseniy Yatsenyuk, 19 January. www.premier.gov.pl/en/news/news/support-for-reforms-in-ukraine.html (accessed 23 August 2016).

Korosteleva, E. A. (2016) 'Eastern partnership and the Eurasian Union: bringing "the political" back in the eastern region', *European Politics and Society*, 17(Supplement 1): 67–81.

Krumm, R. (2012) 'The rise of Realism: Germany's perception of Russia from Gorbachev to Medvedev', in R. Krumm, H. Schröder and S. Medvedev (eds) *Constructing Identities in Europe: German and Russian perspectives*, Baden-Baden: Nomos, pp. 114–23.

Krzyzanowski, M. (2009) 'Europe in crisis: discourses on crisis-events in the European press 1956–2006', *Journalism Studies*, 10(1): 18–35.

—— (2010) *The Discursive Construction of European Identities*, Frankfurt am Main: Peter Lang.

Kundera, M. (1984) 'The tragedy of Central Europe', *New York Review of Books*, 31(7): 33–38.

Laffey, M. and Weldes, J. (1997) 'Beyond belief: ideas and symbolic technologies in the study of international relations', *European Journal of International Relations*, 3(2): 193–237.

Langenbacher, E. (2008) 'Twenty-first century memory regimes in Germany and Poland. An analysis of elite discourses and public opinion', *German Politics and Society*, 26(4): 50–81.

—— (2010) 'The mastered past? Collective memory trends in Germany since unification', *German Politics and Society*, 28(1): 42–68.

Lasas, A. (2012) 'When history matters: Baltic and Polish reactions to the Russo-Georgian War', *Europe-Asia Studies*, 64(6): 1061–75.

Lebow, R. N. (2006) 'The memory of politics in post-war Europe', in R. N. Lebow, W. Kansteiner and C. Fogu (eds) *The Politics of Memory in Post-War Europe*, Durham: Duke University Press, pp. 1–39.

—— (2008a) *A Cultural Theory of International Relations*, Cambridge: Cambridge University Press.

—— (2008b) 'Identity and International Relations', *International Relations*, 22(4): 473–92.

Lebow, R. N., Kansteiner W. and Fogu, C. (eds) (2006) *The Politics of Memory in Post-War Europe*, Durham: Duke University Press.

Legro, J. and Moravcsik, A. (1999) 'Is anybody still a realist?', *International Security*, 24(2): 5–55.

Leonard, M. and Popescu, N. (2007) *A Power Audit of EU–Russia Relations*, London: European Council on Foreign Relations.

Levintova, E. (2010) 'Good neighbours? Dominant narratives about the "Other" in contemporary Polish and Russian newspapers', *Europe–Asia Studies*, 62(8): 1339–61.

Lippert, W. (2011) *The Economic Diplomacy of Ostpolitik: Origins of NATO's energy dilemma*, New York: Berghahn Books.

Liu, J. and Hilton, D. (2005) 'How the past weighs on the present: social representations of history and their role in identity politics', *British Journal of Social Psychology*, 44: 537–56.

Liulevicius, V. G. (2000) *War Land on the Eastern Front: Culture, national identity and German occupation in World War I*, Cambridge: Cambridge University Press.

Lo, B. (2009) 'Medvedev and the European security architecture', Policy Brief, London: Centre for European Reform.

Loew, P. O. (2008) 'Helden oder Opfer. Erinnerungskulturen in Polen nach 1989', *Osteuropa*, 6: 85-102.

Löning, M. (2011) Interview with *Die Welt*, 20 December. www.welt.de/politik/ausland/article13776313/Putin-Gegenteil-eines-lupenreinen-Demokraten.html (accessed 10 August 2016).

—— (2012a) 'Russian draft law discriminates homosexuals', 9 February. www.auswaertiges-amt.de/DE/Infoservice/Presse/Meldungen/2012/120209_MRHH_RUS.html (accessed 10 August 2016).

—— (2012b), 15 May. 'Homosexuals are not second-class citizens'. www.auswaertiges-amt.de/DE/Infoservice/Presse/Meldungen/2012/120515-MRHH_Tag_Homophobie.html (accessed 10 August 2016).

—— (2012c) New Russian NGO law stigmatises civil rights organizations, 13 July. www.auswaertiges-amt.de/DE/Infoservice/Presse/Meldungen/2012/120713_MRHHB_NGO_Gesetz_Russland.html (accessed 10 August 2016).

Luhn, A. (2014) 'The Ukrainian nationalism at the heart of Euromaidan', *The Nation*, 21 January, www.thenation.com/article/178013/ukrainian-nationalism-heart-euromaidan (accessed 26 August 2016).

Makarychev, A. and Meister, S. (2015) 'The modernisation debate and Russian–German normative cleavages', *European Politics and Society*, 16(1): 80–94.

Malesevic, S. (2011) 'The chimera of national identity', *Nations and Nationalism*, 17(2): 272–90.

Mankoff, J. (2012) 'The politics of US missile defence cooperation with Europe and Russia', *International Affairs*, 88(2): 329–47.

March, L. (2011) 'Is nationalism rising in Russian foreign policy? The case of Georgia', *Demokratizatsiya*, 19(3): 187–208.

March, L. (2012) 'The Russian Duma "opposition": no drama out of crisis?', *East European Politics*, 28(3): 241–55.

Marx, C. (1990) *Das Bild der Sowjetunion im westdeutschen Fernsehen: Eine medienkritische Studie zum Reflex des politischen Wandels 1986/87 in der Sowjetunion aus literatursoziologischer Sicht*, Frankfurt: Peter Lang.

Marson, J. (2012) 'Gazprom cuts gas price for Poland', *Wall Street Journal*, 6 November. http://online.wsj.com/news/articles/SB10001424052970204 3494045781022301353 29520 (accessed 11 August 2016).

McManus-Czubinska, C. and Miller, W. (2008) 'European civilization or European civilizations: the EU as a "Christian club"? Public opinion in Poland in 2005', in M. Myant and T. Cox (eds) *Reinventing Poland: Economic and political transformation and evolving national identity*, London: Routledge, pp. 128–49.

Medvedev, S. (1999) 'Russia as the subconsciouness of Finland', *Security Dialogue*, 30(1): 95–107.

Megill, A. (2011) 'History, memory, identity', in J. Olick, V. Vinitzky-Seroussi and D. Levy (eds) *The Collective Memory Reader*, Oxford: Oxford University Press, pp. 193–7.

Meier, O. (2007) 'Europeans split over US missile defence plans', *Arms Control Today*, 2 April, www.armscontrol.org/print/2333 (accessed 18 July 2016).

Meister, S. (2012) 'An alienated partnership. German–Russian relations after Putin's return', FIIA Briefing Paper 105, Helsinki: Finnish Institute of International Affairs.

—— (2014) 'Reframing Germany's Russia policy: an opportunity for the EU', ECFR Policy Brief, London: European Council on Foreign Relations Policy.

Merkel, A. (2008a) Press release of the office of the Federal Chancellor on the NATO summit in Bucharest, 4 April. www.bundeskanzlerin.de/ContentArchiv/DE/Archiv17/Reiseberichte/ro-nato-abschluss-pk.html (accessed 8 August 2016).

—— (2008b) Press release of the office of the Federal Chancellor, 17 August. www.bundeskanzlerin.de/ContentArchiv/DE/Archiv17/Reiseberichte/ge-merkel-tiflis.html (accessed 8 August 2016).

—— (2008c) Press release of the office of the Federal Chancellor, 26 August. www.bundeskanzlerin.de/ContentArchiv/DE/Archiv17/Reiseberichte/ee-lt-merkel-tallinn.html (accessed 8 August 2016).

—— (2008d) Press release of the office of the Federal Chancellor, 1 September. www.bundeskanzlerin.de/ContentArchiv/DE/Archiv17/Reiseberichte/be-kaukasus-gipfel-bruessel.html (accessed 8 August 2016).

—— (2010) Speech at the German Committee on Eastern European Economic Relations, 14 October. www.bundeskanzlerin.de/ContentArchiv/DE/Archiv17/Reden/2010/10/2010-10-14-merkel-ostausschuss.html (accessed 7 August 2016).

—— (2011) Speech at the inauguration of the Nord Stream pipeline, 8 November. www.bundeskanzlerin.de/ContentArchiv/DE/Archiv17/Reden/2011/11/2011-11-08-merkel-lubmin.html (accessed 7 August 2016).

—— (2012a) Joint press conference with Vladimir Putin, 1 June.

—— (2012b) Speech at the German Committee on Eastern European Economic Relations, 25 October. www.bundesregierung.de/Content/DE/

Rede/2012/10/2012-10-25-merkel-60-jahre-ostausschuss.html (accessed 7 August 2016).

—— (2012c) Joint press conference with Vladimir Putin, 16 November.

—— (2012d) Speech at the New Year reception of the German diplomatic corps, 26 January. www.bundesregierung.de/Content/DE/Rede/2012/01/2012-01-26-bkin-dipl-corps.html (accessed 10 August 2016).

—— (2012e) Speech at the plenary conference of the German–Russia Petersburg Dialogue, 16 November. www.bundesregierung.de/Content/DE/Rede/2012/11/2012-11-16-rede-petersberger-dialog.html (accessed 10 August 2016).

—— (2014a) Speech at the Bundestag, 13 March. www.auswaertiges-amt.de/EN/Infoservice/Presse/Meldungen/2014/140314-Merkel-Ukraine.html (accessed 18 August 2016).

—— (2014b) Statement announcing EU economic sanctions against Russia, 29 July. www.bundesregierung.de/Content/EN/Artikel/2014/07_en/2014-07-29-eu-sanktionen_en.html (accessed 18 August 2016).

—— (2014c) Statement at the European Council meeting, 18 December. www.bundesregierung.de/Content/EN/Artikel/2014/12_en/2014-12-18-ukraine-merkel-regierungserklaerung.html (accessed 18 August 2016).

—— (2014d) New Year address, 31 December. www.bundesregierung.de/Content/EN/Artikel/2015/01_en/2014-12-31-merkel-ansprache-ukraine_en.html (accessed 18 August 2016).

—— (2015a) Statement at meeting with NATO Secretary-General in Berlin, 14 January. www.bundeskanzlerin.de/Content/EN/Artikel/2015/01_en/2015-01-14-besuch-nato-gs-stoltenberg_en.html (accessed 18 August 2016).

—— (2015b) Statement following talks in Kiev and Moscow, 5 February. www.bundeskanzlerin.de/Content/EN/Reiseberichte/2015/2015-02-05-merkel-hollande-kiew-moskau_en.html (accessed 18 August 2016).

—— (2015c) Speech at the Munich Security Conference, 7 February. www.bundesregierung.de/Content/EN/Reden/2015/2015-02-07-merkel-sicherheitskonferenz_en.html (accessed 18 August 2016).

—— (2015d) Statements concerning the Minsk-2 agreement, 11 February. www.bundeskanzlerin.de/Content/EN/Reiseberichte/2015/2015-02-11-merkel-minsk_en.html (accessed 19 August 2016).

—— (2015e) Statement on the occasion of Petro Poroshenko's visit to Berlin, 16 March. www.bundeskanzlerin.de/Content/EN/Artikel/2015/03_en/2015-03-16-poroschenko-bei-merkel_en.html (accessed 19 August 2016).

—— (2015f) Speech at the Bundestag, 19 March. www.bundeskanzlerin.de/Content/EN/Artikel/2015/03_en/2015-03-19-ukraine-regierungserklaerung_en.html (accessed 19 August 2016).

—— (2015g) Statements following consultations with Jean-Claude Juncker, 5 March. www.bundeskanzlerin.de/Content/EN/Artikel/2015/03_en/2015-03-05-ukraine_en.html (accessed 19 August 2016).

—— (2015h) Statements at joint press conference with Vladimir Putin in Moscow, 10 May. www.bundeskanzlerin.de/Content/EN/ Reiseberichte/2015/2015-10-05-bkin-zu-gedenken-min-moskau.html (accessed 19 August 2016).

—— (2015i) Statements at the G7 summit, 7 June. www.bundeskanzlerin. de/Content/EN/Artikel/2015/06_en/2015-06-07-auftakt-g7-gipfel-1_ en.html (accessed 19 August 2016).

—— (2015j) Government statement, 15 October. www.bundeskanzlerin.de/ Content/EN/Regierungserklaerung/2015-10-15-regierungserklaerung-bundestag.html (accessed 19 August 2016).

Mickiewicz, A. (1833) *Books of the Polish Nation and Polish Pilgrimage*, London: James Ridgway.

Miller, D. (1997) *On Nationality*, Oxford: Oxford University Press.

Ministry for Foreign Affairs of Finland (2008a) Press release, 21 February. http:// formin.finland.fi/public/default.aspx?contentid=115444andcontentlan=2 andculture=en-US (accessed 9 August 2016).

—— (2008b) Press release, 29 August, http://formin.finland.fi/public/default. aspx?contentid=135644andcontentlan=2andculture=en-US (accessed 9 August 2016).

—— (2012) 'Visa-free travel and the state of civil society sparked discussion during the visit of Russia's Foreign Minister', 23 August. www.formin. fi/public/default.aspx?contentid=255671andcontentlan=2andculture= en-US (accessed 9 August 2016).

Mitzen, J. (2006) 'Ontological security in world politics: state identity and the security dilemma', *European Journal of International Relations*, 12(3): 341–70.

Moeller, R. (2003) *War Stories: The search for a usable past in the Federal Republic of Germany*, Berkeley, CA: University of California Press.

Möller, U. and Bjereld, U. (2010) 'From Nordic neutrals to post-neutral Europeans: differences in Finnish and Swedish policy transformation', *Cooperation and Conflict*, 45(4): 363–86.

Mühle, E. (2003) 'The European East on the mental map of German Ostforschung', in E. Mühle (ed.) *Germany and the European East in the Twentieth Century*, Oxford: Berg, pp. 107–30.

Müller, H. (2004) 'Arguing, bargaining and all that: communicative action, rationalist theory and the logic of appropriateness in international relations', *European Journal of International Relations*, 10(3): 395–435.

Müller, J. (2002) 'The power of memory, the memory of power and the power over memory', in J. Müller (ed.) *Memory and Power in Post-War Europe*, Cambridge: Cambridge University Press, pp. 1–36.

Müller, R. and Ueberschär, G. R. (2009) *Hitler's War in the East: A critical assessment*, Oxford: Berghahn.

Naarden, B. (1992) *Socialist Europe and Revolutionary Russia: Perception and prejudice, 1848–1923*, Cambridge: Cambridge University Press.

Naimark, N. (1995) *The Russians in Germany: A history of the Soviet zone of occupation 1945–1949*, Cambridge, MA: Harvard University Press.

Nau, H. (2002) *At Home Abroad: Identity and power in American foreign policy*, Ithaca, NY: Cornell University Press.

Neumann, I. (1996) 'Self and Other in International Relations', *European Journal of International Relations*, 2(2): 139–74.

—— (1998) *Uses of the Other: The East in European identity formation*, Minneapolis, MN: University of Minnesota Press.

Neumann, I. and Medvedev, S. (2012) 'Identity issues in EU–Russian relations', in R. Krumm, H. Schröder and S. Medvedev (eds) *Constructing Identities in Europe: German and Russian perspectives*, Baden-Baden: Nomos, pp. 9–29.

Niinistö, S. (2012a) Inauguration speech as president of Finland, 1 March. www.eilen.fi/en/1708/?language=en (accessed 11 August 2016).

—— (2012b) Speech to the diplomatic corps in Helsinki, 26 April. www.eilen.fi/en/1775/?language=en (accessed 11 August 2016).

—— (2012c) Speech at the plenary session of Saint Petersburg International Economic Forum, 21 June. www.eilen.fi/en/1785/?language=en (accessed 11 August 2016).

—— (2012d) Speech at the ambassador seminar in Helsinki, 20 August. www.eilen.fi/en/1788/?language=en (accessed 25 August 2016).

—— (2012e) Speech at the Norwegian Institute of International Affairs, 11 October. www.eilen.fi/en/1797/?language=en (accessed 25 August 2016).

—— (2014a) Speech at the dinner for the state visit by President of the Swiss Confederation Didier Burkhalter, 7 April. www.eilen.fi/en/3192/?language=en (accessed 25 August 2016).

—— (2014b) Speech at a dinner for the diplomatic corps at Helsinki City Hall, 29 April. www.eilen.fi/en/3193/?language=en (accessed 25 August 2016).

—— (2014c) Speech at the opening session of the Arctic Circle Assembly 2014, 31 October. www.eilen.fi/en/3241/?language=en (accessed 25 August 2016).

—— (2015) Speech at the diplomatic corps dinner at the Presidential Palace, 23 April. www.eilen.fi/en/3324/?language=en (accessed 26 August 2016).

Nitoiu, C. (2016) 'The Ukraine crisis and the conflict/cooperation dichotomy in EU–Russia relations', *Southeast European and Black Sea Studies*, online first, www.tandfonline.com/doi/full/10.1080/14683857.2016.1193305 (accessed 17 July 2016).

Nolte, E. (1986) 'Die Vergangenheit, die nicht vergehen will', *Frankfurter Allgemeine Zeitung*, 6 June. www.staff.uni-giessen.de/~g31130/PDF/Nationalismus/ErnstNolte.pdf (accessed 29 August 2016).

Nora, P. (1989) 'Between memory and history. Les lieux de mémoire', *Representations*, 26: 7–24.

—— (1992) *Realms of Memory: The construction of the French past*, New York: Columbia University Press.

Oberhuber, F., Bärenreuter, C., Krzyzanowski, M., Schönbauer, H. and Wodak, R. (2005) 'Debating the European Constitution: on representations of Europe/EU in the press', *Journal of Language and Politics*, 4(2): 227–71.

Olick, J. (2007) *The Politics of Regret: On collective memory and historical responsibility*, New York: Routledge.

Olick, J., Vinitzky-Seroussi, V. and Levy, D. (eds) (2011) *The Collective Memory Reader*, Oxford: Oxford University Press.

Onken, E. (2007) 'The Baltic States and Moscow's 9 May commemoration: analysing memory politics in Europe', *Europe–Asia Studies*, 59(1): 23–46.

Orla-Bukowska, A. (2006) 'New threads on an old loom. National memory and social identity in postwar and post-Communist Poland', in R. N. Lebow, W. Kansteiner and C. Fogu (eds) *The Politics of Memory in Post-war Europe*, Durham, NC: Duke University Press, pp. 177–210.

Ostermann, C. F. (ed.) (2001) *Uprising in East Germany 1953: The Cold War, the German question and the first major upheaval behind the Iron Curtain*, Budapest: Central European University Press.

Ozbay, F. and Aras, B. (2008) 'Polish–Russian relations: history, geography and geopolitics', *East European Quarterly*, 42(1): 27–42.

Pakier, M. and Stråth, B. (2010) 'Introduction: a European memory?', in M. Pakier and B. Stråth (eds) *A European Memory? Contested histories and politics of remembrance*, Oxford: Berghahn, pp. 1–20.

Paul, A. (2010) *Katyn: Stalin's massacre and the triumph of truth*, DeKalb, IL: Northern Illinois University Press.

Pieper, C. (2012) 'Statements at the opening of the exhibition "Russen und Deutsche – 1000 Jahre Kunst, Geschichte und Kultur"'. www.auswaertiges-amt. de/DE/Infoservice/Presse/Reden/2012/120620-StM_P_Ausstellung_ St_H_M.html (accessed 10 August 2016).

Pirani, S. (2012) 'Russo-Ukrainian gas wars and the call on transit governance', in C. Kuzmenko, A. Belyi, A. Goldthau and M. F. Keating (eds) *Dynamics of Energy Governance in Europe and Russia*, Basingstoke: Palgrave Macmillan, pp. 169–86.

Poe, M. (2003) 'A distant world: Russian relations with Europe before Peter the Great', in C. Whittaker (ed.), *Russia Engages the World, 1453–1825*, Cambridge, MA: Harvard University Press, pp. 2–23.

Poland's Ministry of Foreign Affairs (2012a) 10th meeting of Polish–Russian Group for Difficult Matters, 17 December. www.mfa.gov.pl/en/ news/10th_meeting_of_polish_russian_group_for_difficult_matters (accessed 11 August 2016).

—— (2012b) Press release of the Polish foreign ministry, 26 July. www.mfa. gov.pl/en/news/foreign_ministers_sikorski_and_lavrov_hold_phone_ talks (accessed 11 August 2016).

Porter, B. (2000) *When Nationalism Began to Hate: Imagining modern politics in nineteenth century Poland*, Oxford: Oxford University Press.

Pouliot, V. (2008) 'The logic of practicality: a theory of practice of security communities', *International Organization*, 62(2): 257–88.

Powers, C. (1990) 'Czech–Polish–Hungarian accord urged: Europe: Havel proposes "spirit of solidarity" in aftermath of Soviet domination', *Los Angeles Times*, 26 January. http://articles.latimes.com/1990-01-26/news/mn-726_1_central-europe (accessed 17 July 2016).

President of Finland (2012) 'President Halonen visited Russia', 17 January. www.presidentti.fi/halonen/Public/defaultf952.html?contentid=238834 (accessed 11 August 2016).

Prizel, I. (1998) *National Identity and Foreign Policy: Nationalism and leadership in Poland, Russia and Ukraine*, Cambridge: Cambridge University Press.

Putin, V. (2007) 'Vladimir Putin's prepared remarks at 43rd Munich Conference on Security Policy', *The Washington Post*, 12 February. www.washingtonpost.com/wp-dyn/content/article/2007/02/12/AR2007021200555.html (accessed 8 August 2016).

Ray, L. (2006) 'Mourning, melancholia and violence', in D. Bell (ed.) *Memory, Trauma and World Politics*, Basingstoke: Palgrave Macmillan, pp. 135–54.

Reeves, C. (2010) 'Reopening the wounds of history? The foreign policy of the "Fourth" Polish Republic', *Journal of Communist Studies and Transition Politics*, 26(4): 518–41.

Reichel, P. (2005) *Schwarz–Rot–Gold: Kleine Geschichte deutscher Nationalsymbole nach 1945*, Munich: C. H. Beck.

Reisigl, M. and Wodak, R. (2001) *Discourse and Discrimination*, London: Routledge.

Reuters (2013) 'Finland's Fennovoima signs reactor deal with Rosatom', 21 December. www.reuters.com/article/us-fennovoima-rosatom-idUSBRE9BK05G20131221 (accessed 25 August 2016).

Reynolds, P. (2008) 'New Russian world order: the five principles', *BBC News*, 1 September. http://news.bbc.co.uk/1/hi/world/europe/7591610.stm (accessed 9 August 2016).

Rich, P. (ed.) (2010) *Crisis in the Caucasus: Russia, Georgia and the West*, London: Routledge.

Ringmar, E. (1996) *Identity, Interests and Action: A cultural explanation of Sweden's intervention in the Thirty Years War*, Cambridge: Cambridge University Press.

—— (1996a) 'Russia: territory and identity crises', *Nations and Nationalism*, 2(3): 453–60.

Risse, T. (2007) 'Deutsche Identität und Aussenpolitik', in S. Schmidt, G. Hellmann and R. Wolf (eds) *Handbuch zur deutschen Aussenpolitik*, Wiesbaden: Verlag für Sozialwissenschaften, pp. 49–61.

—— (2010) *A Community of Europeans? Transnational identities and public spheres*, Ithaca, NY: Cornell University Press.

Risse-Kappen, T. (1996) 'Collective identity in a democratic community. The case of NATO', in P. Katzenstein (ed.) *The Culture of National Security: Norms and identity in world politics*, New York: Columbia University Press, pp. 357–99.

Robertson, G. (2013) 'Protesting Putinism: The election protests of 2011–2012 in broader perspective', *Problems of Post-Communism*, 60(2): 11–23.

Robinson, N. (2013) 'Russia's response to crisis: the paradox of success', *Europe–Asia Studies*, 65(3): 450–72.

Romanova, T. (2016) 'Sanctions and the future of EU–Russian economic relations', *Europe–Asia Studies*, 68(4): 774–96.

Ruchniewicz, K. (2007) *"Noch ist Polen nicht Verloren": Das historische Denken der Polen*, Münster: LIT Verlag.

Ruggie, J. G. (1998) 'What makes the world hang together? Neo-utilitarianism and the social constructivist challenge', *International Organization*, 52(4): 855–85.

Rupnik, J. (1994) 'Europe's new frontiers: remapping Europe', *Daedalus*, 123(3): 91–114.

Sabrow, M. (2009) *Erinnerungsorte der DDR*, Munich: C. H. Beck.

Said, E. W. (1978) *Orientalism*, New York: Vintage Books.

Sakwa, R. (2008) 'New Cold War or twenty years' crisis? Russia and international politics', *International Affairs*, 84(2): 241–67.

—— (2012) 'Conspiracy narratives as a mode of engagement in international politics: the case of the 2008 Russo-Georgian war', *The Russian Review*, 71(4): 581–609.

—— (2015) *Frontline Ukraine: Crisis in the borderlands*, London: I. B. Tauris.

Satjukow, S. (2008) *Besatzer: "Die Russen" in Deutschland 1945–1994*, Göttingen: Vandenhoeck and Ruprecht.

Schetyna, G. (2014a) Speech at the Sejm, 6 November. www.msz.gov.pl/en/news/minister_grzegorz_schetyna_on_polish_foreign_policy_priorities (accessed 23 August 2016).

—— (2015a) Speech at lunch with ambassadors of EU member states, 6 February. www.msz.gov.pl/resource/dde8b343-005e-4e9a-af17-80a5a69eae4f:JCR (accessed 23 August 2016).

—— (2015b) Speech at the Sejm, 23 April. http://msz.gov.pl/en/news/minister_grzegorz_schetyna_addresses_priorities_of_polish_diplomacy (accessed 23 August 2016).

—— (2015c) Speech at the presentation of the ECFR European Foreign Policy Scorecard, 9 February. www.msz.gov.pl/resource/14f87508-729d-45f0-b86b-a1dd91000901:JCR (accessed 23 August 2016).

Schmitt, C. (1976) *The Concept of the Political*, New Brunswick, NJ: Rutgers University Press.

Schildt, A. (2003) 'Mending fences: the Federal Republic of Germany and Eastern Europe', in E. Mühle (ed.) *Germany and the European East in the Twentieth Century*, Oxford: Berg, pp. 153–79.

Schmidt-Felzmann, A. (2011) 'EU Member States' energy relations with Russia: conflicting approaches to securing natural gas supplies', *Geopolitics*, 16(3): 574–99.

Schockenhoff, A. (2011a) Speech at the Heinrich Böll Foundation, 26 October. www.auswaertiges-amt.de/DE/Infoservice/Presse/Reden/2011/111026_KoRus_Boell.html (accessed 10 August 2016).

—— (2011b) Interview with *Der Tagesspiegel*, 27 November. www.auswaertiges-amt.de/DE/Infoservice/Presse/Interviews/2011/111127-Ko_RUS_Tsp.html (accessed 10 August 2016).

—— (2011c) Speech at the German Bundestag, 15 December. www.auswaertiges-amt.de/DE/Infoservice/Presse/Reden/2011/111215-KoRUS-Bundestag.html?nn=336102 (accessed 10 August 2016).

—— (2012a) Statement on harassment of independent election observers before the Russian presidential elections, 26 January. www.auswaertiges-amt.de/DE/Infoservice/Presse/Meldungen/2012/120126-Ko_RUS_Wahlen.html (accessed 10 August 2016).

—— (2012b) Statement on free and fair elections in Russia, 3 February. www.auswaertiges-amt.de/DE/Infoservice/Presse/Meldungen/2012/120203-Wahlen_RUS.html (accessed 10 August 2016).

—— (2012c) Interview with *Der Tagesspiegel*, 9 August. www.tagesspiegel.de/politik/russland-koordinator-schockenhoff-cdu-putin-setzt-auf-repression/6978120.html (accessed 10 August 2016).

Schröder, H. (2012) 'Portraying the "strangest country": evolution of the German image of Russia', in R. Krumm, H. Schröder and S. Medvedev (eds) *Constructing Identities in Europe: German and Russian perspectives*, Baden-Baden: Nomos, pp. 97–113.

Schwirtz, M. (2010) 'Putin Marks Soviet Massacre of Polish Officers', *New York Times*, 7 April, http://www.nytimes.com/2010/04/08/world/europe/08putin.html?ref=europe (accessed 23 January 2017).

Sebenius, J. K. (1992) 'Challenging conventional explanations of international cooperation: negotiation analysis and the case of epistemic communities', *International Organization*, 46(1): 323–65.

Service, R. (2007) *Comrades! A history of world Communism*, Cambridge, MA: Harvard University Press.

Shevtsova, L. (2012) 'Russia under Putin: Titanic looking for its iceberg?', *Communist and Post-Communist Studies*, 45 (3–4): 209–16.

Shiraev, E. (2013) *Russian Government and Politics*, Basingstoke: Palgrave Macmillan.

Shuster, S. (2011) 'Russia–Poland tensions rise with crash report', *The Time*, 19 January 2011, www.time.com/time/world/article/0,8599,2043130,00.html (accessed 19 July 2016).

Siddi, M. (2012) Russia and the forging of memory and identity in Europe. *Studia Diplomatica*, 65(4): 77–103.

—— (2016a) 'German foreign policy towards Russia in the aftermath of the Ukraine crisis: a new Ostpolitik?', *Europe–Asia Studies*, 68(4): 665–77.

—— (2016b) 'The EU's energy union: a sustainable path to energy security?', *The International Spectator*, 51(1): 131–44.

—— (2016c) 'The Ukraine crisis and European memory politics of the Second World War', *European Politics and Society*, online first. http://www.tandfonline.com/doi/full/10.1080/23745118.2016.1261435 (accessed 15 February 2017).

Sidorenko, E. (2008) 'Which way to Poland? Re-emerging from Romantic unity', in M. Myant and T. Cox (eds) *Reinventing Poland: Economic and political transformation and evolving national identity*, London: Routledge, pp. 109–27.

Sikorski, R. (2008a) Transcript of Radoslaw Sikorski's interview for BBC television programme *Hardtalk*, 30 April. www.youtube.com/watch?v=utaUBuwuaSc (accessed 9 August 2016).

—— (2008b) Interview with *The Telegraph*, 20 August.

—— (2008c) Radoslaw Sikorski's speech at the Atlantic Council, 19 November. www.atlanticcouncil.org/news/transcripts/transcript-polish-foreign-minister-radoslaw-sikorski-talks-to-council (accessed 9 August 2016).

—— (2010a) 'The future of EU–Russian relations', *The New York Times*, 16 June. www.nytimes.com/2010/06/17/opinion/17iht-edsikorski.html?_r=0 (accessed 7 August 2016).

—— (2010b) Interview with *Tagesspiegel*, 4 November. www.auswaertiges-amt.de/DE/Infoservice/Presse/Interviews/2010/101104-BM-Sikorski-Tagesspiegel-Int.html (accessed 7 August 2016).

—— (2011a) Interview with *The Wall Street Journal*, 'Nord Stream waste of money, but irrelevant for Poland', 9 November. http://blogs.wsj.com/emergingeurope/2011/11/09/nord-stream-waste-of-money-but-irrelevant-for-poland/ (accessed 7 August 2016).

—— (2011b) Speech at Harvard University, 28 February. www.mfa.gov.pl/resource/f733dba2-09d4-4322-aa0d-e4fb5dfac966:JCR (accessed 11 August 2016).

—— (2011c) Speech at the Sejm, 16 March. www.mfa.gov.pl/resource/86efef22-d645-4dd8-9532-9e244ed41b1e:JCR (accessed 11 August 2016).

—— (2011d) Press release of the Polish foreign ministry, 14 December. www.mfa.gov.pl/en/news/20111214_minister_sikorski_on_a_visit_to_moscow (accessed 11 August 2016).

—— (2011e) 'Sikorski wyraża sympatię dla protestujących w Rosji. "Mówiono nam, że Rosjanie są pasywni"' ['Sikorski expressed sympathy for the protesters in Russia. "They told us that the Russians are passive"'], *Polska Times*, 14 December.

—— (2012a) Press release of the Polish foreign ministry, 29 February. www.mfa.gov.pl/en/news/weimar_triangle_foreign_ministers_meeting_in_berlin (accessed 11 August 2016).

—— (2012b) Transcript joint press conference with Hilary Clinton, 7 March.

—— (2012c) Interview with *Le Monde*, 21 March. www.lemonde.fr/europe/article/2012/03/21/radek-sikorski-la-pologne-n-acceptera-pas-de-revenir-sur-l-acquis-de-schengen_1673286_3214.html (accessed 11 August 2016).

—— (2012d) Speech at the European Council on Foreign Relations, 22 March. www.mfa.gov.pl/resource/6c250265-3db6-4912-aaef-b2f2a9d027ef:JCR (accessed 11 August 2016).

—— (2012e) Speech at the Sejm, 29 March. www.msz.gov.pl/resource/db6d43cf-cd4a-4993-a08b-ce578440f0cd:JCR (accessed 11 August 2016).

—— (2012f) Transcript of interview at BBC television programme *Hardtalk*, 14 November.

—— (2012g) Transcript of interview with French television channel France24, 13 December.

—— (2012h) Press release of the Polish foreign ministry, 17 December. www.msz.gov.pl/en/news/minister_sikorski_in_moscow___meeting_of_the_committee_for_polish_russian_cooperation_strategy (accessed 29 August 2016).

—— (2014a) Interview with *Washington Post*, 18 April. www.washingtonpost.com/opinions/talking-with-polands-foreign-minister-about-the-ukraine-crisis-and-russias-next-moves/2014/04/17/f1811e84-c5ad-11e3-bf7a-be01a9b69cf1_story.html?utm_term=.325294e861d1 (accessed 22 August 2016).

—— (2014b) Interview with CNN, 16 March. http://cnnpressroom.blogs.cnn.com/2014/03/16/radek-sikorski-russia-is-leaving-the-european-council-no-choice-on-monday/ (accessed 22 August 2016).

—— (2014c) Interview with Euractiv, 12 September. www.msz.gov.pl/en/news/they_wrote_about_us/minister_radoslaw_sikorski_discusses_european_union_and_ukraine_conflict_with_euractiv__12_september_2014;jsessionid=17517406CD51F0C34681CC15BD27E432.cmsap1p (accessed 22 August 2016).

—— (2014d) Interview with *Spiegel*, 10 March. www.spiegel.de/international/europe/polish-foreign-minister-discusses-weak-eu-position-in-ukraine-crisis-a-957812.html (accessed 22 August 2016).

Sikorski, R., Olex-Szczytowski, M. and Rostowski, J. (2007) 'Russian gas pipeline would be geopolitical disaster for EU', *Financial Times*, 28 May. www.ft.com/intl/cms/s/0/db259cf2-0cb7-11dc-a4dc-000b5df10621.html (accessed 7 August 2016).

Sivan, E. and Winter, J. (1999) 'Setting the framework', in E. Sivan and J. Winter (eds) *War and Remembrance in the Twentieth Century*, Cambridge: Cambridge University Press, pp. 6–39.

Smith, A. D. (1988) 'The myth of the "modern nation" and the myths of nations', *Ethnic and Racial Studies*, 11(1): 1–26.

—— (1991) *National Identity*, Reno, NV: University of Nevada Press.

—— (1992) 'National identity and the idea of European unity', *International Affairs*, 68(1): 55–76.

—— (1994) 'The problem of national identity: ancient, medieval and modern?', *Ethnic and Racial Studies*, 17(3): 375–99.

—— (1996a) 'Opening statement: nations and their pasts', *Nations and Nationalism*, 2(3): 358–65.

—— (1996b) 'Memory and modernity: reflections on Ernest Gellner's theory of nationalism', *Nations and Nationalism*, 2(3): 371–88.

—— (2004) 'History and national destiny: responses and clarifications', *Nations and Nationalism*, 10(1/2): 195–209.

—— (2011) 'National identity and vernacular mobilisation in Europe', *Nations and Nationalism*, 17(2): 223–56.

Smith, H. (2012) 'Russian foreign policy and energy: the case of the Nord Stream as pipeline', in P. Aalto (ed.) *Russia's Energy Policies: National, interregional and global levels*, Cheltenham: Edward Elgar, pp. 117–35.

Smyth, R., Sobolev, A. and Soboleva, I. (2013) 'A well-organised play. Symbolic politics and the effect of the pro-Putin rallies', *Problems of Post-Communism*, 60(2): 24–39.

Snyder, T. (2003) *The Reconstruction of Nations: Poland, Ukraine, Lithuania, Belarus, 1569–1999*, New Haven, CT: Yale university Press.

Sobczyk, M. and Wasilewski, P. (2014) 'Poland's new premier signals shift in Ukraine policy', *The Wall Street Journal*, 1 October. www.wsj.com/articles/poland-to-update-foreign-policy-1412155939 (accessed 23 August 2016).

Soini, T. (2015) Statement at the meeting of the Barents Euro-Arctic Council, 15 October. www.eilen.fi/en/3394/?language=en (accessed 26 August 2016).

Spanger, H. (2011) 'Die deutsche Russlandpolitik', in T. Jäger, A. Höse and K. Oppermann (eds) *Deutsche Außenpolitik*, Wiesbaden: Verlag für Sozialwissenschaften, pp. 648–72.

Spiegel Online (2008) 'Merkel redet Medwedew ins Gewissen', 15 August 2008. www.spiegel.de/politik/ausland/georgien-krise-merkel-redet-medwedew-ins-gewissen-a-572360.html (accessed 8 August 2016).

Spohn, W. (2005) 'National identities and collective memory in an enlarged Europe', in W. Spohn and K. Eder (eds) *Collective Memory and European Identity*, Aldershot: Ashgate, pp. 1–14.

Standard Eurobarometer 83 (2015), Tables of Results, QD1.1 and QD4, pp. T112 and T123. http://ec.europa.eu/public_opinion/archives/eb/eb83/eb83_anx_en.pdf (accessed 17 July 2016).

Stauter-Halsted, K. (2001) *The Nation in the Village: The genesis of peasant national identity in Austrian Poland 1848–1914*, Ithaca, NY: Cornell University Press.

Steinmeier, F. W. (2006a) Interview with RBB Inforadio, 14 October.

——— (2006b) Speech at Viadrina European University, 26 October. www. auswaertiges-amt.de/DE/Infoservice/Presse/Reden/2006/061026-Viadrina.html (accessed 7 August 2016).

——— (2007a) Interview with Wirtschaftswoche, 22 January.

——— (2007b) 'Verflechtung und Integration', *Internationale Politik*, 1 March. https://zeitschrift-ip.dgap.org/de/ip-die-zeitschrift/archiv/jahrgang-2007/maerz/verflechtung-und-integration (accessed 7 August 2016).

——— (2007c) Interview with Gazeta Wyborcza, 10 December.

——— (2007d) Speech at the lower house of the German parliament (Bundestag), 21 March. www.auswaertiges-amt.de/DE/Infoservice/Presse/Reden/2007/070321-Abruestung-Btg.html (accessed 8 August 2016).

——— (2008a) Speech at the French Institute of International Relations, 1 February. www.auswaertiges-amt.de/EN/Infoservice/Presse/Reden/2008/080201-Erler-IFRI-Europa-Energie.html (accessed 7 August 2016).

——— (2008b) Speech at the lower house of the German parliament (Bundestag), 20 February. www.auswaertiges-amt.de/DE/Infoservice/Presse/Reden/2008/080220-Steinmeier-BT-Kosovo.html (accessed 8 August 2016).

——— (2008c) Speech at the Institute of International Relations of Yekaterinburg Ural University, 13 May. www.auswaertiges-amt.de/DE/Infoservice/Presse/Reden/2008/080513-BM-Russland.html (accessed 8 August 2016).

——— (2008d) Interview with *Süddeutsche Zeitung*, 27 August.

——— (2008e) Interview with *Welt am Sonntag*, 17 August.

——— (2008f) Speech at the opening of the ambassadors' conference at the German foreign ministry, 8 September. www.auswaertiges-amt.de/DE/Infoservice/Presse/Reden/2008/080908-Rede-BM-Boko-Eroeffnung.html (accessed 8 August 2016).

——— (2008g) Speech at the Heinz Schwarzkopf Foundation, 11 December. www.auswaertiges-amt.de/DE/Infoservice/Presse/Reden/2008/081210-schwarzkopf.html (accessed 8 August 2016).

——— (2008h) Interview with *Rheinische Post*, 23 August.

——— (2008i) Speech at the lower house of the German parliament, 18 December. www.auswaertiges-amt.de/DE/Infoservice/Presse/Reden/2008/081218-BM-BundestagER.html (accessed 8 August 2016).

——— (2009a) Interview with *Gazeta Wyborcza*, 17 June.

——— (2009b) Interview with *Rzeczpospolita*, 9 February.

——— (2014a) Speech at the German–Russian Forum, 19 March. www.auswaertiges-amt.de/EN/Infoservice/Presse/Reden/2014/140319-BM_dtrus-Forum.html (accessed 18 August 2016).

——— (2014b) *Frankfurter Allgemeine Zeitung*, 6 May. www.auswaertiges-amt.de/EN/Infoservice/Presse/Interview/2014/140506-BM_UKR_FAZ.html (accessed 18 August 2016).

—— (2014c) Speech at the Bundestag, 7 May. www.auswaertiges-amt.de/EN/Infoservice/Presse/Reden/2014/140507-BM_BT_Ukraine.html (accessed 18 August 2016).

—— (2014d) Interview with *Frankfurter Allgemeine Zeitung*, 30 May. www.auswaertiges-amt.de/EN/Infoservice/Presse/Interview/2014/140530-BM_FAZ.html (accessed 18 August 2016).

—— (2014e) Interview with *Rzeczpospolita*, 22 July. www.auswaertiges-amt.de/EN/Infoservice/Presse/Interview/2014/140722-BM_Rzesczpospolita.html (accessed 18 August 2016).

—— (2014f) Interview with *Deutschlandfunk*, 27 July. www.auswaertiges-amt.de/EN/Infoservice/Presse/Interview/2014/140727_BM_DLF.html (accessed 18 August 2016).

—— (2014g) Interview with *Bild*, 26 March. www.auswaertiges-amt.de/EN/Infoservice/Presse/Interview/2014/140326-BM_Bild.html (accessed 18 August 2016).

—— (2014h) Interview with *Spiegel*, 28 July. www.auswaertiges-amt.de/EN/Infoservice/Presse/Interview/2014/140728-BM_Spiegel.html (accessed 18 August 2016).

—— (2015a) Interview with *Neue Osnabrücker Zeitung*, 4 June. www.auswaertiges-amt.de/EN/Infoservice/Presse/Interview/2015/150604_NOZ.html (accessed 19 August 2016).

—— (2015b) Interview with *Handelsblatt*, 5 March. www.auswaertiges-amt.de/EN/Infoservice/Presse/Interview/2015/150305-BM_Hbl.html (accessed 19 August 2016).

—— (2015c) Speech at Volgograd to commemorate the end of the Second World War, 7 May. www.auswaertiges-amt.de/EN/Infoservice/Presse/Reden/2015/150507_Wolgograd.html (accessed 19 August 2016).

—— (2015d) Interview with *Neue Westfälische*, 4 November. www.auswaertiges-amt.de/EN/Infoservice/Presse/Interview/2015/151104_NeueWestfaelische.html (accessed 19 August 2016).

—— (2015e) Interview with *Bild am Sonntag*, 22 November. www.auswaertiges-amt.de/EN/Infoservice/Presse/Interview/2015/151122_BamS.html (accessed 19 August 2016).

Stewart, S. (2012) 'Coherence in EU policy towards Russia: identities and interests', in R. Krumm, H. Schröder and S. Medvedev (eds) *Constructing Identities in Europe: German and Russian perspectives*, Baden-Baden: Nomos, pp. 185–204.

Stubb, A. (2008a) 'Georgia on my mind'. Reprinted in *Bluewings*, October, p. 46. http://digipaper.fi/bluewings/18582/index.php?pgnumb=3 (accessed 9 August 2016).

—— (2008b) Speech at the annual meeting of the heads of Finnish diplomatic missions abroad, 25 August. http://formin.finland.fi/public/default.aspx?contentid=135322andcontentlan=2andculture=en-US (accessed 9 August 2016).

—— (2008c) Press release of the Finnish Ministry of Foreign Affairs, 26 August. http://formin.finland.fi/public/default.aspx?contentid=135447an dcontentlan=2andculture=en-US (accessed 9 August 2016).

—— (2008d) Press release of the Finnish Ministry of Foreign Affairs, 8 August. http://formin.finland.fi/public/default.aspx?contentid=134721an dcontentlan=2andculture=en-US (accessed 9 August 2016).

—— (2008e) Press release of the Finnish Ministry of Foreign Affairs, 12 August. http://formin.finland.fi/public/default.aspx?contentid=134838an dcontentlan=2andculture=en-US (accessed 9 August 2016).

—— (2008f) Speech at the United Nations' Security Council, 26 September. http://formin.finland.fi/public/default.aspx?contentid=137874andcontent lan=2andculture=en-US (accessed 9 August 2016).

—— (2008g) Speech at the London School of Economics, 20 November. www.eilen.fi/se/307/?language=en (accessed 9 August 2016).

—— (2008h) Interview with *Ulkopolitiikka*, 18 December. http://formin. finland.fi/public/default.aspx?contentid=153423andcontentlan=2andcult ure=en-US (accessed 9 August 2016).

—— (2009a) 'Europe's gas dilemma'. Reprinted in *Bluewings*, October 2009, p. 49. www.digipaper.fi/bluewings/33117/index.php?pgnumb=49 (accessed 8 August 2016).

—— (2009b) Speech at the Pohjola-Norden Seminar, 10 November 2009, http://formin.finland.fi/public/default.aspx?contentid=180523andcontent lan=2andculture=en-US (accessed 8 August 2016).

—— (2011) Statements before the representatives of the Finnish media, 16 December. http://formin.finland.fi/public/default.aspx?contentid=23666 3andcontentlan=2andculture=en-US (accessed 11 August 2016).

—— (2012) 'Russia remains the most interesting but also the hardest market for Finnish companies', 5 November. http://formin.finland.fi/public/default. aspx?contentid=261755andcontentlan=2andculture=en-US (accessed 11 August 2016).

—— (2014) Speech at the Körber-Stiftung in Berlin, 29 September. www. eilen.fi/en/3247/?language=en (accessed 25 August 2016).

Suny, R. G. (1994) *The Making of the Georgian Nation*, Bloomington, IN: Indiana University Press.

Telegraph (2015) 'Minsk agreement on Ukraine crisis: text in full', 12 February. www.telegraph.co.uk/news/worldnews/europe/ukraine/11408266/ Minsk-agreement-on-Ukraine-crisis-text-in-full.html (accessed 15 August 2016).

Thumann, M. (1997) 'Vom Einmarsch in der Tschechoslowakei bis zum Moskauer Vertrag. Das Russlandbild westdeutscher Zeitschriften 1968–1970', in K. Meyer (ed.) *Deutsch, Deutschbalten und Russen: Studien zu ihren gegenseitigen Bildern und Beziehungen*, Lüneburg: Nordostdeutsches Kulturwerk, pp. 201–27.

Tiilkainen, T. (1998) *Europe and Finland: Defining the political identity of Finland in Western Europe*, Aldershot: Ashgate.

—— (2006) 'Finland — an EU Member with a small state identity', *Journal of European Integration*, 28(1): 73–87.

Timmins, G. (2011) 'German–Russian bilateral relations and EU policy on Russia: between normalisation and the "multilateral reflex"', *Journal of Contemporary European Studies*, 19(2): 189–99.

Torbakov, I. (2011) 'History, memory and national identity: understanding the politics of history and memory wars in post-Soviet lands', *Demokratizatsiya*, 19(3): 209–32.

Torfing, J. (2005) 'Discourse theory: achievements, arguments and challenges', in D. Howarth and J. Torfing (eds) *Discourse Theory in European Politics*, Basingstoke: Palgrave Macmillan, pp. 1–32.

Treaty on European Union (as amended by the Treaty of Lisbon). HYPERLINK "http://register.consilium.europa.eu/pdf/en/08/st06/st06655.en08.pdf" http://register.consilium.europa.eu/pdf/en/08/st06/st06655.en08.pdf (accessed 24 August 2016).

Tsygankov, A. (2008) 'Self and Other in International Relations theory: learning from Russian civilizational debates', *International Studies Review*, 10(4): 762–75.

Tuomioja, E. (2006) Speech at the seminar 'Visegrád Group and Finland', 31 May. http://formin.finland.fi/public/default.aspx?contentid=68999andcontentl an=2andculture=en-US (accessed 8 August 2016).

—— (2011) Speech at the OSCE ministerial council, 6 December. www.eilen. fi/en/467/?language=en (accessed 11 August 2016).

—— (2012a) Speech at the opening ceremony of the Visa Service Centre in Kouvola, 18 September. www.eilen.fi/en/1825/?language=en (accessed 11 August 2016).

—— (2012b) Speech at the seminar 'Changing security environment – challenges in the North', 12 April, http://formin.finland.fi/public/default. aspx?contentid=246548andcontentlan=2andculture=en-US (accessed 11 August 2016).

—— (2014a) Speech at the meeting of the Council of Europe Foreign Ministers, 6 May. www.eilen.fi/en/3211/?language=en (accessed 25 August 2016).

—— (2014b) Opening words at Helsinki Policy Forum, 2 June. http://formin. finland.fi/public/default.aspx?contentid=307277&contentlan=2&culture =e (accessed 25 August 2016).

—— (2014c) Speech at the Diplomatic Academy of Vienna, 27 May. http:// formin.finland.fi/public/default.aspx?contentid=307075&contentlan=2& culture=en-US (accessed 25 August 2016).

—— (2014d) Speech at the Fifth Annual Forum of the EU Strategy for the Baltic Sea Region, 4 June. www.eilen.fi/en/3206/?language=en (accessed 26 August 2016).

—— (2014e) Speech at the final seminar of the EU Arctic Information Centre, 11 September. http://www.eilen.fi/en/3280/?language=en (accessed 26 August 2016).

—— (2015) Speech at a seminar on the Arctic in Helsinki, 18 March. www.eilen.fi/en/3329/?language=en (accessed 26 August 2016).

Tusk, D. (2008a) Interview with *Novaya Gazeta*, 'Donald Tusk: turning backs upon each other is the worst we can do', 19 February. http://en.novayagazeta.ru/politics/8522.html (accessed 7 August 2016).

—— (2008b) Interview with *Neue Osnabrücker Zeitung*, 5 September. http://www.noz.de/deutschland-welt/politik/artikel/390240/ukraine-braucht-von-eu-klare-perspektive (accessed 9 August 2016).

—— (2008c) Interview with the *Financial Times*, 8 December.

—— (2009) Joint press conference with Vladimir Putin in Gdansk, 1 September.

—— (2010) Transcript of interview with *Financial Times*, 27 January. www.ft.com/cms/s/0/9ad8793a-0b74-11df-8232-00144feabdc0.html (accessed 7 August 2016).

—— (2014a) Speech at Sejm, 5 March. www.premier.gov.pl/en/news/news/prime-minister-tusk-at-the-sejm-on-ukraine.html (accessed 22 August 2016).

—— (2014b) Statements after the European Council, 6 March. www.premier.gov.pl/en/news/news/european-council-in-brussels-discussion-results-in-line-with-polands-postulates.html (accessed 22 August 2016).

—— (2014c) Press conference, 4 March. www.premier.gov.pl/en/news/news/donald-tusk-on-ukraine-our-strategy-does-bring-results.html (accessed 22 August 2016).

—— (2014d) 'A united Europe can end Russia's energy stranglehold', *Financial Times*, 21 April. www.ft.com/cms/s/0/91508464-c661-11e3-ba0e-00144feabdc0.html (accessed 22 August 2016).

—— (2014e) Press conference, 25 July. www.premier.gov.pl/en/news/news/the-prime-minister-on-european-union-sanctions-against-russia-weaker-sanctions-of-the.html (accessed 22 August 2016).

Vajda, M. (1989) 'Who excluded Russia from Europe?', in G. Schoepflin and N. Wood (eds) *In Search of Central Europe*, Cambridge: Polity, pp. 168–82.

Van Dijk, T. (2002) 'Multidisciplinary CDA: a plea for diversity', in R. Wodak and M. Meyer (eds) *Methods of Critical Discourse Analysis*, London: Sage, pp. 95–120.

Vanhanen, M. (2006a) Key note speech at the European Business Leaders Convention, 7 July. www.eilen.fi/en/579/?language=en (accessed 8 August 2016).

—— (2008a) Speech at the Japan National Press Club, 9 June. www.eilen.fi/en/788/?language=en (accessed 8 August 2016).

—— (2008b) Speech at the Finnish Centre Party foreign and security policy seminar, 2 April. www.eilen.fi/se/774/?language=en (accessed 9 August 2016).

Vehviläinen, O. (2002) *Finland in the Second World War: Between Germany and Russia*, Basingstoke: Palgrave Macmillan.

Vihavainen, T. (2006) 'Does history play a role in Finnish–Russian relations?', in H. Smith (ed.) *The Two-level Game: Russia's relations with Great Britain, Finland and the European Union*, Helsinki: Aleksanteri Institute, pp. 27–48.

Volkov, D. (2012) 'The protesters and the public', *Journal of Democracy*, 23(3): 55–62.

Von Haxthausen, A. (1972) *Studies on the Interior of Russia*, Chicago: University of Chicago Press.

Von Herberstein, S. (2010) *Notes upon Russia: A translation of the earliest account of that country, entitled Rerum moscoviticarum commentarii*, Cambridge: Cambridge University Press.

Waltz, K. (1979) *Theory of International Politics*, Reading: McGraw-Hill.

Wæver, O. (1992) 'Nordic nostalgia: Northern Europe after the Cold War', *International Affairs*, 68(1): 77–102.

—— (2002) 'Identity, communities and foreign policy: discourse analysis as foreign policy theory', in O. Wæver and L. Hansen (eds) *European Integration and National Identity: The challenge of the Nordic states*, London: Routledge, pp. 20–49.

—— (2005) 'European integration and security: analysing French and German discourses on state, nation and Europe', in D. Howarth and J. Torfing (eds) *Discourse Theory in European Politics*, Basingstoke: Palgrave Macmillan, pp. 33–67.

Webber, M. (2009) 'Russia and the European security governance debate', in J. Gower and G. Timmins (eds) *Russia and Europe in the Twenty-first Century: An uneasy partnership*, London: Anthem Press, pp. 267–88.

Weidenfeld, W. (2001) 'Geschichte und Identität', in K. Korte and W. Weidenfeld (eds) *Deutschland-Trendbuch: Fakten und Orientierungen*, Opladen: Leske and Budrich, pp. 29–58.

Weitz, R. (2009) 'Russia and NATO maneuver over Georgia', *Central Asia–Caucasus Institute Analyst*, 11(9): 6–8.

Wendt, A. (1994) 'Collective identity formation and the international state', *American Political Science Review*, 88(2): 384–96.

—— (1995) 'Constructing international politics', *International Security*, 20(1): 71–81.

—— (1999) *Social Theory of International Politics*, Cambridge: Cambridge University Press.

Westerwelle, G. (2010a) Speech at the German Council on Foreign Relations Berlin, 21 October. www.auswaertiges-amt.de/DE/Infoservice/Presse/Reden/2010/101021-BM-dgap-grundsatzrede.html (accessed 7 August 2016).

—— (2010b) Interview with *Tagesspiegel*, 4 November. www.auswaertiges-amt.de/DE/Infoservice/Presse/Interviews/2010/101104-BM-Sikorski-Tagesspiegel-Int.html (accessed 7 August 2016).

—— (2011) Speech at the OSCE ministerial council, 6 December. www.auswaertiges-amt.de/EN/Infoservice/Presse/Reden/2011/111206-BM_OSZE.html (accessed 10 August 2016).

—— (2012a) Interview with *Welt am Sonntag*, 4 March. www.auswaertiges-amt.de/DE/Infoservice/Presse/Interviews/2012/120304-BM_BamS.html (accessed 10 August 2016).

—— (2012b) Interview with *Neue Passauer Presse*, 10 March. www.auswaertiges-amt.de/DE/Infoservice/Presse/Interviews/2012/120310-BM-Neue-Presse.html (accessed 10 August 2016).

—— (2012c) Interview with *Frankfurter Allgemeine Zeitung*, 12 November. www.auswaertiges-amt.de/DE/Infoservice/Presse/Interviews/2012/121112-BM_FAZ.html (accessed 10 August 2016).

Westphal, K. (2008) 'Germany and the EU–Russia energy dialogue', in P. Aalto (ed.) *The EU–Russian Energy Dialogue*, Aldershot: Ashgate, pp. 93–118.

—— (2011) 'The Energy Charter Treaty revisited', *SWP Comment*, 8, Berlin: Stiftung Wissenschaft und Politik.

Whitman, R. and Wolff, S. (2010) 'The EU as a conflict manager? The case of Georgia and its implications', *International Affairs*, 86(1): 1–21.

Wilds, K. (2000) 'Identity creation and the culture of contrition: recasting "normality" in the Berlin Republic', *German Politics*, 9(1): 83–102.

Wilkinson, C. (2014) 'Putting "traditional values" into practice: the rise and contestation of anti-homopropaganda laws in Russia', *Journal of Human Rights*, 13(3): 363–79.

Wilson, A. (2014) *Ukraine Crisis: What it means for the West*, New Haven, CT: Yale University Press.

Winkler, H. A. (1996) 'Rebuilding of a nation: the Germans before and after unification', in M. Mertes, S. Muller and H. A. Winkler (eds) *In search of Germany*, New Brunswick, NJ: Transaction Publishers.

Wittlinger, R. (2008) 'The Merkel government's politics of the past', *German Politics and Society*, 26(4): 9–27.

—— (2011) *German National Identity in the Twenty-first Century: A different republic after all?*, Basingstoke: Palgrave Macmillan.

Wodak, R. (1996) *Disorder of Discourses*, London: Longman.

—— (2002a) 'What CDA is about: a summary of its history, important concepts and its developments', in R. Wodak and M. Meyer (eds) *Methods of Critical Discourse Analysis*, London: Sage, pp. 1–13.

—— (2002b) 'The discourse–historical approach', in R. Wodak and M. Meyer (eds) *Methods of Critical Discourse Analysis*, London: Sage, pp. 63–94.

—— (2009) *The Discourse of Politics in Action: Politics as usual*, Basingstoke: Palgrave Macmillan.

WTO (2011) 'Ministerial Conference approves Russia's WTO membership', 16 December. www.wto.org/english/news_e/news11_e/acc_rus_16dec11_e.htm (accessed 11 August 2016).

—— (2012) 'WTO membership rises to 157 with the entry of Russia and Vanuatu', 22 August. www.wto.org/english/news_e/pres12_e/pr671_e.htm (accessed 11 August 2016).

Yle (2015a) 'Finnish exports to Russia down more than 35 percent', 25 August. http://yle.fi/uutiset/finnish_exports_to_russia_down_more_than_35_percent/8251837 (accessed 25 August 2016).

—— (2015b) 'More Finns on the fence over NATO membership', 26 October. http://yle.fi/uutiset/more_finns_on_the_fence_over_nato_membership/8408782 (accessed 25 August 2016).

Zagorski, A. (2009) 'The Russian proposal for a treaty on European security: from the Medvedev initiative to the Corfu Process', in *OSCE Yearbook 2009*, Hamburg: Institute for Peace Research and Security Policy, pp. 43–59.

Zarycki, T. (2004) 'Uses of Russia: the role of Russia in the modern Polish national identity', *East European Politics and Societies*, 18(4): 595–627.

—— (2011) 'On the contemporary Polish perception of Russian intelligentsia', in I. Novikova (ed.) *Europe–Russia: Contexts, discourses, images*, Rīga: Lu Dzsc – Levira, University of Latvia, pp. 130–41.

Zehfuss, M. (2001) 'Constructivism and identity', *European Journal of International Relations*, 7(3): 315–48.

—— (2006) 'Remembering to forget, forgetting to remember', in D. Bell (ed.) *Memory, Trauma and World Politics*, Basingstoke: Palgrave Macmillan, pp. 213–30.

Zito, A. R. (2001) 'Epistemic communities, collective entrepreneurship and European integration', *Journal of European Public Policy*, 8(4): 585–603.

Zürcher, C. (2007) *The Post-Soviet Wars: Rebellion, ethnic conflicts and nationhood in the Caucasus*, New York: New York University Press.

Index

dominant discourses,
identification in 30, 32, 36, 39,
65–6
fieldwork in 29, 41
identity construction data in *29*
longue durée approach in 41, 64,
66, 160
sources used in 36–9, 41
textual analysis in 29–30, 38,
39–40
'the Other', use in 10–13, 22–3,
157, 158
see also case studies: Nord
Stream pipeline; Russia
2011–12 street protests;
Russian-Georgian war (2008);
Ukraine crisis (2013–15);
under Finland; Germany;
Poland;
Fotyga, A. 56, 77, 80 n.9, n.10
France 10, 12, 25, 33, 34, 46, 47, 52,
114, 131, 138, 139, 144, 145
French Institute of International
Relations 73, 74
French Revolution 5, 6

Gazprom 68, 69, 75, 90
Georgia 14, 91–114
Abkhazia/ South Ossetia separatist
conflict 91–114
and NATO membership 92–3, 96,
101ff., 105
see also Russian-Georgian war
(2008)
German Council on Foreign
Relations 74
Germany
as Berlin Republic 41–2
Berlin Wall, fall of (1989) 43–4
*Bundesstiftung Flucht, Vertreibung,
Versöhnung* 45
energy provision in 68–76, 140
Nord Stream project 68–76,
89–90

Nord Stream-2 140
see also Nord Stream pipeline
discourses analysis
Institute for International and
Security Affairs 37
national identity in 19, *29*, 41–5, *49*,
64, 68–76, 89–90, 115, 160
and antimilitarism 19, *49*, *66*, 98,
115, 141, 164
EU framework in 42, 43, *49*, *66*,
89, 100, 123, 160
historical construction of 42–5
Holocaust/WW2 memory in 43,
44, 45, 47, 97, 160
multilateralism, support for 42,
49, 64, *66*, 98, 100, 115, 141,
160, 164
reunification, effect on 43–4,
48, 65
Russia, policy analysis 2, 14, 23,
29, 34, 45–9, *66*, 68–76, 89–90,
91, 94–101, 114, 115, 120–7,
160, 164, 168
cooperation/partnership in 45,
89, 95–6, 97, 120, 122–3, 124,
125, 141, 160
dominant identity discourses 45,
49, *66*, 160
energy/economic policies 34,
49, 96
historical perceptions in 45–8,
66, 115
human rights/democracy
discourses 48, 49, *66*, 75–6,
121, 123, 124, 126, 160
as modernisation partnership 94,
95–6, 120, 122–3
Ostpolitik discourse in 45–6,
47–8, *49*, 65, *66*, 70, 71, 89,
97, 124, 141, 153, 160, 164
as significant Other 14, 25, 45,
47, 48, 65
see also case studies: Nord
Stream pipeline; Russia

www.ingramcontent.com/pod-product-compliance
Lightning Source LLC
Chambersburg PA
CBHW021815270326
41932CB00007B/201